Our readers are invited to view and download the exhibits this book. The materials are available FREE with the purchase of this book at www.wiley.com/go/pangarkar

The Trainer's Balanced Scorecard

A COMPLETE RESOURCE
FOR LINKING LEARNING
TO ORGANIZATIONAL STRATEGY

Ajay M. Pangarkar and
Teresa Kirkwood

Foreword by
Dr. David Norton

Pfeiffer
A Wiley Imprint
www.pfeiffer.com

CONTENTS

List of Figures, Tables, and Exhibits   xi

Contents of the Website   xix

Foreword   xxiii

Preface   xxv

Acknowledgments   xxix

About the Learning Scorecard Website   xxxi

Introduction   1

What You Can Expect from This Book   4
How This Book Is Organized   6
Some Advice When Reading This Book   15

ONE Defining Organizational Strategy   19

The Importance of Strategy: What It Is   20
Types of Strategy   22
Corporate Strategy Versus Business Strategy   24
Factors Affecting Strategy   25
What Management Wants to Know   32
Workplace Learning and Its Role in Strategy Development   33
Fostering a Learning Culture to Move Beyond ROI   36
Moving Beyond ROI and Toward Strategy   37
Making Learning Relevant to Management   39
Last Thoughts   40

TWO The Balanced Scorecard | 43

The Evolution of the BSC | 44
History of the Balanced Scorecard | 45
The Scope of the Balanced Scorecard | 45
The Strategic Framework | 48
Strategy Maps | 52
Going Deep: Defining the BSC Perspectives and Metrics | 57
Cascading Scorecards: Delivering a Strategic Message to the Masses | 68
Potential Pitfalls of the Balanced Scorecard | 72
Last Thoughts | 73

THREE Alignment with Management's Expectations | 75

Management's View: From Performance Measurement to Strategic Management | 76
Management's Expectations Versus Learning's Concerns | 80
Closing the Communication Gap | 98
Answering Management's Questions | 103
Last Thoughts | 110

FOUR Business Data and Performance Metrics | 111

Using Business Data to Develop Strategic Learning Solutions | 112
The Role of Workplace Learning and Performance | 113
Non-Financial Performance Measures | 120
Specific Factors That Drive Performance | 128
Last Thoughts | 132

FIVE Business Processes and Performance Measures | 133

The Organizational Value Chain: Providing Real Value | 134
The Value Chain's Proposition to the Customer | 136
Deconstructing the Value Chain | 139
Building the Learning and Performance Value Chain | 148
Last Thoughts | 150

SIX Workplace Learning in Relation to Financial Performance   153

How Management Differentiates Between Investment
and Expense   154
The Value of an Organization's Financial Statements   154
How to Tie Financial Statements to Management Objectives   155
Last Thoughts   165

SEVEN Developing the Learning and Growth Perspective   167

Learning and Growth Perspectives   168
Traditional Performance Thinking Versus the Balanced
Scorecard   169
An Organizational Perspective of Learning in the BSC   171
Applying the Learning and Growth Performance Metrics   188
Last Thoughts   191

EIGHT An Application of the Learning and Growth Perspective   193

Developing Learning and Growth Perspectives   194
Executing Learning Strategy   196
Demonstrating Results for Learning   205
Facilitating the Development of Learning and Growth Metrics   207
Last Thoughts   207

NINE The Case of Sky Air Limited   215

A Quick Review of the Basics   215
Case Application: Sky Air Limited   217
The Steps for Resolving the Case   219
Last Thoughts   252

TEN The Learning Department's Balanced Scorecard   253

Purpose of a Learning Department Scorecard   253
The Learning Department BSC: A Different Perspective   256
A Rapid Development Process for the Learning Scorecard   266
Last Thoughts   271

ELEVEN Factors Affecting Strategy, Balanced Scorecard, and
Workplace Learning   273

    The New Variables: Technology, Workers, and the World   275
    Expectation of Return on Workplace Investment   276
    Managing Learning for a Generational Workforce   284
    Developing the Entrepreneurial Employee   285
    Developing Specialists, Not Generalists   286
    Increasing Trend for Customer Intimacy   286
    Managing Knowledge for Maximum Benefit   287
    Final Thoughts   288

Conclusion   291

Appendices   295

    Appendix A: The Case of Dofasco, Inc.   297
    Appendix B: The Case of TD Bank's Enterprise
Balanced Scorecard: A Performance Measurement   305
    Appendix C: The Case of The Canadian
Physiotherapy Association   319
    Appendix D: The Case of United Way of
Kitchener-Waterloo and Area   339
    Appendix E: The Case of Bell Canada   345
    Appendix F: The Case of CMA Canada: Linking
Strategy to Competency   351
    Appendix G: The Case of Infosys: Competency
Development as a Business Imperative   363

Resources   371

References   375

Index   379
About the Authors   387

LIST OF FIGURES, TABLES, AND EXHIBITS

List of Figures

Figure I.1. The Organizational Change Process   4

Figure 1.1. The Three Basic Forms of Strategy   22

Figure 1.2. Focal Points of Strategy   28

Figure 1.3. Primary Points of Strategy   29

Figure 1.4. How the Strategic Framework
Links to the Organization   38

Figure 2.1. Balanced Scorecard Template   47

Figure 2.2. The Strategic Framework   49

Figure 2.3. The Balanced Scorecard Perspectives   50

Figure 2.4. Sample Strategy Map   54

Figure 2.5. Summary of External Performance
Perspectives   60

Figure 2.6. Summary of Internal Performance
Perspectives   62

Figure 2.7. Sample Balanced Scorecard   67

Figure 2.8. Cascading Scorecards   70

Figure 3.1. The Balanced Scorecard as a Strategic
Framework for Action   77

Figure 3.2. Casual Relationship Within the Four Perspectives   79

Figure 3.3. The ADDIE Model   100

Figure 4.1. WLP's Impact on Organizational Decision Making   117

Figure 4.2. The Flow of KPIs from Strategic Objectives   130

Figure 5.1. Organizational Value Chain   135

Figure 5.2. Value Chain Aligned with the BSC Perspectives   135

Figure 5.3. Value Chain Aligned with the Learning and Growth Perspective   136

Figure 5.4. Deconstructing the Value Chain Around the BSC and Learning   137

Figure 5.5. Reconciling Business and Learning Needs   139

Figure 5.6. Management's Perspective of the Value Chain   140

Figure 5.7. Relationship Between the Value Chain and Employee Skills   146

Figure 5.8. Sample Value Chain for a Production Business Unit   150

Figure 7.1. Reskilling Matrix   172

Figure 8.1. Sample Strategy Map for Widgets Inc.   197

Figure 8.2. Sample Balanced Scorecard for Widget Inc.   200

Figure 8.3. Sample Completed Balanced Scorecard for Widget Inc.   203

Figure 9.1. Incomplete Sky Air Strategy Map and Balanced Scorecard   220

Figure 9.2. Sky Air Strategy Map   221

Figure 9.3. Sample Completed Sky Air Balanced Scorecard and Strategy Map   251

Figure 10.1. Cascading Scorecard Development Process   254

Figure 10.2. Sample Balanced Scorecard Performance Metrics   257

Figure 10.3. Sample Learning Scorecard Performance
Metrics   258

Figure 10.4. Questions to Help Develop the Learning
Department's Scorecard   270

Figure 11.1. ROI   276

Figure A.1. Dofaseo's L&D Strategy Map   300

Figure B.1. The Enterprise Reporting Hierarchy   307

Figure B.2. Sample Tracking Form   310

Figure B.3. Business Partner Satisfaction Index   311

Figure B.4. Sample BPSI Scorecard   312

Figure B.5. Corporate Timeline for Implementing
the Model   314

Figure C.1. External Requests for Participation   333

Figure C.2. Letters of Support from Outside Sources   334

Figure C.3. Number of Discussion/Position Statements   334

Figure C.4. Aggregate Number of Sites Participating in
CPA Teleconference Program   335

Figure C.5. Congress Registration Numbers   336

Figure C.6. Submissions to PT Canada for Publication   336

Figure C.7. Number of CPA-Accredited Organizations   337

Figure C.8. Total Nominations and Awards, 2002–2006   337

Figure C.9. Shirley Sahrmann Course Participants   338

Figure D.1. United Way of Kitchener-Waterloo and
Area 2007 Strategy Map   341

Figure F.1. CMA's Balanced Scorecard   352

Figure F.2. Sample Personal Scorecard   354

Figure F.3. Sample Competency-Based Position Description   357

Figure G.1. Four Dimensions of Competency   365

Figure G.2. Translating Strategies to Business Units   367

List of Tables

Table 1.1. The Differences Between Strategy and Tactics   23

Table 1.2. The Three Basic "Value Disciplines"   26

Table 1.3. Sample of Fundamental Questions   27

Table 2.1. Value Proposition Strategies   59

Table 2.2. Sample Objectives   63

Table 2.3. Sample Measures   64

Table 2.4. Sample Targets   65

Table 2.5. Sample Initiatives   66

Table 3.1. Defining Your Target Audience and Their Needs   93

Table 6.1. Structure of a Balance Statement   156

Table 6.2. Structure of an Income Statement   160

Table 6.3. Structure of a Cash Flow Statement   164

Table 7.1. Performance Measures and Targets   181

Table 7.2. Skills Gaps for Manufacturing   182

Table 7.3. Skills Gaps for Customer Support   182

Table 7.4. Performance Targets   183

Table 8.1. Summary of Basic Principles   196

Table 8.2. Steps with Corresponding Exhibits   208

Table 9.1. Summary of the Steps with the Corresponding Templates   216

Table 9.2. Customer Perspective   231

Table 9.3. Internal Process Perspective   232

Table 9.4. Customer Perspective Past Performance Matrix   233

Table 9.5. Internal Process Perspective Past
Performance Matrix   233

Table 9.6. Customer Perspective Performance
Target Improvements   234

Table 9.7. Internal Process Perspective Performance
Target Improvements   235

Table 9.8. Customer Perspective Performance
Target Improvements   237

Table 9.9. Internal Process Perspective Performance
Target Improvements   238

Table 9.10. Financial Perspective Initiative Type   239

Table 9.11. Customer Perspective Initiative Type   239

Table 9.12. Internal Process Perspective Initiative Type   239

Table 9.13. Financial Perspective Initiative Type   240

Table 9.14. Customer Perspective Initiative Type   240

Table 9.15. Internal Process Perspective Initiative Type   241

Table 9.16. Customer Perspective   244

Table 9.17. Internal Process Perspective   245

Table 9.18. Customer Perspective   245

Table 9.19. Internal Process Perspective   246

Table 9.20. Customer Perspective   247

Table 9.21. Internal Process Perspective   248

Table 10.1. Sample Learning Department Balanced Scorecard   271

Table 11.1. Kirkpatrick's Four Levels of Evaluation   279

List of Exhibits

Exhibit 1.1. Are You Able to Define Your
Organization's Strategy?   31

Exhibit 1.2. Defining Your Organization's Expectations   34

Exhibit 2.1. Cause-and-Effect Relationships to
Learning and Growth   69

Exhibit 3.1. Critical Questions   82

Exhibit 3.2. Thinking Like They Do   83

Exhibit 3.3. WLP Concerns   97

Exhibit 3.4. External Perspectives   102

Exhibit 3.5. Internal Perspectives   103

Exhibit 3.6. What Is Management Asking you?   108

Exhibit 3.7. Responses to Management's Questions   109

Exhibit 4.1. Learning Based on Strategic, Tactical,
and Operational Data   117

Exhibit 4.2. Key Performance Measures   131

Exhibit 5.1. Define Your Organization's Value
Proposition   142

Exhibit 5.2. Identifying Your Value Chain   142

Exhibit 5.3. Assessing Employee Skills and Knowledge   146

Exhibit 6.1. Balance Sheet Value Creation   158

Exhibit 6.2. Income Statement Value Creation   162

Exhibit 7.1. Initiative Selection Template   185

Exhibit 7.2. Initiative Prioritization Template   186

Exhibit 7.3. Sample Initiative Prioritization Template   186

Exhibit 7.4. Initiative Description Template   187

Exhibit 7.5. Improving and Creating Value   191

Exhibit 8.1. Identifying Strategically Critical Areas   209

Exhibit 8.2. Strategic Linkages Analysis   210

Exhibit 8.3. Identifying Objectives   210

Exhibit 8.4. Customer Perspective Performance
Measures   211

Exhibit 8.5. Internal Process Perspective Performance
Measures   211

Exhibit 8.6. Financial Perspective Performance Measures   212

Exhibit 8.7. Balanced Scorecard Initiatives   213

Exhibit 8.8. Balanced Scorecard Initiatives and
Learning Initiatives   214

Exhibit 8.9. Balanced Scorecard Learning Initiatives and
Performance Metrics   214

Exhibit 9.1. Identifying Strategically Critical Areas   222

Exhibit 9.2. Strategic Linkages Analysis   227

Exhibit 9.3. Customer Perspective Performance Measures   229

Exhibit 9.4. Internal Process Perspective Performance
Measures   230

Exhibit 9.5. Sky Air Learning and Growth Analysis   242

Exhibit 9.6. Sample Completed Balanced Scorecard
Learning Initiatives and Performance Metrics: Customer   249

Exhibit 9.7. Completing Sky Air's Learning and
Growth Perspective   250

Exhibit 10.1. Financial Perspective: "How Do We Look
to Our Stakeholders?"   260

Exhibit 10.2. Customer Perspective: "How Do Our
Customers See Us?"   262

Exhibit 10.3. Internal Process Perspective: "What Must
We Excel At?"   265

Exhibit 10.4. Learning and Growth Perspective:
"How Can Learning Continue to Improve and
Create Value?"   267

CONTENTS OF THE WEBSITE

You are invited to view and download the supplementary materials listed below. The materials are available FREE with the purchase of this book at www.wiley.com/go/pangarkar.

Exhibit 1.1. Are You Able to Define Your Organization's Strategy?	31
Exhibit 1.2. Defining Your Organization's Expectations	34
Exhibit 2.1. Cause-and-Effect Relationship to Learning and Growth	69
Exhibit 3.1. Critical Questions	82
Exhibit 3.2. Thinking Like They Do	83
Exhibit 3.3. WLP Concerns	97
Exhibit 3.4. External Perspectives	102
Exhibit 3.5. Internal Perspectives	103
Exhibit 3.6. What Is Management Asking You?	108
Exhibit 3.7. Responses to Management's Questions	109
Exhibit 4.1. Learning Based on Strategic, Tactical, and Operational Data	117
Exhibit 4.2. Key Performance Measures	131
Exhibit 5.1. Define Your Organization's Value Proposition	142
Exhibit 5.2. Identifying Your Value Chain	142
Exhibit 5.3. Assessing Employee Skills and Knowledge	146

Exhibit 6.1. Balance Sheet Value Creation   158

Exhibit 6.2. Income Statement Value Creation   162

Exhibit 7.1. Initiative Selection Template   185

Exhibit 7.2. Initiative Prioritization Template   186

Exhibit 7.3. Sample Initiative Prioritization Template   186

Exhibit 7.4. Initiative Description Template   187

Exhibit 7.5. Improving and Creating Value   191

Exhibit 8.1. Identifying Strategically Critical Areas   209

Exhibit 8.2: Strategic Linkages Analysis   210

Exhibit 8.3. Identifying Objectives   210

Exhibit 8.4. Customer Perspective Performance
Measures   211

Exhibit 8.5. Internal Process Perspective Performance
Measures   211

Exhibit 8.6. Financial Perspective Performance
Measures   212

Exhibit 8.7. Balanced Scorecard Initiatives   213

Exhibit 8.8. Balanced Scorecard Initiatives and Learning
Initiatives   214

Exhibit 8.9. Balanced Scorecard Learning Initiatives and
Performance Metrics   214

Exhibit 9.1. Identifying Strategically Critical Areas   222

Exhibit 9.2. Strategic Linkages Analysis   227

Exhibit 9.3. Customer Perspective Performance
Measures   229

Exhibit 9.4. Internal Process Perspective Performance
Measures   230

Exhibit 9.5. Sky Air Learning and Growth Analysis   242

Exhibit 9.6. Sample Completed Balanced Scorecard
Learning Initiatives and Performance Metrics: Customer   249

Exhibit 9.7. Completing Sky Air's Learning and
Growth Perspective   250

Exhibit 10.1. Financial Perspective: "How Do We Look
to Our Stakeholders?"   260

Exhibit 10.2. Customer Perspective: "How Do Our
Customers See Us?"   262

Exhibit 10.3. Internal Process Perspective:
"What Must We Excel At?"   265

Exhibit 10.4. Learning and Growth Perspective:
"How Can Learning Continue to Improve and
Create Value?"   267

FOREWORD

by David P. Norton

When Bob Kaplan and I developed the concept of a Balanced Scorecard in the 1990s, we had a very simple message to improve performance:

1. Understand your organization strategy

2. Translate your strategy to measures and target (a "Balanced Scorecard")

3. Align your people (their competencies, goals and incentives) to the measures and, hence, to the strategy.

While the message may have been simple, the realization was anything but. We found that there was no generally accepted way to describe an organization's strategy. If you can't describe a phenomenon, you certainly can't *measure* it and without measures, you can't *align* the organization.

We had two important breakthroughs in our thinking as the Balanced Scorecard evolved from a measurement technique to a performance management system. The first was the development of the "Strategy Map." The map provided a visual way to show the relationship among desired outcomes (financial success and customer satisfaction) and the strategic drivers (internal business processes and human capital).

The second breakthrough was the role of *alignment* as a creator of value. The Strategy Map defined the strategic priorities of the organization. These priorities became the targets for all organization investments including training, development, technology, reengineering, etc. With the strategy map as the target, all organization activity could be aligned to the strategy.

One of the most important activities in this alignment process is the training and development of the work force. Human assets that are trained to meet the requirements of the strategy are worth more than those that are not. Conversely, the ROI of investments in workplace learning will be greater if the investments develop the competencies required by the strategy than if they are focused elsewhere. In other words, alignment is a source of value.

It was the recognition of this need and opportunity that caused the authors, Ajay Pangarkar and Teresa Kirkwood, to develop this excellent work, "The Trainer's Balanced Scorecard." They begin with a call for members of the Training and Development community to "be strategic." Being strategic is a state of mind–a way of looking at the big picture of the business and creating a context for your individual actions. This is not a remedy that is limited to TD professionals–strategy is everyone's job. But the leverage and impact that Human Capital has on the organization is unique.

From this starting point, the authors do an excellent job of tailoring the Balanced Scorecard approach that has been used successfully around the world to the needs of training and development community.

I applaud the work of the authors and urge you to develop the competencies defined here and to apply them in your organizations. And remember, you are not alone. There are thousands of professionals like you going through this experience in their own organizations. Reach out and join them through communities and your professional organizations. Based on my own experience, I can tell you that if you succeed, the results for both you and your organizations will be profound.

Good luck,
David P. Norton
Founder, The Balanced Scorecard Collaborative
Director, The Palladium Group
Boston, MA
November 2008

PREFACE

We hope that this book inspires you to develop effective learning initiatives and strategies that deliver a tangible contribution toward the success of your organization. It is a pleasure to have the unique opportunity of writing this book and helping you, our colleagues, to truly make learning relevant in a strategic context.

For many years, we have struggled to make workplace learning relevant to management, to gain credibility in the workplace, and to be held accountable for its intangible results in a tangible business world. Our story began over fifteen years ago as we both held management roles within our respective organizations. We did not have responsibility over training, but were accountable for our employees' and departments' performance. Regularly, our bosses would come to us and mandate that we send our staff to the "flavor of the month" training course. These were the days when "bums in seats" was the measure of a successful training program, and so everyone, without question, was expected to attend and hopefully participate in the training program proudly acclaimed by senior management. Most of you can relate to this, since each time a new business trend comes along the management bandwagon begins to roll and everyone is expected to learn and apply the new skills. What usually happens, as it did in our cases, is that very little learning took place, as it was not necessarily relevant to the participants or, as in the words all learning professionals today recognize: telling participants what they need to know isn't the same as them actually learning the topic. For lower-level managers like ourselves at the time, it also meant that our staff had to take valuable time away from their jobs, our budgets were reduced, and our performance objectives rose. All in all, it was a recipe for failure and blame. And that is exactly what happened.

Even though management pushed the training onto everyone in the company, training took the blame when it didn't work. Go figure how that happened.

Being young and on the fast track for management, we asked ourselves why we couldn't obtain the training that would help our staffs to maximize their abilities. Why did everyone in the company have to attend training on a specific topic that was not relevant to their responsibilities? And why would we not be allowed to determine the needs of our departments' performance and maximize the business investment we made in our employees? These all seem to be common sense questions, but as we all know, these questions were rarely, if ever, asked. And if you were courageous enough to question senior management as we did then, it was closely equivalent to career-ascension suicide.

Much has changed in the last decade as a result of three specific drivers: (1) economic factors and competitive environments require management to change and adapt much faster than ever before (a primary driver for the need for learning); (2) as a result of limited resources, every business investment incurred, including workplace learning, must be held accountable for its contribution to meeting organizational goals; and (3) learning, like every other business activity, must be held to the same standards and prove that their intangible outcomes produce in some way tangible results.

Some of you will equate "results" with the common term "return on investment." This is not appropriate. As we will demonstrate, what senior management believes to be more relevant is how investments in learning contribute to longer-term organizational objectives. Both Dr. Kaplan and Dr. Norton recognized that strategy was the primary preoccupation of senior managers. They also recognized that within a knowledge-driven environment, return on investment, albeit valuable, is an event-based measure. Traditionally, ROI is a financial measure of tangible outcomes. It is also viewed as a lagging measure or indicator of performance. Senior management may be skeptical of learning ROI measures and may find more from using the balanced scorecard, which has connections to the strategic goal, the organization's mission, and what needs to be accomplished to achieve it. The balanced scorecard also clearly demonstrates how intangible efforts such as organizational learning contribute to the organization's goals. Before you begin reading this book, clear your head of any pre-concepts about learning ROI and look toward leading thinking solutions rather than lagging financial measures.

As you read through this book, we hope that you will see our passion for the topic of learning and its relationship with organizational strategy. We believe this is what many of the people who have supported us and contributed to the book see. We attempted to provide you with a way to align every learning effort with your organization's business needs and seamlessly incorporate them with the organization's balanced scorecard.

INTENDED AUDIENCE FOR THE BOOK

Essentially, anyone who is involved with workplace learning should read this book. *The Trainer's Balanced Scorecard* is a resource for your own professional development and continuous learning. Ideally, all internal learning professionals responsible for managing learning and employee development as well as chief learning officers and directors for learning and training would read this book. It is also a must read for all learning and performance consultants. Others who could benefit from this book include senior managers, specifically those responsible for strategic planning, change management staff, human resource professionals, and all lower-level managers within these organizations.

ACKNOWLEDGMENTS

We need to acknowledge the contribution and unconditional support of many people in our efforts to create this book. They include:

Case Contributors

- Theresa O'Halloran, Manager, Development, ArcelorMittal Dofasco

- Tracy MacPherson, Learning and Development Specialist, ArcelorMittal Dofasco

- Steve Vieweg, MBA, C.Dir., CMA, FCMA, President and CEO, The Society of Management Accountants of Canada (CMA Canada)

- Mathieu Campeau, Associate Director–Awareness/Knowledge Management/ Initial and Continuous Training, Bell Canada Enterprise (BCE)

- Ed Orendorff, CMA, Director, Finance and Administration, for the Canadian Physiotherapy Association, Canadian Physiotherapy Association (CPA)

- Connie Karlsson, CTDP, Manager, Instructional Design and Measurement, Learning and Development, TD Bank Financial Group

- V. Ganapathy Subramanian, Group Manager–Corporate Planning and Corporate Performance Management, Infosys Technologies Ltd.

- Srikantan (Tan) Moorthy, Vice President and Head, Education and Research, Infosys Technologies Ltd.

- Cam Scholey, MBA, CMA, Ph.D., faculty member at The University of Waterloo

- Jan Varner, CEO, United Way of Kitchener, Waterloo and Area

Supporting Contributors

Eric DaSilva, CMA. Thank you for your efforts in researching topics in this book and for your dedication in reviewing the chapters. Chao Ling Pan, CMA. Thank you for providing research and support for the content of parts of this book and for helping us review some of book content. Thank you to both of you for your patience and involvement.

We want to thank Dr. David Norton, founder of the Balanced Scorecard Collaborative, for his support and generous endorsement to The Trainer's Balanced Scorecard. Both his and Dr. Robert Kaplan's efforts in aligning strategy to performance are now essential for every organization's existence and growth within a rapidly evolving economic environment.

To Matt Davis, our acquisitions editor at Pfeiffer. Thank you, Matt, for believing in our idea and encouraging us to write this book. It started with that one cup of coffee after our presentation of this topic at ASTD ICE 2006. You really know how to make things happen, and we look forward to many future projects together. We would also like to thank the professional and punctual support of the Pfeiffer staff who helped put this book together. A thank you to Lindsay Morton, Dawn Kilgore, Susan Rachmeler, Rebecca Taff, and Kathleen Dolan Davies for their professional expertise and helping us look great.

A special thank you goes to my co-author, partner, and wife, Teresa, for believing in this project and for her patience and understanding, which was extensively put to the test during the writing of the book. Her objectivity and clarity helped to keep this book going in the right direction and focused on our objectives.

And a thank you to you, our readers and audience, for pushing yourselves to make workplace learning not only relevant but truly accountable for helping organizations and people be successful . . . that is what our role as learning professionals is all about.

Go forth and become a true learning strategist!

ABOUT THE LEARNING SCORECARD WEBSITE

The Balanced Scorecard is a challenging topic for many to implement properly. Those involved in developing scorecards at various levels and those incorporating specific strategies across scorecards face significant challenges. At the same time, these individuals encounter many opportunities to contribute to their organization's growth and help it to meet its strategic objectives. As learning professionals, those responsible for employee development are fortunate to be included in the new strategic alignment of an organization's growth. For the fist time in recent business history, the learning function is considered a strategic component for an organization's growth, critical for its survival.

In an effort to provide you with the required resources and support to help you develop and leverage the learning and growth perspective of the Balanced Scorecard, we want you to become part of the Learning Scorecard web community at http://learningscorecard.centralknowledge.com. This unique workplace learning web portal provides you with areas to develop your skills and share your experiences with others. By becoming a member of this web portal you will have access to:

- All of the learning scorecard tools and templates in the book
- All of the new tools and templates the authors develop
- The learning strategy scorecard blog and pod-casts
- Workplace learning and scorecard discussion groups
- Case studies and white papers of actual applications

- The learning strategy scorecard newsletter
- Access to learning strategy scorecard certification program
- Articles and editorials from major publications
- Opportunities to be included in the next edition of this book
- Certification opportunities through the learning scorecard certification process
- Free books, discounts, and exclusive meetings with the authors

So if you are serious about making a difference in your organization and would like to maximize the benefit of the opportunities represented in this book, sign up with http://learningscorecard.centralknowledge.com web portal.

We want to wish you much success in aligning your learning solutions with your balanced scorecard or other strategic management scorecard tool. We both look forward to seeing you as a member on the CentralKnowledge Learning Scorecard Portal. You can contact us by email at: learning@centralknowledge.com

Ajay M. Pangarkar
President, Senior Learning Strategist
Learning Scorecard Portal
CentralKnowledge Inc.

Teresa Kirkwood
Vice President, Associate Learning Strategist
Learning Scorecard Portal
CentralKnowledge Inc.

It is safe to say that Ford's ability to harness his people's knowledge led to lasting innovations. It can also be said that Ford "learned" the knowledge required to achieve his vision. This is an early and relevant example of how learning can directly influence and impact an organization's strategy leading to growth and product leadership. The Ford story demonstrates the importance human knowledge has on the development of an organization, especially profit-driven companies seeking to maintain their competitive advantage. Every organization's single most underestimated and powerful attribute is its people. People are the minds, or specifically the knowledge, that drives an organization forward. It is the raison d'etre for an organization's existence. Surprisingly, you wouldn't know it by seeing how organizational performance is measured and currently valued.

Organizations are traditionally valued based on financial performance. These results are perceived as credible because they are tangible and supported by physical assets. The investments organizations make contribute to or support the production of goods and services and are considered capital expenditures. This type of valuation model is familiar to businesspeople and is an integral and accepted model of corporate performance. More importantly, it is also human nature to value what can be seen and touched because it is difficult to value non-tangible items such as employee knowledge.

Similar to the industrial revolution of the late 19th century, the 21st century ushers in another significant economic and market evolution. Currently, there is a transition from an industrial and very tangible environment to an information-driven, intangible one dominated by intangible assets such as intellectual capital and knowledge. These two items are significantly valued by information-dependent, knowledge-driven organizations that want to survive and compete in this new age and strays from the tangible and traditional value-based approach described previously.

Many questions are being asked during this economic transition. Because knowledge and information are the new competitive drivers of our economy, why do organizations still value their business and growth as they have in the past? How can we measure the impact of these intangible drivers on a balance sheet? More importantly, how can an organization correlate and link the intellectual capital it possesses to leverage, measure, and harness it to the benefit of the organization's growth and long-term success? How does management support the value of these intangibles in the eyes of their shareholders expecting short-term results? And how can an organization correlate the need for tangible financial performance measures with intangible asset values? These are just some of the many questions being asked that become clear through a strategic tool called the Balanced Scorecard (BSC).

The BSC, first develop by Dr. Robert Kaplan and Dr. David Norton in the early 1990s, outlined a method to define and link traditional performance measures, usually lagging type and financial outcomes, with non-tangible performance results. The balanced scorecard appropriately accommodates both the evolving economic conditions and the market forces affecting organizations within a complete performance measurement and change management framework. Prior to this, the traditional value-based approach was directly linked to the past or lagging performance outcomes of the organizations and their capital asset intensity.

The change in market conditions and many economic factors resulted in significant and intense competition. No longer can the leadership of an organization afford to judge itself based on past performance; they need to know immediately, or as close to real-time as possible, how their organization is doing to effectively compete in a constantly changing business world. In the business "jungle," it is survival of the fittest. The business lions of the past must rethink how and what they are doing to compete with the new and much younger cheetahs and other more versatile predators. This is the reality of business that leads us to a second lesson—courtesy of Henry Ford.

Early in the 20th century, Henry Ford built a dominant leadership in the automotive sector using the knowledge and talent of his people. Ford's complacency, and arguably his arrogance, was the downfall of the company's market dominance and industry monopoly. At the same time, Ford's competition, a coalition of fledgling companies forming what we currently know as General Motors, watched Ford's experiences and quickly learned what buyers wanted. Ford's famous statement of having the "Model T in any color as long as it was black" quickly returned to haunt him. One of the first lessons learned about competitive advantage by the coalition was to offer a choice of colors. This simple lesson illustrates how knowledge and "learning" are powerful instruments and can have a dramatic impact on business.

This is what this book is all about. This book will help you to link and integrate learning and performance with business and organizational strategic objectives. We will show you the importance that workplace learning has on strategy and how both must work together for an organization's long-term viability. Over one hundred years after Ford's experience, we are currently in the infancy of another

Figure I.1. The Organizational Change Process

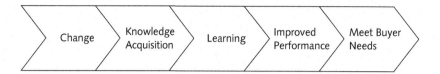

significant economic change. Both hold similar challenges: the significant increase in the pace of business, rapid changes in market conditions, and continual technological advances. The differences are also clear. During the industrial revolution, one could expect some stability in business and market conditions for extensive periods of time. The rules, at least in appearance, were set for a period of time, and most changes were relatively minor.

The same cannot be said for the current economic evolution. All industries live with the reality of "constant change" and are often unable to discern between major and minor changes. Even the largest and mightiest of global corporations are rethinking how they do business, where they do it, and whom they compete against—all the while meeting buyer expectations. In the current economic environment, major corporations do not necessarily have control and influence over the market, as they once did; they are unable to dictate market needs. The marketplace now requires a more formalized approach to acquiring and leveraging knowledge. This is where workplace learning and performance come in. The role of the learning professional is becoming increasingly prominent. Figure I.1 illustrates how change impacts the organization. Clearly, workplace learning has a significant role in the change process.

WHAT YOU CAN EXPECT FROM THIS BOOK

We did not write this book to promote the importance of workplace learning and performance or to explain why management must begin to take it more seriously. As much as we believe in the crucial role workplace learning plays, the primary reason we wrote this was to bring together two perspectives: that of workplace learning and that of business.

Workplace learning is a way to ensure that every employee is capable of working with the organization to achieve its strategic objectives. The organization is only accountable for meeting its strategic objectives, specifically through its employees. If employees do not possess the appropriate knowledge to be effective, the organization will certainly not meet its objectives—let alone survive. Is this enough weight on the shoulders of workplace learning? Are you feeling pressure? Don't worry. Reading this book and building your business and strategic acumen will help you to help your organization in its efforts to meet its strategic objectives.

Our intention is simple—to help those responsible for learning to connect directly with their business, align with organizational strategy, and effectively communicate with management. As learning professionals, we are concerned about the role of learning and how it is perceived within an organization. But we are equally concerned about how disconnected the learning function is from the business environment, especially in an economic environment in which change is constant. Our goal is to empower HR and workplace learning professionals to demonstrate the strategic value learning and performance play in a knowledge-driven organization.

We targets two groups: organizational decision-makers, often referred to in the book as the C-level or C-suite (CEO, COO, CFO, etc.), and our peers in the learning and HR profession, especially those responsible for workplace learning and talent development.

As mentioned in our last book, *Building Business Acumen for Trainers: Skills to Empower the Learning Function,* training and development (T&D) is just like any other business unit, functional or operational. T&D is an investment in the organization's current and future performance. In the "good old days," T&D would receive a lump sum allocation of funds and be told to spend it. It was treated physically and psychologically as a line expense. This is no longer the case. Even though learning remains a line expense on the profit-and-loss statement, those in charge of administering the learning are now accountable not only for how budgets are allocated but also to justify to decision-makers how learning helps the organization reach its strategic objectives. This concept is often foreign to learning professionals; however, being accountable and demonstrating results are business realities. Now workplace learning and performance are experiencing the same level of scrutiny as other business units and function face.

Does this sound overwhelming, disconcerting, or simply foreign to you? Don't worry. This book will help to answer your questions and make your learning initiatives accountable and results-driven.

We want to you to learn about:

- The relevance and importance of strategy on the organization and learning and performance's role within this context;
- The Balanced Scorecard and the relationship workplace learning and performance (WLP) has within its framework and strategy;
- How to develop the learning and growth perspective of the BSC and connecting to the other BSC perspectives while answering the needs of the organization;
- How to develop a learning department balanced scorecard that fits within the organization's scorecard and corporate mission; and
- Other factors that may play a significant role in workplace learning.

One question is, "Does this replace existing models of learning evaluation and ROI measures?" The short answer is no, it does not replace current models of measurement and evaluation. The question you should be asking instead is, "How do the current learning measurement, evaluation, and ROI models fit into the BSC environment?" We will address this important question throughout the book. To answer it properly, you must read this book from a holistic business approach, rather than with the predominant measurement, evaluation, and ROI models (or whatever model you follow) in mind.

HOW THIS BOOK IS ORGANIZED

This book is rooted in both workplace learning and in business and organizational strategic subjects. Our goal is to provide you with a systematic process to understand fundamental business and strategic concepts and how to apply a learning strategy within a simple but powerful framework called the Balanced Scorecard. In the following twelve chapters, you will go from learning about the importance of strategy to developing a learning strategy that aligns with the organization's strategy and completes the learning and growth perspective of the scorecard.

Chapter 1: Defining Organizational Strategy

In this chapter we lay the foundation for the primary strategic concepts and components essential to organizational effectiveness and survival. In this chapter we introduce and explain the fundamental business and strategic concepts that will be the basis of applying learning solutions within the balanced scorecard framework.

This is not a chapter to skim over or skip. This is a critical chapter in developing an understanding of why strategy, more than ever, is at the heart of every organization's success or demise and the foundation to your efforts in working with the balanced scorecard. Formulating a sensible strategy facilitates a number of specific actions and desired strategic results that would be difficult for the organization to accomplish otherwise. Formulating a systematic strategy forces an organization to assess and properly examine the prospect of changing and evolving factors in the foreseeable future. The strategy process allows an organization to prepare for the changes rather than to passively wait until the market forces it to change. The strategic formulation process is significant, as it allows an organization to plan its use of the resources it has available, especially financial resources.

On the other hand, an organization without a clear strategic plan gives its decision-makers no direction other than maintenance of the status quo. The organization becomes purely reactive to external pressures and less effective at dealing with change. In highly competitive markets, a firm without a coherent strategy is likely to be outmaneuvered by its rivals and face declining market share or declining sales.

In Chapter 1 you will learn about:

- The importance of strategy
- Types of strategy
- Factors affecting strategy
- What management wants to know
- Workplace learning and its role in strategy development
- Fostering a learning culture to move beyond ROI
- Making learning relevant to management

These points help you to build a strong foundation. This is your starting point to build a sustainable learning strategy directly connected to the organizational mission and vision.

Chapter 2: The Balanced Scorecard

Chapter 2 introduces the Balanced Scorecard (BSC) and the components surrounding this powerful management tool, including the strategy map. The BSC is a strategic business tool helping management to effectively translate their mission into tactical and tangible performance measures and processes. By using a BSC, every employee is able to align with the organization's long-term direction. Prior to the BSC, organizations were challenged by not having the ability to link short-term business objectives to long-term corporate vision. By recognizing and grasping the concepts presented in the BSC, you will gain an appreciation for how learning fits within the framework and give you the knowledge you require to develop performance-driven learning solutions.

Chapter 2 begins our journey to reconciling learning within the balanced scorecard. Through the scorecard framework, you will discover the need to shift from a "training and development" perspective to seeing workplace learning as a performance tool within the business and strategic context. The chapter will explain the four elements of the BSC—financial, customer, internal business processes, and learning and growth—and demonstrate how performance improvement and strategic alignment fit into these elements. The chapter focuses specifically on the "learning and growth" perspective of the balanced scorecard and the perspective's relationship and connection with the other components of the scorecard.

Chapter 2 provides a comprehensive overview of the balanced scorecard and explains the following:

- The evolution of the BSC
- History of the balanced scorecard
- Strategy maps
- Cascading scorecards
- Potential pitfalls of the balanced scorecard

Chapter 2 is where you will begin to see the role that workplace learning holds within the balanced scorecard and its impact on performance management and organizational strategy.

Chapter 3: Alignment with Management's Expectations

Chapter 3 continues a discussion about the balanced scorecard and organizational strategy and how workplace learning fits into this new strategic paradigm. Before we jump into how to develop a learning strategy within the balanced scorecard, it is crucial to recognize what type of audience you are addressing. Workplace learning professionals must see that they live and work within a business environment. This is not to disparage learning professionals, but for too long workplace learning lived in isolation from the rest of the organization. This is partially because business leaders did not understand and/or see the relevance of workplace learning and also because learning professionals were uncomfortable in demonstrating business results for their efforts. Learning professionals remained a secluded business unit mainly communicating among themselves about the learning initiatives developed. The reality, however, is that all management must be concerned about how their finite resources are being maximized to achieve the results they expect.

This chapter addresses this issue directly. Our objective is to help learning professionals understand and communicate with their business counterparts. It also provides business leaders with information about how learning professionals arrive at effective learning solutions.

By the end of this chapter, you will be better able to:

- Understand management's views on performance and strategic management
- Compare management's expectations with learning's concerns
- Correlate WLP thinking with C-level thinking characteristics
- Answer management's questions
- Close the communication gap between management and workplace learning

In the end, however, it is learning's responsibility to be sure their efforts are relevant to management and stakeholders. A learning solution is a means to an end, not an end itself.

Chapter 4: Business Data and Performance Metrics

Chapter 4 stresses the need for and importance of the business data produced by an organization and the data existing in the respective competitive environment. To fully align and integrate with an organization's strategy, learning professionals must develop learning solutions that adapt and respond quickly to rapidly changing markets and customer needs. The power and effectiveness of the BSC is the inter-relationships existing within its framework. You will discover that forming strategic internal partnerships helps you to achieve the organization's strategic aspirations; you become the learning and performance "department" for each business unit by leveraging its subject-matter knowledge and experiences and aligning them with your learning expertise.

This is a golden opportunity for workplace learning and performance. This is also the "secret" of "smart" organizations—getting people to learn how to recognize relevant business data and using it to your advantage.

In this chapter you will learn about:

- The growing need for business data in an increasingly competitive business environment
- Leveraging business data and metrics to develop targeted learning interventions
- The difference between financial and non-financial performance measures
- The limitations to using non-financial performance measures
- Specific factors that drive performance in an organization

Workplace learning and performance must interpret the business data available and allow employees to use it to their advantage. This will lead to more aligned learning interventions and holistic learning strategies.

Chapter 5: Business Processes and Performance Measures

In Chapter 5 we examine the business processes of organizations in more detail. In the past, learning solutions were developed only after the business processes were established and finalized. With increasing competition and customer demands, an organization must become more agile and flexible. Rather than simply being reactive and waiting for a market response, the organization has to make adjustments as early as possible in the process.

Learning professionals are now literally thrown into the mix to facilitate the changes that take place. Whether it is a minor change in a production procedure or a full-scale innovative prototype development initiative, learning must be comfortable with every segment of the organization's business processes. In this chapter you will discover how an organization creates value for its customers and its own long-term growth from its internal processes and how workplace learning and performance can deliver tangible value.

By the end of this chapter your will learn about:

- The organizational value chain: providing real value
- The value chain's proposition to the customer
- Building the learning and performance value chain

Workplace learning must align with the organization's business processes. Workplace learning professionals must develop relevant learning opportunities that connect directly to the business and contribute to achieving the organization's strategic objectives.

Chapter 6: Workplace Learning in Relation to Financial Performance

The reality is that business performance is and will always be measured against financial results. All businesses, profit or non-profit, have to account for their financial well-being and how well they manage their financial resources. Opportunities exist for learning professionals to find new ways to help the organization gain these benefits. Learning professionals can align their learning initiatives with results management wants. This will increase their credibility with business leaders and stakeholders of the organization.

Don't be intimidated by the subject of this chapter. Financial results and performance is a business reality and something learning professionals must address if they want to be included in management discussions. This chapter provides you with an opportunity to gain a fundamental understanding of this process. In this chapter you will learn:

- How management differentiates between investments and expense
- The value of an organization's financial statements
- How to tie financial statements to management objectives

Including a financial perspective solves more than half of your battle in gaining management support for learning solutions. Because it contains a financial component, the balanced scorecard framework links your efforts to expected financial performance.

Chapter 7: Developing the Learning and Growth Perspective

The balanced scorecard is a unique strategic tool that encompasses both the tangible and intangible factors of executing an organization's strategy. But to paraphrase Dr. Kaplan, learning and growth is the enabler of the other three perspectives of the balanced scorecard without which none of the perspectives can flourish.

Business leaders are quickly realizing that their competitive advantage comes not from frivolous initiatives or new product introduction but in the knowledge of their people. The leading organizations of our time have learned to harness and leverage their intellectual capacity to their advantage, delivering significant gains for the stakeholders. But how do they do this? What is their secret?

In the previous chapters we addressed many of the elements that compose the balanced scorecard and their relationships to the organization's strategy. In Chapter 7, we focus solely on the learning and growth perspectives of the balanced scorecard to help you to build performance measures that completely align with the scorecard's other perspectives.

In this chapter you will learn about:

- Why learning and growth are relevant in the balanced scorecard
- The difference between traditional performance thinking and performance in the balanced scorecard
- How management perceives workplace learning
- Developing the performance metrics for the learning and growth perspective
- Applying the learning and growth performance metrics

Chapter 7 provides the foundation for both Chapter 8, An Application of the Learning and Growth Perspective, and Chapter 9, an actual case we ask you to complete to build your abilities in this critical step.

Chapter 8: An Application of the Learning and Growth Perspective

In this chapter we present to you a sample application and the steps to complete in developing the learning and growth perspective of the scorecard. We provide a systematic process and some tools to demonstrate that completing the learning and growth perspective does not need to be complex or onerous. By completing this chapter you will be able to:

- Follow the basic principles for developing the learning and growth perspective
- Learn the steps for learning strategy execution
- Learn some methods to demonstrate results for learning
- Facilitate the development of learning and growth metrics

This chapter is focused on learning how to develop the learning and growth perspective utilizing a sample company's strategy map and balanced scorecard.

Chapter 9: The Case of Sky Air Limited

At this point you have learned what is required to properly complete the learning and growth perspective (Chapter 7) and have experienced an actual example of an application (Chapter 8). In Chapter 9 we work together to complete an actual application. You are introduced to Sky Air Limited, which recently shifted its corporate strategy and completed a balanced scorecard. Management, however, did not complete the learning and growth perspective of the scorecard, a critical issue. Management provides you, the learning director, with its strategy map and balanced scorecard. Equipped with this information, you are mandated to complete the perspective, align your proposed performance metrics with the performance requirements of the other perspectives, and help management meet its strategic objectives.

As you complete each step, we provide you with our proposed solution. By the end of the chapter you will have completed the learning and growth perspective of Sky Air's balanced scorecard by following five key principles and applying a six-step process.

Chapter 10: The Learning Department's Balanced Scorecard

In Chapter 2 we explained that a balanced scorecard is only the starting point to translating the strategy within the organization into results. The utility of the scorecard is in how it can disseminate the performance measures of the strategic objectives to all organizational levels. Its power is in its ability to ensure that every employee recognizes how his or her role connects to the mission and how his or her performance is interrelated to other areas of the organization. This is what Kaplan and Norton term as "cascading" the scorecard.

The learning balanced scorecard links to the corporate level scorecard. The learning department perspectives are completed as if you are completing a corporate scorecard, except that departmental scorecard performance metrics must align and support the superseding and lateral scorecards.

In Chapter 10, we explain the process of developing a balanced scorecard for the learning department of your organization. Working through each of the four perspectives, we emphasize the uniqueness of the learning scorecard, compared with any other departmental scorecard. In this chapter you will learn:

- The purpose of the learning balanced scorecard
- The types of questions to ask management when completing the learning scorecard
- How the learning department's scorecard is different from other departmental scorecards
- To develop a learning scorecard through a rapid development process

By using a thorough analysis, learning professionals will discover that the learning scorecard is often one of the key underpinnings of the corporate-level scorecard and increasingly a significant influence on the success of organizational strategy.

Chapter 11: Factors Affecting Strategy, Balanced Scorecard, and Workplace Learning

The factors that affect strategy, the balanced scorecard, and workplace learning are varied and often unpredictable. Some variables affect the performance of these factors. Compensating for these variables may be possible, although it is not possible to assess their impact within the strategic or balanced scorecard framework.

We will not attempt to predict what business variables will impact an organization's strategy, nor will we predict what challenges or opportunities will come up, except to say that change will most likely be required. The following areas are significant factors affecting an organization's strategy and its workplace environment:

- The new variables: technology, workers, and the world
- Expectation of return on workplace investments

- Managing learning for a generational workforce
- Developing the entrepreneurial employee
- Developing specialists, not generalists
- Increasing trend for customer intimacy
- Managing knowledge for maximum benefit

SOME ADVICE WHEN READING THIS BOOK

For some, balanced scorecards may be a new topic, especially those not directly involved with the business operations of their organizations. Even for those actively involved in business management and strategic planning, the topic of workplace learning and managing intellectual capital may be unfamiliar. Your level of experience is not relevant when reading this book. Whether you are a senior business leader, new to the management role, a novice learning professional, or one with years of experience, reading this book is essential for your professional development. The objective of this book is to bring the two sides, business leaders and those responsible for employee development, closer together. To do so, we recommend the following:

Take a Holistic Approach

This book covers some very critical and deep topics, including strategy, business, learning, and the balanced scorecard. Reading this book should only be one part for your journey when developing each of these areas. It is your responsibility to learn as much as possible about the "business side" of learning. This includes the processes, business concerns, and strategy concepts not necessarily directly associated with learning. Learning professionals have a significant responsibility to continuous professional development, not just in learning topics but in all other topics that affect your organization. For those readers who are business professionals and leaders, everyone recognizes that you must be aware of and a part of a business "system" and process. However, to be an effective leader you must possess a proper understanding of the components of the system. This means that you should value all functions, including the learning function, and discover how you can integrate their solutions into the fabric of the organization's strategy.

The learning department is the key to unlocking the potential that exists within the minds of your people and to giving you that elusive sustainable competitive advantage you desperately seek. The balanced scorecard is pushing you to make it happen.

Read Related Material on the Topic

This book is far from the last word on any of the topics addressed. We are only providing you with the basics to help you get started in building a learning organization. We strongly recommend that you read further on each of these topics. The topic of strategy alone is continually debated among scholars, business leaders, and thought leaders. The balanced scorecard is one of a variety of types of scorecarding and strategic tools available. We provide a list of resources and suggested readings at the end of this book.

Take Some Risks

Those who only read are cheating themselves and only gaining part of the experience. Those who actually do something with what they read learn. This book is more than a reference or a must-read about an upcoming trend; we believe it is an experiential tool. We tried to balance theoretical concepts, real-life experiences, case applications, and tools to provide you with enough information to actually implement what we talk about. Apply what is presented and experience it within your environment. It takes trial and error to find what actually works for you and practice to make yourself comfortable in this new strategically aligned world. Take some risks and actually apply what you learn from reading this book.

Experiment with the Skills and Tools

Build your own learning "laboratory" and experiment with the tools and techniques presented in each chapter. Develop scenarios as to what would occur if you actually were to develop solutions within the scorecard. Just as a computer simulation tests an engineering concept, you can work through a simulation by creating various scenarios and evaluating what is best for your organization.

Face Your Fears

It is human nature to avoid what we are unfamiliar with or fear. If you feel confused and fearful after completing this book, accept it as a natural part of your learning process. There is a saying that you should do one thing every day that scares you. If this topic frightens you, then the only way to overcome it is to face it head on. Issue yourself a personal challenge and summon those around you to work through and apply what is presented in this book. Learning is about facing the unknown, so it is time to face this unknown. You are not alone. We are providing a web-based resource to support your efforts and a community where you can share your experiences and best practices with others. In all of our workshops, we ask participants for a commitment to using the new knowledge and skills they gain. We hold all the participants accountable and expect results. We expect the same level of commitment from you. Accept our challenge and be part of your organization's improved performance. As it is often stated, nothing is ever gained by not trying, so it is time for you to try it.

We wish you much success in your journey to being part of a fully aligned and strategically focused organization. Make workplace learning a strategic component for your organization.

improved performance and because workplace learning professionals become more valuable to an organization in flux.

This chapter is the first step in understanding the process. In this chapter on strategy you will read about…

- The importance of strategy: what it is
- Types of strategy
- Corporate strategy versus business strategy
- Factors affecting strategy
- What management wants to know
- Workplace learning and its role in strategy development
- Fostering a learning culture to move beyond ROI
- Moving beyond ROI and toward strategy
- Making learning relevant to management.

THE IMPORTANCE OF STRATEGY: WHAT IT IS

One of the most respected strategists and economists of our time, Michael Porter, in his article "What Is Strategy?" (Porter, 1996, p. 3) stated, "A company can outperform rivals only if it can establish a difference it can preserve." He continues, "The essence of strategy is choosing to perform activities differently than rivals do." This can be seen as the definition of strategy.

No longer can organizations, especially private-sector companies, afford to compete in overcrowded markets. A company's existence is due to its unique position in the market—a result of a mix of products and services that differ from what others currently offer. While holding a unique position in the market is adequate for an initial start-up, a more formal direction is required as a company matures and evolves. The company must focus on how it intends to develop and grow.

In a study of 108 new business ventures, 86 percent were line extensions—incremental improvements to existing offerings—and only 14 percent focused on creating new markets (Blue Ocean Strategy). Even though the companies with improved product lines accounted for 62 percent of the revenues, they only delivered 39 percent of the total profits. By contrast, the companies that created a new market space accounted for more than 61 percent of total profits. (Kim & Mauborgne, 2004, p. 4)

Why is this the case? It is safe to reason that those organizations that sought out a simple method to building the business were not truly building sustainable performance but seeking a way to temporarily sustain market leadership. This is a strategy relegated to organizations that live in a past glory. In the book *Blue Ocean Strategy* (Kim & Mauborgne, 2004), the origin of strategy is described clearly. The authors explain that "Corporate strategy is heavily influenced by its roots in military strategy. The very language of strategy is deeply imbued with military references— chief executive 'officers' in 'headquarters,' 'troops' on the 'front lines.' Described in this way, strategy is about true head-on competition. It is about confronting an opponent and driving him off the battlefield of limited territory."

Organizations that intend to build a sustainable market presence develop a "leading performance" strategy. Management also learns early that attaining their strategic objectives requires a new set of assets—specifically intellectual and knowledge-based assets. Today's intellectual assets—competencies, processes, and people—are the primary drivers of long-term success. Knowledge and how it is leveraged to improve performance is the weapon of choice for every organization. It underpins an organization's worth, fuels profitable growth, and drives stakeholder value (Tanaszi & Duffy, 2000).

One of the earliest references of strategy was recorded in the *Art of War* written in the 6th century BC by military strategist Sun Tzu. This book is required reading for many military schools and also many business and economic schools. The book details warfare tactics that can also be applied in business today. In order to successfully bring down the competition, both for-profit and not-for-profit organizations must have a strategy. Strategy is a long-term plan to achieve a desired goal and is the foundation of all actions that an organization will take. It describes the organization's vision and short-term objectives.

New technologies, trends, and challenges often change some aspect of the business and force management to revise their strategy. The world is evolving at an increasingly rapid pace, and the way we do business is changing as well. Because the market is moving faster than ever, it is even more important for managers to lay down a plan, a road map, as some will call it.

A strategy is a set of values that the company wants to pursue. It has to be distinctive, different from competitors. With a proper strategy set down, managers as well as employees have a definition of the main value that the organization is pursuing. When this set of values is properly communicated and mutually understood, it then becomes the basis for making decisions and taking action.

TYPES OF STRATEGY

Keep one ear open in almost any business environment and the term "strategy" is sure to come up. Often there is no proper or comprehensive understanding of the term and a failure to define it on the speaker's part. Nor do those hearing it verify how it is being used and whether it's in the appropriate context. As a result, conversations about strategy can become confusing and misleading.

There are at least three basic forms of strategy in the business world and it is important that you have a clear understanding of each. It is important to distinguish among the three forms: (1) strategy, (2) corporate strategy, and (3) business strategy (Figure 1.1).

The many definitions of strategy found in management literature fall into one of four categories: plan, pattern, position, and perspective. According to these definitions, strategy is

1. A *plan*, a "how," a means of getting from here to there.

2. A *pattern* in actions over time; for example, a company that regularly markets very expensive products is using a "high end" strategy.

Figure 1.1. The Three Basic Forms of Strategy

3. A *position*, that is, it reflects decisions to offer particular products or services in particular markets.

4. A *perspective*, that is, a vision and direction, a view of what the company or organization is to become.

As a practical matter, strategy evolves over time as intentions accommodate reality. Thus, one starts with a given perspective, concludes that it calls for a certain position, and then sets about achieving it by way of a carefully crafted plan. Over time, things change. A pattern of decisions and actions marks movement from starting point to goal. This pattern of decisions and actions is called "realized" or "emergent" strategy.

Strategy, in the broadest terms, refers to how a given objective will be achieved. Consequently, strategy is concerned with the relationships between ends and means, that is, between the results we seek and the resources at our disposal. Strategy and tactics are both concerned with formulating and then carrying out courses of action intended to attain particular objectives. For the most part, strategy is concerned with deploying the resources at your disposal, whereas tactics are concerned with employing them. Together, strategy and tactics bridge the gap between ends and means.

Strategy and tactics are often confused with each other by even the most experienced managers. Although tactics are the instruments to achieving strategy, it is next to impossible to say something about one without also saying something about the other. Table 1.1 summarizes some of the more important differences noted about strategy and tactics.

Table 1.1. The Differences Between Strategy and Tactics

Aspects	Strategy	Tactics
Scale of the Objective	Grand	Limited
Scope of the Action	Broad and General	Narrowly Focused
Guidance Provided	General and Ongoing	Specific and Situational
Degree of Flexibility	Adaptable, but not hastily changed	Fluid, quick to adjust and adapt in minor or major ways
Timing in Relation to Action	Before Action	During Action
Focus of Resource Utilization	Deployment	Employment

Both of these factors, changing economic environments and the increasing need for knowledge, provide learning and performance with opportunities as well as new challenges. The opportunity is to take on a more prominent role in the development and execution of an organization's strategy. The challenge, however, is to understand how learning interventions link to business dynamics and strategic context. Learning professionals must begin with the five forces of the marketplace on their journey to strategic integration. Through Porter's five forces model, opportunities exist for internal learning groups to enable knowledge encapsulation and transfer to ensure results are delivered when and as they are needed.

FACTORS AFFECTING STRATEGY

Other writers on the subject of strategy point to several factors that can serve as the basis for formulating corporate and competitive strategy. These factors include:

- Products/services offered
- Customers/users served
- Market types and needs
- Production capacity/capability
- Technology
- Sales/marketing methods
- Distribution methods
- Natural resources
- Size/growth goals
- Return/profit goals.

This is not an exhaustive list of factors, but they are the key elements in determining strategy performance. These factors are also the primary concerns of managers in their daily business decisions, as well as elements of the framework of the balanced scorecard. Performance measurement and management occur in a variety of ways, but for management it is about improving financial performance.

To further accentuate the importance of strategy, specific "value disciplines" are sought by an organization to further differentiate it from its competitors and to

Table 1.2. The Three Basic "Value Disciplines"

Operational Excellence	Strategy is predicated on the production and delivery of products and services. The objective is to lead the industry in terms of price and convenience.
Customer Intimacy	Strategy is predicated on tailoring and shaping products and services to fit an increasingly fine definition of the customer. The objective is long-term customer loyalty and long-term customer profitability.
Product Leadership	Strategy is predicated on producing a continuous stream of state-of-the-art products and services. The objective is the quick commercialization of new ideas.

develop true business strategy uniqueness. The three basic "value disciplines" utilized in forming business strategy are operational excellence, customer intimacy, and product leadership (Treacy & Wiersema, 1993), as shown in Table 1.2.

Similar to Porter's five forces, the value disciplines are part of the overall subtleties of effective strategy formulation. Which value discipline an organization decides to pursue will greatly influence the direction of any learning strategy. The strategic context of the organization drives how it will function and dictates the elements of business strategy and operational elements. Learning is no exception. Learning professionals must work in the strategic planning framework.

Understanding the Questions

Regardless of how an organization defines strategy, or the variety of factors affecting the choice of corporate or business strategy, managers must be able to ask and answer fundamental questions. The higher the manager's rank, the more influence he or she will have on the broader context of the strategy. Managers who are closer to the business will have greater influence related to the overall question asked. The learning professional's relationship to the questions will vary, but should be focused on the means to help managers and the business reach the "ends." Some examples of these questions are shown in Table 1.3.

Strategy, essentially, is about where an organization aspires to be. Strategy is not only the destination but, more importantly, the map of how to achieve these objectives. Corporate strategy is concerned with choices and commitments

Table 1.3. Sample of Fundamental Questions

Related to Mission and Vision	Who are we?
	What do we do?
	Why are we here?
	What kind of company are we?
	What kind of company do we want to become?
	What kind of company must we become?
Related to Strategy in General	What is our objective? What are the ends we seek?
	What is our current strategy, implicit or explicit?
	What courses of action might lead to the ends we seek?
	What are the means at our disposal?
	How are our actions restrained and constrained by the means at our disposal?
	What risks are involved and which ones are serious enough that we should plan for them?
Related to Corporate Strategy	What is the current strategy, implicit or explicit?
	What assumptions have to hold for the current strategy to be viable?
	What is happening in the larger, social, political, technical, and financial environments?
	What are our growth, size, and profitability goals?
	In which markets will we compete?
	In which businesses?
	In which geographic areas?
Related to Business Strategy	What is the current strategy, implicit or explicit?
	What assumptions have to hold for the current strategy to be viable?
	What is happening in the industry, with our competitors, and in general?
	What are our growth, size, and profitability goals?
	What products and services will we offer?
	To what customers or users?
	How will the selling/buying decisions be made?
	How will we distribute our products and services?
	What technologies will we employ?
	What capabilities and capacities will we require?
	Which ones are core?
	What will we make, what will we buy, and what will we acquire through alliance?
	What are our options?
	On what basis will we compete?

Figure 1.2. Focal Points of Strategy

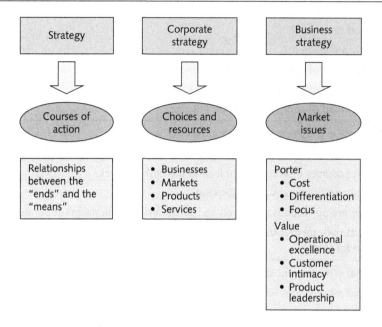

regarding markets, business, and the very nature of the company itself, where business strategy is concerned with the business and market factors itself as illustrated in Figure 1.2.

Every organization must have a strategy that encompasses some key elements. Learning professionals can ensure they are adequately prepared to participate in strategic conversations by recognizing and understanding the primary elements of strategy. A summary of these points is found in Figure 1.3.

In Exhibit 1.1 you will clearly see the relationship of the various forms of strategy beginning with the overall strategic vision subsequently divided first into the corporate level strategy and then into business strategy tactics to accomplish the overall strategy.

Learning and Performance Relationship to Strategy

We highly recommend that learning professionals learn as much as they can about strategy, as this is now at the fundamental core of every organization's survival. But as you can see, what we presented opens up many opportunities for WLP to

Figure 1.3. Primary Points of Strategy

What You Need to Know

Strategy is described as:

- **How an organization intends to create sustained value for its shareholders, customers, and citizens.**
  - Organizations must leverage intangible assets to create value.
  - The BSC relies on an understanding of the linkages between strategic objectives and the metrics.
- **Strategy is not a stand-alone management process.**
  - It is one step in a logical continuum moving an organization from mission statement to the work of the employees.
  - The mission statement and vision are the starting points, defining why the organization exists and where it's going.
- **Strategy is developed and evolved over time.**
  - To help meet changing conditions posed by external environment and internal capabilities.

Every strategy includes an:

- **Organizational mission statement**
  - Is a concise, internally focused statement for the organization's existence.
  - Specifies which activities to focus on and the values that guide employee activities.
- **Organizational vision**
  - Is a concise statement defining mid- to long-term goals.
  - Is focused on the external factors and is market-oriented.
  - Describes how the organization wants to be seen in the market.

—

- As objective as T&D tries to make ROI evaluations, there is still a degree of subjectivity and bias, reducing the credibility and impact of the training initiative;

- There is too much focus on "accomplishing" training initiatives successfully, rather than on aligning expected results with organizational needs and strategic objectives; and

- Return on investment is a financial measure, a lagging indicator demonstrating past performance. What is required are leading indicative performance measures.

Exhibit 1.1. ARE YOU ABLE TO DEFINE YOUR ORGANIZATION'S STRATEGY?

After reading the previous definition of strategy, answer the following questions to see if you are able to recognize your organization's strategic context and environment.

1. In your own words, elaborate your organization's strategy.

   _____

   _____

2. What is the key success factors defined within your organization's strategy? (Key success factors are the specific aspects that will ensure the organization meets its strategic goals and are possibly differentiating competitive factors.)

   _____

   _____

3. Clearly state your organization's mission and vision as stated by management. If there isn't any then state what is the implicit mission and vision.
   Mission:

   _____

   _____

4. Vision:

   _____

   _____

◆　◆　◆

Many senior directors and managers are finding workplace learning professionals overly concerned and preoccupied with evaluating training delivery outcomes, rather than with measuring the effectiveness, or impact, it has on the organization. WLP's focus is to demonstrate some type of proof of its success. This is not to say that return on investment is not a relevant factor in measuring significant training investments, but financial payback alone, specifically ROI, is not enough to gain management support.

For any type of training to be considered successful, it must have some type of impact on the business delivering specific business results (Kirkpatrick Level 4). (For an explanation of Kirkpatrick's model, refer to Kirkpatrick's Levels of Evaluation in the book *Building Business Acumen for Trainers: Skills to Empower the Learning Function*. Refer to Chapter 8. In recent years, the way to demonstrate Level 4 return has been to evaluate in financial terms (Phillips' Level 5), believing that this will instill support for workplace learning. These criteria have not necessarily helped to build a case for workplace learning.

It is time for workplace learning and performance to move beyond return on investment and financial performance measures and learn how to integrate measurement and evaluation techniques that connect with organizational and strategic objectives. This is now possible with the balanced scorecard.

WHAT MANAGEMENT WANTS TO KNOW

In the current business reality, developing a strong business case and aligning with strategy are more important. Financial results are becoming irrelevant in areas related to intangible, human issues as well as for longer-term strategic outlooks. C-level mangers require performance indicators that look toward the future (strategic) and not the past (reactive). Moving beyond simply delivering an ROI figure and, instead, connecting to qualitative business indicators relevant to decision-makers should be your ultimate objective.

WLP professionals must not focus on indicators captured solely at the course level. Participant reaction (Level 1) and participant learning (Level 2), as well as other metrics such as average participant cost, are relevant; however, training success begins when the individuals return to their jobs and actually apply what they learned (Level 3, behavior). Once we identify how the participants are applying the new knowledge, we can ascertain the impact the training has on the business.

How can you define and track these indicators? Through specific metrics. This is quite simple, as many of the indicators already exist. Tracking them over a period of time will help you to determine what areas are being applied and where improvement is required. Examples of metrics that help you to connect with management needs include the following:

- Job productivity (items in the job that were meant to improve after training)
- Skill requirements measured against initial skills possessed
- Efficiency rates (time or methods of completing a task)
- Compliancy levels
- Proficiency standards measured against eligibility and initial base knowledge
- Learning skills application measures
- Demand on support needs such as a reduction of calls to the help desk
- Number of employees trained in a specific skill set over time
- Training costs per employee
- Enrollment rates and attendance rates
- Employee retention rates
- Employee motivation and team cohesion

This is far from an exhaustive list. These types of indicators allow managers at all levels to measure training results and witness behavioral change, further supporting the need for continuous learning. Many of the metrics listed above certainly exist in your organization and some, such as productivity, may already be used by managers to measure performance. Use Exhibit 1.2 to define your organization's expectations.

WORKPLACE LEARNING AND ITS ROLE IN STRATEGY DEVELOPMENT

How do we define workplace learning and performance? One accepted definition is "the integrated use of learning and other interventions for the purpose of improving human performance and addressing individual and organizational needs.

Exhibit 1.2. DEFINING YOUR ORGANIZATION'S EXPECTATIONS

Are you/Is everyone in the organization connected to the strategy?

Yes _____ No _____

How/Why Not?

_____

_____

What are the long-term objectives (three to five years) of the organization?

1. _____

2. _____

3. _____

What are the short-term objectives (six to twenty-four months) of the organization?

1. _____

2. _____

3. _____

What are the priorities of the organization (C-level thinking)?

1. _____

2. _____

3. _____

4. _____

5. _____

◆ ◆ ◆

It uses a systematic process of analyzing and responding to individual, group, and organizational performance issues. It creates positive, progressive change within organizations by balancing humanistic and ethical considerations" (Rothwell, Sanders, & Soper, 1999, p. 121).

This definition states the significance of how learning and performance impact the current workplace. Learning is now at the forefront of building organizational strategies, which was not true previously. Profit or non-profit, public or private, small or large, organizations of all types are recognizing the contribution workplace learning and performance has on helping them to achieve specific objectives. Building a sustainable learning environment is no longer based on the "insert training here" mentality. Organizations must clearly define what it means to be a learning organization and how that connects to business results.

Through a well-developed workplace learning and performance strategy, every organization can become a learning organization. Keep in mind that the terms "workplace learning and performance" and "learning organization" have evolved considerably since their entry into our lexicon several years ago. Workplace learning and performance, commonly referred to as WLP and quickly becoming known as talent management (TM), is gaining significant attention from those responsible for the operations and growth of organizations.

Thanks to those actively involved in the evaluation of learning, the learning community and its professionals have been actively striving to connect learning to what we often refer to as Kirkpatrick's Level 3—the participants' change in behavior or, more appropriately, the application to their responsibilities. In recent times, WLP is regarded as an opportunity to gain and sustain a competitive advantage. WLP is being pushed to align more strategically, in essence, striving to reach Kirkpatrick's Level 4, having an impact on the business.

Although anecdotal, we are increasingly hearing about organizations becoming more innovative and creative. Where does this stem from? It comes from knowing what your people already know, what they need to know, and leveraging their skills, knowledge, and competencies for the future. Still not convinced? Look at the current market and industry leaders. They are names we are all very familiar with, including General Electric, Apple, Microsoft, Wal-Mart, Toyota, and Google, to name a few. What do they have in common? They know what their people know, clearly know where they want to go, and are able to reconcile both to make things happen. What are the outcomes? Great and innovative products and services! These results came from effectively capitalizing on the knowledge their people possess. Let's face it. In the end, every organization is about its people, not about who has the most assets.

Another reason for the increasing importance of WLP is the advent of the "information age." The industrial age of the 20th century has passed; the 21st century is truly about knowledge and information sharing. It has become so important to our economies that information is being valued as much as any monetary measures of the past. Some claim that knowledge and information are even more valuable than any rare natural resource.

What does this mean for professionals in WLP? Learning and talent management professionals must become more accountable for the solutions they develop and how those solutions connect knowledge and information to organizational performance and strategic objectives. They are the new superintendents of the most valuable resource organizations have at their disposal—intellectual assets. We can probably say that WLP's role is secure for the immediate future.

FOSTERING A LEARNING CULTURE TO MOVE BEYOND ROI

Organizational culture is the foundation for a successful and strategically aligned learning environment. Culture, however, is not under the control of WLP professionals. Simply, organizational culture is comprised of the behaviors, attitudes, and processes of the organization that may influence organizational strategy. Behavior and attitudes are people-related, and organizational process is how things are conducted. To build a learning-centered culture and foster positive behaviors and attitudes, C-level managers must demonstrate their commitment to learning initiatives. Senior management support will facilitate employee buy-in.

The third component of culture, internal processes, is often considered a "sacred cow." The saying "If it ain't broke, don't fix it" applies here. People will protect how they do their jobs and tasks for fear of losing control. To overcome these attitudes, you must demonstrate the benefits of new ways of doing things. The challenge for WLP professionals is to support the integration of learning as a business process.

Another way to move beyond measuring training ROI is to integrate a continuous monitoring process post-training. Through sampling smaller groups over time, training departments can quickly gain valuable insights on the effects of their learning initiatives. This may sound time-consuming and involved, but it can be as simple as conducting surveys and forming focus groups. Level 3 issues (application) can be measured through productivity and efficiency metrics, and Level 4 (business results) can be shown through business-related metrics (customer satisfaction, goal attainment, and so forth). Success comes only if you build this capacity into your training organization, reduce your dependence on ROI, and allow yourself to make Levels 3 and 4 as natural a part of your evaluation regimen as gathering smile sheets.

MOVING BEYOND ROI AND TOWARD STRATEGY

Management is becoming more focused on clearly communicating and connecting, in tangible and realistic terms, strategic objectives to all levels within the organization, demonstrating to employees how they contribute to attaining these objectives. WLP professionals have a critical role in helping stakeholders attain strategic expectations by linking learning solutions to organizational strategy.

WLP professionals must help management connect employees to the organizational strategy in an effective manner. One strategic performance tool they can use is the balanced scorecard (BSC) to translate the strategic plan and mission of an organization into tangible non-financial and financial performance measures.

Before we jump into defining the balanced scorecard and elaborating further on how learning fits into it, we'll first explain the strategic framework and how it links through the organization. Figure 1.4 illustrates the relationship clearly.

At the top of the pyramid in Figure 1.4 is the organizational mission. As mentioned earlier, the mission is the strategic direction the organization is pursuing. Everything is driven from the mission statement. From the mission, an organization can define its core values and how employees should conduct themselves. Culture and decision-making processes are part of the value component. (Think back on some of the recent major corporate scandals. The mission was implicit: to unethically make investors and key shareholders wealthy at the expense of the company, employees, and its customers. This fostered a decision-making capacity and an internal culture that led to questionable, unethical, and at times illegal considerations.) Once the mission and values are defined, the organization can develop its vision of what it wants to become.

The strategy map and the balanced scorecard can be described as two sides of the same coin. The strategy map is developed first in order to provide the structure to create the elements of the balanced scorecard. The primary purpose of the strategy map is to illustrate the linkages and connections among the primary business drivers. It provides a clear picture of how a corporate strategy can be translated into tangible business objectives. Anyone looking at a strategy map should be able to discern the overall mission of the company immediately—this is its simplicity.

The balanced scorecard is an extension of a strategy map. While the strategy map defines the business objectives within the four perspectives of the BSC framework, the BSC itself sets up the management process to achieve the objectives that lead to

Figure 1.4. How the Strategic Framework Links to the Organization

achieving the mission. Broken down into tangible and measurable metrics, the BSC provides manager and employees with clear directives that lead to a successful strategy. These metrics are set forth in the next step—"targets and initiatives." The targets and initiatives, along with the objectives (directly from the strategy map) and measures, are integrated within the BSC but are the core to realizing the strategy. Targets provide a specific focus on what everyone in the organization needs to strive for, whereas initiative is what will actually be taken to reach the targets. Once the targets and initiatives are outlined, employees know exactly what they need to do (within their responsibilities) to achieve the business objectives. Personal objectives are the next step within the pyramid. The real strength of an organization's management is the capacity to align the employees' personal objectives, specifically career and skills development, with their growth in the organization. This leads us to the final step, an effective strategy.

Outcomes are related to the "owners" or "stakeholders" of each of the four perspectives of the BSC. You can begin to see the strategic relevance of learning and how many benefits are realized through increased employee satisfaction and retention. Chapter 2 contains more in-depth information on the strategy map and the BSC.

An organization functions best when its departments and divisions work toward a common goal. Within the BSC many of these parts (financial, internal processes, and customer) must have very tangible objectives, measures, and initiatives. One component of the BSC often left alone is "Learning and Growth." There is a lack of understanding between management and the employee development (training and HR) departments, resulting in poor communication.

In the past, training and HR were excluded because they were perceived as not contributing directly to the business's strategic objectives. In the current business context, learning is perceived as an integral part of achieving the organizational strategy, but there is still a significant communication gap between learning professionals and management. Thus, it is important that learning professionals communicate their efforts in terms management will relate to and understand.

MAKING LEARNING RELEVANT TO MANAGEMENT

Why is it important to speak in business and strategic terms and possess business acumen? Most managers use terms when communicating with colleagues and peers that are not always understood by workplace learning professionals. C-level executives do not necessarily share learning professionals' knowledge nor do executives have much passion about workplace learning. Because of this, they want to focus primarily on corporate and business strategy that leads to improved performance.

We need to speak a common language because we live in their world, the business world. This is why the term "performance" has crept into our learning vocabulary, because this is the term understood and accepted in the business environment.

Management often underestimates the impact of their intellectual assets, specifically people, and the value of learning. Their main concern is naturally on financial growth, future success, and end results (attaining strategic objectives). Management's focus on how to achieve the results is changing as they come to realize the importance of intellectual capital in an information-based economy. Early in his study of business and strategy, Peter Drucker recognized that innovations guided by creative people provide the best chance of long-term success, because every other activity can be duplicated by competitors.

What does this mean for organizations wanting to grow for the future? It means that learning is the foundation of success. What employees learn and how they apply new knowledge and skills is a core asset of any company. Management understands that, in order to prosper, employees must fully understand what they need to do, how they are to do it, and how what they do impacts the organization as a whole.

The most innovative and powerful organizations in the world recognize that their most valuable assets are not buildings or equipment but their employees. The knowledge employees possess is likely the single most valuable asset that any company can possess. Managers must endeavor to retain these employees and their knowledge.

In order for an organization to build upon this asset, workplace learning plays a crucial role. Workplace learning directly contributes to the success or failure of a company. It is critically important that learning connect their efforts to the organization's business strategy. WLP professionals need to start thinking "outside the course" to connect learning with business concerns and strategy objectives and to develop the relevant performance measures.

LAST THOUGHTS

Since the beginning of the industrial age, increasing competitive market forces required companies to begin thinking differently to maintain an advantage over their competitors. Although competition was limited, these new companies needed some way to differentiate themselves. They had to begin thinking in a focused and directed manner unique from their competitors. This was the early inception of organizational strategy, which eventually became the cornerstone of modern day organizations.

Up to this point, organizational strategy was not given much thought because the needs were met by few and specialized providers of products and services.

Customers had limited choices of what they could obtain. The rapid development of technology throughout the 20th century provided for increased production capacity, which led to consumers' access to abundant supply, giving them the power to select based on preferences.

Granted, for the better part of the 20th century, strategy gained attention solely from America's growing corporate sector. Eventually, strategic concepts plateaued in their importance as large U.S. multinationals dominated the world market with their products and services. But we know that real change only occurs when there is a challenge or threat to the status quo. This challenge to business began in the latter half of the 20th century with the dramatic advances in technology and the growing strength of other world markets, fueled and supported by the United States. The need and focus for every large company became developing effective long-term strategies or face a quick demise due to complacency.

The change has been dramatic. For the last ten to fifteen years, we have been experiencing a significant shift in our economic thinking. We refer to this new evolution as the "information age."

Why is this important for learning professionals? Ask yourself what happens when there is any type of change. There is a need to learn something new, specifically what the change will lead to. Also, at this time in our economic evolution, change is not a temporary or one-time event. Fortunately for WLP, change is constant, placing organizational learning at the top of corporate leaders' to-do list. The third and most significant reason for WLP to pay attention to these changes is their growing role in the strategy development and planning process. Because change is constant and knowledge and information are becoming more valuable than traditional hard assets, WLP professionals are becoming part of the process and are no longer an afterthought.

Understanding organizational strategy and how you can leverage it is the first step as you seek initiatives that will lead to achievement of your organization's goals. WLP can become credible in the eyes of their leadership by becoming more holistic in their approach and proposing new learning solutions. In our more than fifteen years in the learning and performance field, learning professionals from all organizational backgrounds have complained to us that they are not being heard or recognized by the leadership of their organizations. In the past, senior leadership has not truly realized the value and potential of developing employees' skills. Add to this the fact that senior leadership may lack understanding of the learning organization;

they see it primarily as training and development processes and programs. Although senior management's perception is changing, it will take time and we must support the effort. Always remember that we (WLP) live in *their* world and need to communicate in *their* language. It is our responsibility to work in their terms, which means developing our business acumen and looking at the organization as a whole.

Organizations are about people. The products and services they provide are to meet the needs of people. Organizational survival in these times is knowledge driven, although many organizations still fight the trend and stick to more traditional ways of doing things. That is okay. These companies will quickly realize their error or simply fade away. Look at the marketplace and you will see that the most successful companies of this century are the ones that understand the new reality and attempt to fully leverage and maximize the potential of their people.

This chapter gives an overview of the balanced scorecard. At the end of this chapter we recommend a few books for those of you who would like to learn more about the intricacies of the balanced scorecard or strategy map. This chapter covers the following:

- The evolution of the BSC
- History of the balanced scorecard
- The scope of the balanced scorecard
- The strategic framework
- Strategy maps
- Going deep: defining the BSC perspectives and metrics
- Cascading scorecards: delivering a strategic message to the masses
- Potential pitfalls of the balanced scorecard

THE EVOLUTION OF THE BSC

In recent years there has been an evolution in performance measurement systems. First, the use of non-financial measurements, combined with more traditional financial measures, has come to be used much more since the 1990s. Second, all levels of management are stressing the relationship between the strategic planning process and performance. These two points characterize what is usually called a strategic management system, and the balanced scorecard fits perfectly.

The balanced scorecard gained popularity in the past fifteen years through the innovative and progressive work of Dr. Robert Kaplan and Dr. David Norton. Through their research with the Harvard Business School and their work with KPMG in the early 1990s, Kaplan and Norton were determined to help organizations effectively translate their strategic plans and objectives into tactical and tangible results. They wanted to ensure that an organization's strategic message would not get lost as it was filtered down through the ranks and that those on the front lines would be able to connect to the strategy while performing their daily responsibilities. Now the balanced scorecard is not only accepted in many Fortune 1000 companies, but the concept was selected by the editors of *Harvard Business Review* as one of the most influential management ideas of the past seventy-five years. The term "balanced scorecard" is now an integral part of modern business lexicon and an essential educational component of just about every MBA and business program in Western education.

HISTORY OF THE BALANCED SCORECARD

Some authors and academics suggest that the Balanced Scorecard originated in France inspired by what the French call the "tableau de bord," which has been used in the field of management since the 1930s. In French, "tableau de bord" is translated as the "dashboard," and the manager is thus metaphorically compared to a pilot. According to this tradition, the tableau de bord is "a tool for the top management of the firm, allowing it a global and quick view of its operations and of the state of its environment" (Bourguignon, Malleret, & Nørreklit, 2001, p. 6). It was used by French companies to see how a business was doing in real time and thus allowed companies to react quickly to critical business issues. The tableau provides business data and information through key performance measures, which help managers to manage the company's performance.

Of course, the concept of developing a strategic management system that aligns with daily operational activities and performance has been around for much of the modern business age. Furthermore, many managers are not satisfied with using traditional management and financial measurements that reflect only past performance. The "lagging" measures are unable to guide managers on how they should manage for the future. Today's business leaders want more non-financial performance measures.

Specifically, Kaplan and Norton explained the BSC as a way to measure a company's activities in terms of its vision and strategies, to give managers a comprehensive view of the performance of the business. The new element in the BSC is the focus also on the human issues that drive outcomes, so that organizations focus on the future and act in their long-term best interests.

THE SCOPE OF THE BALANCED SCORECARD

The BSC is widely acknowledged to have moved beyond the original ideology. It has now become a strategic change management and performance management process. Let's first clearly understand what it is. Dr. Robert Kaplan and Dr. David Norton define it as follows:

> "The balanced scorecard retains traditional financial measures. But financial measures tell the story of past events, an adequate story for industrial age companies for which investments in long-term capabilities and customer relationships were not critical for success.

> "These financial measures are inadequate, however, for guiding and evaluating the journey that **information age** companies must make to create future value through investment in customers, suppliers, employees, processes, technology, and innovation." (Kaplan & Norton, 1996, p. 6)

The list below provides an overview of traditional management measures versus the balanced scorecard.

The Balanced Scorecard Versus Traditional Management Processes
- Traditional context of the management process:
  - Measures governed by a financial reporting process
  - Anchored to an accounting model based on tangible assets
  - Measures based on internal performance and short-term outlook
  - Performance witnessed through the balance sheet
  - Financial measures reflect passed performance
- Current and future needs:
  - Valuation of intangible and intellectual assets
  - Measures required to account for these assets
  - Holistic performance measures (internal/external/360)
  - Performance based on qualitative over quantitative
  - Less dependence on past; more focused on future performance
- The BSC:
  - Complements financial measures of past performance with measures of the drivers of future performance

- The objectives and measures of the BSC are derived from vision and strategy
- The objectives and measures view organizational performance from four perspectives

The Balanced Scorecard demonstrates all of the critical variables for operating an organization in one-page diagram. An overview of the balanced scorecard structure is reflected in Figure 2.1, illustrating its four primary perspectives and the performance metrics within each perspective.

The term "scorecard" has been around for some years, but the word "balance" is recent. In an organizational and business context, balance represents six areas critical to strategic development:

- Leading and lagging performance measures
- Financial and non-financial measures
- Internal and external concerns and environments
- Tangible and intangible "assets" and resources

Figure 2.1. Balanced Scorecard Template

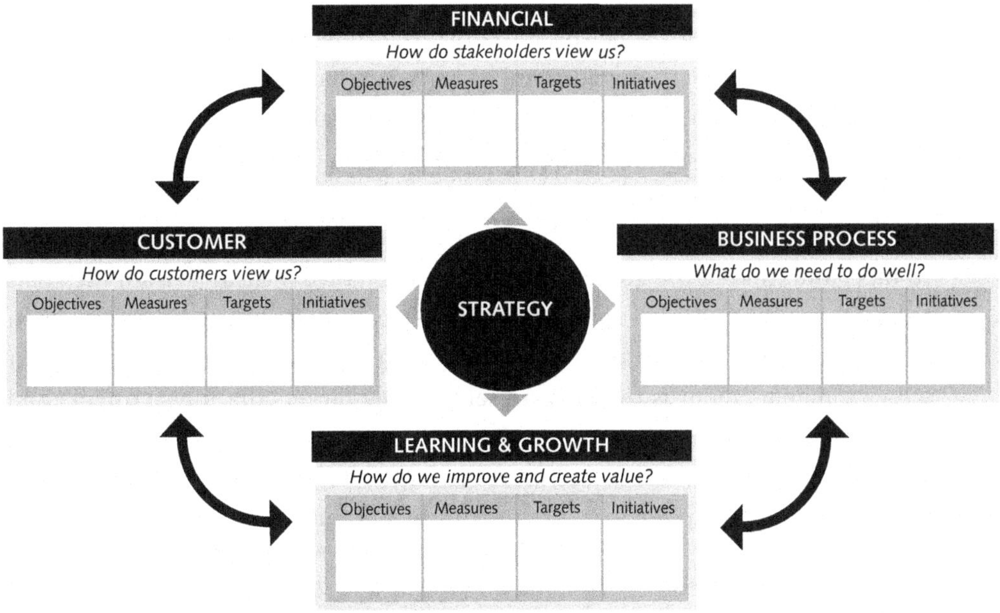

- Past and future performance
- Short- and long-term objectives

Senior and operational managers are now recognizing the significance of non-financial, or leading, performance measures.

According to surveys by the Institute of Management Accountants (IMA) (www.imanet.org), more than 50 percent of the large companies in the United States are using some form of balanced scorecard. This is reflective of the power and simplicity of the BSC.

The scorecard is similar to a dashboard in a car. You can glance down to obtain real-time information such as how much fuel remains, the speed you are traveling, the distance you've traveled, etc. The BSC provides similar information to all levels of the organization through performance measures connected to specific business areas. The scorecard communicates to managers in clearly defined terms how well the business is meeting its strategies and goals.

THE STRATEGIC FRAMEWORK

Every organization works within a strategic framework that allows it to more effectively manage it resources and meet its objectives. Figure 2.2 provides a visual overview of a strategic framework. An organization begins by stating its strategic purpose, by clarifying its mission, and by ensuring that everyone understands and is working toward the revenue objectives. It is essential that learning professionals be clear on what the mission is, because this will influence the direction that their learning interventions take.

Management then communicates their objectives by setting goals for people to meet and linking the goals to specific performance measures. Both the goals for each area and the rewards for good performance are starting points when developing a learning strategy. Once they have been communicated, the next step for management is to plan and set tangible targets that departments and employees have to strive to meet. Within these targets are milestones to make sure that everyone is on track to meet the targets. A learning professional's role is to find ways to help the various areas of the organization meet the milestones and targets.

Figure 2.2. The Strategic Framework

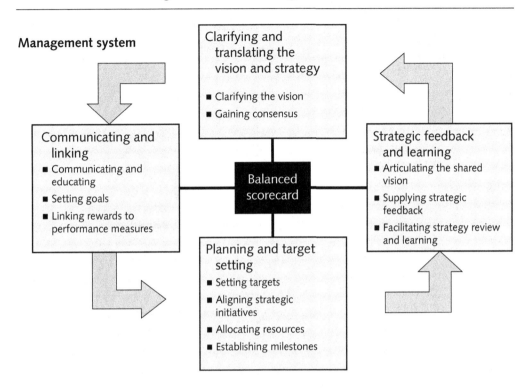

Fundamentally, the BSC is about performance measures. This is also what our role as learning professionals has become (hence, the word "performance" in workplace learning and performance). The BSC does incorporate traditional financial performance metrics. In the past this information would have been sufficient; however, the current reality dictates something more comprehensive.

The appeal of the BSC is its ability to include both traditional financial metrics and non-financial performance measures, hence the term "balanced." Managers can obtain information on metrics such as customer satisfaction, cost per new hire, percent of jobs that meet schedule, percent of errors in budget predictions, and so forth.

Figure 2.3. The Balanced Scorecard Perspective

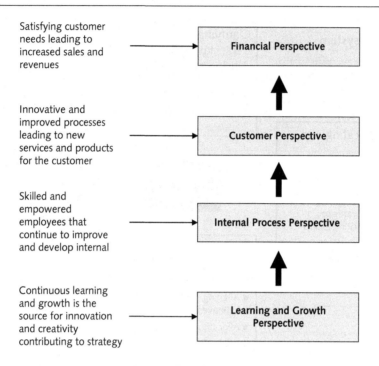

Satisfying customer needs leading to increased sales and revenues → **Financial Perspective**

Innovative and improved processes leading to new services and products for the customer → **Customer Perspective**

Skilled and empowered employees that continue to improve and develop internal → **Internal Process Perspective**

Continuous learning and growth is the source for innovation and creativity contributing to strategy → **Learning and Growth Perspective**

The BSC, as shown in Figure 2.1, is divided into four primary business and strategic areas upon which an organization must focus in order to gain a complete picture of how the enterprise is performing:

- The financial perspective
- The internal process perspective
- The customer perspective
- The learning and growth perspective

Within each of these perspectives are four performance metrics to achieve the perspective:

- Objectives
- Measures

- Targets
- Initiatives

We will discuss the metrics later in the chapter in more detail. First we need to understand the purpose of the four perspectives (see Figure 2.3):

- *Financial Perspective:* The question is: "How do we look to our stakeholders?" The objective of every organization is to deliver maximum value to stakeholders. For profit-oriented companies these are the shareholders and customers; for non-profits it many be government, taxpayers, or the community. Achieving financial results is a balance between investing for long-term growth and cutting costs for superior short-term results. In many mature companies, it is about obtaining maximum value from every dollar of investment.

- *Customer Perspective:* This is the specific value proposition an organization provides to its customers. The question is: "How do we look to our customers?" All organizations, profit and non-profit, have customers. To survive and grow, an organization must be able to deliver quality goods and/or services resulting in customer satisfaction. There are three major value propositions:
  - Lowest total cost of ownership (operational excellence)
  - Superior products or services (product leadership)
  - Offering complete customer solutions (customer intimacy)

- *Internal Business Processes:* These are the various internal processes by which products and services are prepared and delivered to customers. The question here is: "What must we excel at?" The reason for an organization's existence is what it produces or delivers. Identifying the key business processes at which an organization must excel is essential if it is to meet strategic goals and customer expectations. Internal processes can be clustered into four groups:
  - Operations management—producing and delivering
  - Customer management—relationship building
  - Innovation—next-generation products or services
  - Regulatory and social—complying with the law

- *Learning and Growth Perspective:* These are the organizational intangible assets (people, technology, culture) that enable more added value to be created in the

—

strategy map, the balanced scorecard can derive its other measure, targets, and initiatives. Combining a strategy map with a balanced scorecard allows constant monitoring of strategies, with the goal of closing any gaps between targeted performance and actual results. In short, when used in combination with a balanced scorecard, a strategy map helps organizations execute more effectively.

Strategy maps are built around the structure of the four BSC perspectives. The map ensures that the organization's objectives in each of these perspectives are consistent and internally aligned, which means that the organization is focused and performing at an optimum level. Strategy maps clarify all cause-and-effect relationships.

Conceptually, a strategy map links the high-level goals of the organization—its mission, values and vision—with meaningful and actionable steps each employee can take. This helps learning professionals identify specific learning opportunities to connect strategy to operational concerns. Strategy maps also provide balance between the various competing dynamics every organization faces:

- Whether to invest in intangible assets that will generate strong long-term revenue growth or focus on cutting costs more aggressively so as to boost short-term results

- How to differentiate yourself from competitors by clarifying your value strategy, which usually involves one of the three different approaches already mentioned:

  - Operational excellence—offering the lowest total cost to customers

  - Product leadership—always offering superior products

  - Customer intimacy—making available complete customer solutions

- Which internal processes to focus on and optimize and which to outsource

- How to balance the allocation of resources between the various internal processes in such a way that different benefits are delivered at various points of time

- How to align everything the organization does in such a way that the efforts of one part of the company don't have a negative impact on the results achieved elsewhere

- How to make good management decisions about investments in intangible assets as the drivers of organizational growth in the future

Figure 2.4. Sample Strategy Map

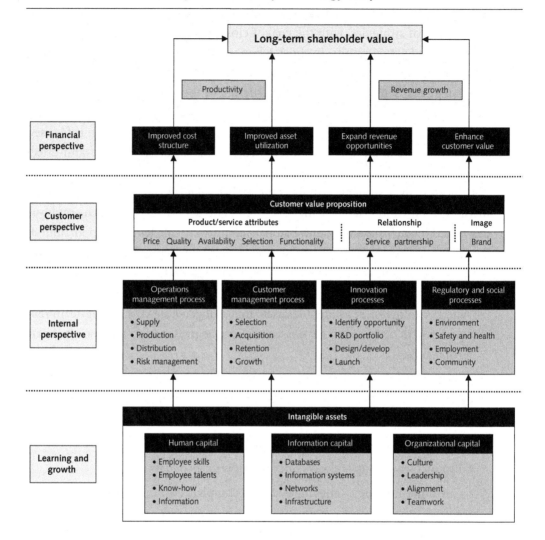

A strategy map is a diagram (see Figure 2.4) that describes how an organization creates value by connecting strategic objectives in explicit cause-and-effect relationships. Strategy maps can be produced at organizational, departmental, and even project levels. They provide an excellent snapshot of strategy and are supported by measurable objectives and initiatives.

Strategy maps enable organizations to:

- Clarify strategies and communicate them to employees
- Identify the key internal processes that drive success
- Align investments in people, technology, and organizational capital for maximum impact
- Expose gaps in strategies so that early corrective action can be taken

There are five main principles behind strategy maps:

- Strategy balances contradictory forces;
- Strategy is based on a differentiated customer value proposition;
- Value is created through internal business processes;
- Strategy consists of simultaneous complementary themes; and
- Strategic alignment determines the value of intangible assets.

How to Use a Strategy Map

Strategy maps are exceptionally useful, as they help to create a "dynamic" action plan rather than a passive view of what the company intends to do. Even though the strategy map and balanced scorecard are two components of the same process, the power is in looking at a strategy map and understanding what the organization's strategic objectives are. Organizations that use a strategy map and balanced scorecard together effectively in this way follow a six-step process:

1. *Establish and define what the current value gap is for shareholders.* This means setting the financial objectives, measures, and targets. Determine how much long-term revenue growth and how many short-term productivity improvements you will work toward achieving. These should be stretch targets that will challenge the organization.

2. *Reconcile the current value proposition.* Identify current target customer segments, clarify the value proposition in use, select measures, and reconcile customer objectives to financial growth goals. A new customer proposition may result that will generate the growth desired by the strategic objective.

3. *Establish a projected time line.* Knowing how quickly new internal processes are developed can help you to begin to generate the kinds of outcomes and results

—

map, balanced scorecard, and action plan is consistency. Instead of a fragmented approach, everyone uses the same overall strategy. The vision is consistent, along with the strategy for getting there. People can be inspired to action because they see that it is feasible to get to where management wants to go.

GOING DEEP: DEFINING THE BSC PERSPECTIVES AND METRICS

As mentioned earlier, the strategy map and balanced scorecard focus solely on four primary and critical perspectives: financial, customer, business process, and learning and growth. Managers ask themselves:

- How do we look to our stakeholders? (financial perspective)
- How do our customers see us? (customer perspective)
- What must we excel at? (business process perspective)
- How can we continue to improve and create value? (learning and growth perspective)

All four perspectives must be examined equally. The balanced scorecard cuts down on the number of areas and measures used and allows a focus on the relevant performance measures required to achieve results. Within each perspective are four performance metrics—objectives, measures, targets, and initiatives. Each of these metrics identifies a maximum of four performance outcomes. Let's define each of the perspectives and performance metrics in greater detail.

Financial Perspective: "How Do We Look to Our Stakeholders?"

Financial measures are an essential part of any organization and an important part of the balanced scorecard. This is also one of the two perspectives considered externally focused. The objectives and measures of this perspective tell us whether our strategic plan is adding to our bottom-line results and productivity improvements. This perspective communicate important measures such as market value, profitability, and production efficiencies. A company can either focus on increasing revenues or on asset utilization, but the optimal aim is to increase profitability through improved performance.

Examples of items that are of relevance to the financial perspective include:

- Financial statements of the organization
- Sales/revenue of the organization
- Profitability of the organization
- Other financial analysis and reporting

To learn more about financial ratios and reporting, please reference *Building Business Acumen for Learning Professionals: Skills to Empower the Learning Function* (Gargiulo, Pangarkar, Kirkwood, & Bunzel, 2006). Other reporting mechanisms can be included to track production performance and operational efficiencies.

Customer Perspective: "How Do Our Customers See Us?"

The customer perspective is tricky because we need to place ourselves in the customers' shoes and ask critical questions. To devise effective measures for this perspective, managers must ask, "How can we demonstrate we are delivering the value customers expect?" Too many organizations tend to rely on customer satisfaction surveys and indexes as their sole measures of performance. This is insufficient. Other measures are required, including customer retention, market share, and share of the customer's business in a particular product or service. Leading organizations become creative and develop performance indicators focused around their specific requirements and market needs. For example, one Fortune 100 company that leads in bringing innovative products to market developed an innovation index. This index compiles information from various sources, including R&D, focus groups, and test market data, to indicate whether their new products are successful in their market space.

Organizations are concerned primarily with being able to meet and, preferably, exceed market needs and demands. Customer needs quickly change, making it a challenge for an organization to predict what product or service will be successful. The key questions to begin asking include:

- Who are our target customers?
- What is our value proposition in serving them?
- What do our customers expect and demand from us?

Table 2.1. Value Proposition Strategies

Value Proposition	Points of Differentiation
Operation Excellence	Competitive pricing
	Product quality and selection
	Speedy order fulfillment
	On-time delivery
Customer Intimacy	Exceptional customer service
	Completeness of solutions offered
Product Leadership	Focus on functionality, features, and overall performance of its products or services

These three questions are only a starting point. The answers can differentiate an organization from competitors and show an organization how to attract and create loyalty among customers. A company must select one of the three generally accepted strategies: operational excellence, customer intimacy, or product leadership (see Table 2.1) on which to focus.

The above questions and market strategies apply equally to internal customers. We will come back to this later. What is important is for learning professionals to comprehend the external perspectives, as they will dictate how the internal areas function and require learning support at various levels. Answering the questions above will really assist in knowing what customers expect. This will also help you to focus all learning initiatives to internal clients in a way the organization needs to address its external ones. The external performance perspectives are summarized in Figure 2.5.

Business Process Perspective: "What Must We Excel At?"

This perspective highlights the key processes the organization needs to achieve in order to continually add value for the customer. Managers must ask, "What must we excel at to deliver value to our customers?" To achieve any of the three value discipline strategies, the organization will need to identify the specific internal operations that link to the customer and financial perspective performance measures. Since the objective is to satisfy customers, it may be necessary to identify new

FINANCIAL PERSPECTIVE
"How do we look to stakeholders?"

- Financial performance measures indicate whether a company's strategy is contributing to bottom-line improvement
- Relates to profitability through measures on financial statements

CUSTOMER PERSPECTIVE
"How do our customers see us?"

- Customer performance measures indicate specific value propositions the company will deliver to customers
- This perspective articulates to managers the customer/market strategy delivering future financial returns

→ Alignment of action and capabilities with the customer value proposition is the core of strategy execution

→ Customer perspective directly contributes to the financial performance

defines the core competencies and skills, the technologies, and the corporate culture needed to support an organization's strategy. After the other perspectives have been defined, there will certainly be some discrepancies between the required organizational output and employee skills and technologies. This is when learning strategies must be developed to help reduce any skills gaps. Notable performance measures in this perspective are

- Employee skills development and retention,
- Employee satisfaction,
- Availability of information, and
- Alignment with drivers, personal growth, and the organization.

Through learning and growth performance measures, organizations are able to determine the methods they will use to meet new requirements of the other perspectives.

Many organizations fail in identifying learning and growth measures properly or dedicate little if any importance to them whatsoever. This perspective has to be the last one developed, but it is the foundation. In developing a scorecard, many organizations overlook this perspective, leaving it to be developed by Human Resources. Leading organizations, often labeled "learning organizations," never neglect this perspective. They recognize the importance of a strong foundation of knowledge disseminated through various learning methodologies to ensure and enhance their competitive position.

Kaplan and Norton say that learning and growth should be thought of as the roots of a tree, followed by the trunk, which are the internal processes, followed by the branches, which represent the customer results, and finally the leaves of financial returns. Niven (2006) says that the learning and growth perspective measures "are the enablers of all measures on your scorecard."

Figure 2.6 is a summary of the internal performance perspectives.

Each of the balanced scorecard perspectives contains specific performance metrics that encompass a list of what managers and employees need to do to achieve the corporate strategy. The BSC works in multiples of four; as there are four perspectives, there are also four performance metrics:

- Objectives ("Where do we want to be?")
- Measures ("How will we measure what we are doing?")

INTERNAL BUSINESS PROCESS
"What must we excel at?"

- IB performance measures identifies critical processes expected to have the greatest impact on strategy
- Incorporates innovation into the business strategy

LEARNING PERSPECTIVE
"How can we continue to improve and create value?"

- Learning identifies the intangible and intellectual assets most important to the strategy
- Identifies which jobs, which systems, and what climate to support a value-creating internal process

→ Alignment of learning with the internal business process is the key to attaining external growth and contributes to the core of strategy execution

→ Learning and Internal Processes are the foundation of strategy

Table 2.2. Sample Objectives

BSC Perspective	Objective
Financial perspective	Increase sales by 20 percent in fourteen months
Customer perspective	Develop client relationships
	Develop product options and accessories
Internal business process	Increase customer support
	Lower cost structures
	Increase R&D efforts and expenditure
Learning and growth	Offer customer service training
	Develop/deliver new product training
	Production efficiency and cost management training
	Creativity and innovation learning tools and training

to take a trip and your destination were Florida (objective) then your methods of measure might be your automobile odometer, fuel gage, schedule, and a map. Table 2.3 shows an example of measures for the objectives previously shown in Table 2.2.

Targets: "How Will We Know When We Arrive?"

Once you have set your objectives for each perspective, you must establish specific targets, precise goals you want to reach for each objective, to guide you in your efforts to achieving the objectives. Targets must be realistic but also help to push the organization forward, so managers will often set achievable targets and stretch targets that move them beyond the initial target goal. Targets also act as benchmarks, indicating where a perspective needs to be in a period of time and guiding it in the right direction. Continuing with our previous example, you will now see a column labeled "targets" in Table 2.4.

Initiatives: "What Are We Going to Do to Get Where We Want to Be?"

Initiatives are the things you are going to do to achieve your objectives and meet your targets. Simply put, initiatives are the executable actions you need to take to help the organization move toward its strategic objectives. It is important not to jump directly

Table 2.4. Sample Targets

BSC Perspective	Objective	Measures	Targets
Financial perspective	Increase sales by 20 percent in fourteen months	Sales and revenue statements and forecasts	20 percent increase in fourteen months
Customer perspective	Develop client relationships	Develop product options and accessories	New customer acquisition and customer satisfaction reports
	Competitor product information	15 percent new customers based on last year	Provide two new product options and match competitor offering
Internal business process	Increase customer support	Customer satisfaction surveys	Increase customer satisfaction by 10 percent
	Lower cost structures	Reduce costs by 20 percent	Production costing reports
	Increase R&D development by 25 percent	Increased R&D	R&D innovation reports
Learning and growth	Offer customer service training	Develop/deliver new product training	80 percent acceptance from participants and management
	Production efficiency and cost management training	Benchmark percentage reduction from existing levels	10 percent cost reduction in six months
	Creativity and innovation learning tools and training	Testing and assessment results	Pilot program evaluation
	New idea and innovation reports (number of new product ideas)	Min. 85 percent testing results	Fifteen new product ideas and five prototype products

Figure 2.7. Sample Balanced Scorecard

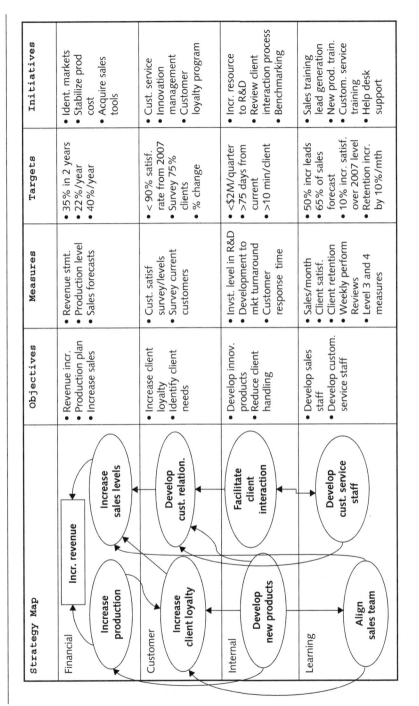

Strategy Map	Objectives	Measures	Targets	Initiatives
Financial **Incr. revenue** **Increase sales levels** **Increase production**	• Revenue incr. • Production plan • Increase sales	• Revenue stmt. • Production level • Sales forecasts	• 35% in 2 years • 22%/year • 40%/year	• Ident. markets • Stabilize prod cost • Acquire sales tools
Customer **Develop cust. relation.** **Increase client loyalty**	• Increase client loyalty • Identify client needs	• Cust. satisf survey/levels • Survey current customers	• < 90% satisf. rate from 2007 • Survey 75% clients • % change	• Cust. service • Innovation management • Customer loyalty program
Internal **Facilitate client interaction** **Develop new products**	• Develop innov. products • Reduce client handling	• Invst. level in R&D • Development to mkt turnaround • Customer response time	• <$2M/quarter • >75 days from current • >10 min/client	• Incr. resource to R&D • Review client interaction process • Benchmarking
Learning **Develop cust. service staff** **Align sales team**	• Develop sales staff • Develop custom. service staff	• Sales/month • Client satisf. • Client retention • Weekly perform Reviews • Level 3 and 4 measures	• 50% incr leads • 65% of sales forecast • 10% incr. satisf. over 2007 level • Retention incr. by 10%/mth	• Sales training lead generation • New prod. train. • Custom. service training • Help desk support

develop their selling abilities (learning and growth perspective). Moving horizontally through each perspective, you can see the linkages within each of the performance metrics. For example, if the objective in the financial perspective is to increase revenues, then the measure may be using the revenue statement/forecast, the target would be to increase revenues by 35 percent in two years, and this would be accomplished (initiative) by identifying new markets.

Now you try to make the linkages. We encourage you to not only attempt to make the connections from what is presented but if you consider other options not presented to add them to the scorecard. Exhibit 2.1 is designed to help you to think in terms of developing linkages through a cause-and-effect process in the same way the balanced scorecard is set up.

CASCADING SCORECARDS: DELIVERING A STRATEGIC MESSAGE TO THE MASSES

The strength of the balanced scorecard is in its ability to translate the organization's mission and the strategy into tangible performance driven measures and initiatives. The scorecard can be used to disseminate this message in a relevant way and to tie in directly to each manager's objectives and each employee's specific responsibilities. But simply developing one corporate level scorecard is insufficient. Developing scorecards throughout the organization, or cascading scorecards from the corporate level, is required to ensure a connection to the overall strategy.

Once senior-level management completes a corporate-level balanced scorecard, they next have to assist each business unit to devise scorecards that complement the corporate one. By cascading scorecards in this manner, managers of each division, department, and functional area develop their scorecards.

It is important that as many of the managers as possible at various levels are involved to ensure that high-level strategic objectives are translated into relevant and tangible objectives in all areas. Enlisting a cross-section of managers and functional teams, especially the internal learning group, will ensure a high level of energy and engender the commitment of a wide cross-section of employees. Figure 2.8 shows the connections among the scorecards.

When properly done, each cascaded scorecard aligns everyone's efforts because they are relevant, understandable, and controllable at the local level (The Society of Management Accountants of Canada, 1999). For example, a senior-level manager

Exhibit 2.1. Cause-and-Effect Relationship to Learning and Growth

If the company is to increase sales, what would be affected in the other perspectives?

_____

_____

_____

If the company is to develop new innovative products, what would you include in the performance measures?

_____

_____

_____

What would be an initiative for this company to reduce client handling (list others if you wish)?

_____

_____

_____

If one of the initiatives under the customer perspective is to develop and implement a customer loyalty program, how can learning and growth link to it?

_____

_____

_____

What would be the expected target for learning and growth if they are to help develop the skills of the customer service staff?

_____

_____

_____

◆　◆　◆

may have an objective to seek efficiency improvements of greater than 20 percent. The production staff may translate this to an objective of reducing production defects and waste by 30 percent. In this way, production workers can relate the higher-level objectives to their specific work responsibilities.

This is what we term as "granularization" of strategic objectives within the cascading process. Granularizing high-level objectives into tangible and relevant

Figure 2.8. Cascading Scorecards

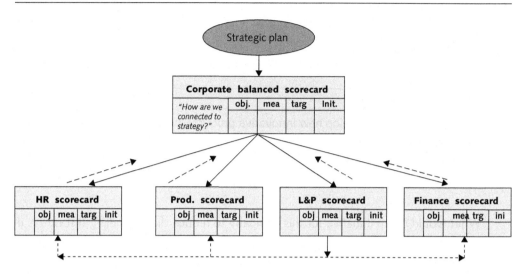

components is the key to achieving corporate-level results. For the organization's learning group, this is important in two ways. First, you will certainly be asked to develop a scorecard cascaded from the corporate level or from the level directly above you (possibly HR) with your departmental objectives. Second and more importantly, this gives learning groups the ability to work closely with each departmental scorecard to assist in developing initiatives to build knowledge and skills of their staff. As each department "granularizes" its objectives, specific needs begin to be obvious. Department managers then seek help from learning and HR to help them ascertain and meet employee needs. This is where the learning group can help to close competency gaps. For example, let's say that one of the chief financial officer scorecard objectives requires a reduction in operational and working capital of 25 percent. This may granularize to the billing department staff as a 40 percent reduction in invoicing errors. The department manager then needs to determine whether this requires skill development for his staff. The internal learning group can partner with the billing department to conduct a needs assessment to determine the appropriate learning solutions so that the billing department staff can meet their stated objectives.

The process of cascading scorecards is relatively simple as long as the objectives that become granularized have a logical and cohesive relationship to the scorecards they are derived from. Keep this in mind as you develop a scorecard for the learning department, as the intended strategic objective of your department must support the corporate-level scorecard strategic objectives and also align with the other operational concerns of the organization.

The following example will help you in the process:

1. Let's say your company, ABC Inc., has a growth financial strategy and you want to examine the financial objectives and apply them to your department. The first thing is to ask yourself, "Can this department have an effect on this objective?" If this answer is "no," you will continue to the next objective.

2. However, if your answer is "yes," then you must determine the appropriate measure to track your progress. It is recommended that, for consistency, you use the exact measures as outlined in the high-level BSC. While ABC Inc.'s growth strategy will probably measure earnings per share, it would be impossible for your department to come up with the same measure. Instead, you might measure budget variance, where you would argue that controlling costs can have a direct impact on the overall ABC Inc. objectives of improved earning per share.

3. Now that you have created your objectives and measures, you will set targets and initiatives for your department, setting individual goals for each departmental employee based on past results and future goals.

4. At this stage you will work through all the other objectives on the strategy map that affect your department, following Steps 1, 2, q and 3 above.

5. Now that you have worked on every objective, you should have a strategy map reflecting your own department.

Learning will gain the most credibility and value for the organization in its ability to partner closely with the various operational areas of the organization and clearly understand their strategic objectives. In this way, learning will play an operational rather than a functional role in developing solutions that benefit the organization as a whole. As we like to say in our workshops, "Become the training department of each operational area, not simply the training department of the company."

Cascading to Personal Scorecards

Dr. Kaplan and Dr. Norton state that it is important to "make strategy everyone's job" (2006, p. vii). One way of doing this is by cascading the scorecard down to the *personal* level. The individual personal scorecard is the final step in the process. This is relevant to learning and performance because proposed learning should not only impact the organization but also support every employee's personal growth and also fully align with the objectives of the enterprise.

Once a strategy is set by management, the skill areas that employees possess are not necessarily the ones that will take the organization to where it wants to go. These skills gaps lead to personal development plans tied to the performance expectations put in place by management, often tied in to the individual's performance incentives, evaluation reviews, and salary. Thus, personal learning plans benefit the organization in achieving its objectives and benefit the employees with personal and professional growth.

POTENTIAL PITFALLS OF THE BALANCED SCORECARD

For every tool, there are pitfalls, and the balanced scorecard is no different. Any tool is only as reliable as how effectively it has been developed and the information provided for inclusion. Three primary pitfalls those developing scorecards tend to fall into are (1) a lack of a well-defined strategy, (2) the use of only lagging performance measures, and (3) the use of generic performance metrics.

Lack of a Well-Defined Strategy

When asked, many organizations will probably say they have well-defined strategies to achieve their missions. In many instances, however, this is not the case. Many managers confuse daily activities and tactical objectives with the organization's strategic imperative or, worse, believe they have a strategy where none actually exists. For the balanced scorecard to be truly effective, a well-defined organizational mission and a well-laid-out strategic plan are essential. By having both, managers at all levels can break the strategy into manageable objectives.

Use of Only Lagging Performance Measures

Unfortunately, many managers rely solely on financial performance measures to drive their organizations. But financial performance measures only demonstrate past or historical performance and do not provide any guidance for long-term objectives. This is not to say that financial performance measures are not important, but for the scorecard to work it must "balance" both leading and lagging performance measures to provide a complete picture.

Use of Generic Metrics

Those who criticize the ineffectiveness of the balanced scorecard are often the same ones who try to "shortcut" the developmental process by using very generic and unspecific metrics. The power of the balanced scorecard is in the detailed nature of performance metrics: listing specific objectives, identifying the proper measurement tools, setting attainable targets, and outlining appropriate initiatives to make the objectives happen.

The following are some pitfalls to avoid when implementing the BSC:

- *Lack of a well-defined strategy:* The BSC relies on an understanding of the linkages between strategic objectives and the metrics.

- *Using only lagging measures:* Care should be taken to identify not only lagging measures but also leading measures that can be used to plan for future performance.

- *Use of generic metrics:* Each firm should put forth the effort to identify the measures that are appropriate for its own strategy and competitive position.

LAST THOUGHTS

The balanced scorecard is a powerful but simple strategic tool. This is why so many organizations are embracing it with enthusiasm. By laying the framework within limited and defined perspectives, an organization can now easily have all managers and employees understand how they are connected with and relevant to achieving the corporate mission.

The simplicity of the scorecard is in its design. By encompassing four primary perspectives, the tool allows an organization to turn its attention to external concerns, such as the financial outcomes and its customers' expectations, and internal areas, which include its internal processes to meet external requirements and its integration of learning and growth, to successfully meet its strategic expectations.

Each of the four perspectives encompasses four areas of performance measures and indicators. Each objective is driven by attainable targets and set forth by outlining specific initiatives to ensure that objectives are met. Further, beginning with corporate-level objectives, managers are able to derive departmental objectives and link them directly and tangibly to every employee's areas of responsibility.

This chapter has provided you with a comprehensive overview of the balanced scorecard. Combined with what you learned in the previous chapter on strategy, you are now in a better position to begin to recognize management's expectations and to discover new ways to build value for workplace learning and performance within your organization.

—

- Understand management's perspective
- Compare management's expectations with learning's concerns
- Close the communication gap between management and workplace learning
- Answer management's questions in a way they understand

While you read and work through this chapter, place yourself in a new paradigm. Don't think of yourself as only a learning professional but as part of the business and management mindset. Go a step further if possible. Try to place yourself in the position of the senior managers, stakeholders, and decision-makers of your organization. This type of thinking will help you to build credibility for learning within your organization.

MANAGEMENT'S VIEW: FROM PERFORMANCE MEASUREMENT TO STRATEGIC MANAGEMENT

Let's get started on how management views the balanced scorecard. You must be able to understand the balanced scorecard as management sees it. The goal of every organization today is to achieve its strategic objectives by effectively executing its strategy and being able to manage change within the organization. As stated earlier, the balanced scorecard creates a balance between the historical measures (lagging indicators) and the drivers of future value of the organization (leading indicators). But as more and more organizations apply the balanced scorecard, they notice it is also a crucial tool in aligning short-term actions with strategy (Niven, 2006).

The BSC also aligns strategic activities and objectives with the organization's operational functions. Thus, all parts of the organization are linked to the balanced scorecard and all members of the organization can find how their roles fit. For example, when disseminated properly, the BSC allows a greeter at a Wal-Mart store to understand in a broad context exactly how his or her role as a greeter corresponds to the organization's overarching goals.

As shown in Figure 3.1, management uses the balanced scorecard as a strategic framework. Executives can use it to clarify and translate the vision and strategy, communicate strategy down through the organization, plan and set targets for the business, and encourage feedback that will provide the organization with information that can change the strategy so that it is in line with the company vision. Each

Figure 3.1. The Balanced Scorecard as a Strategic Framework for Action

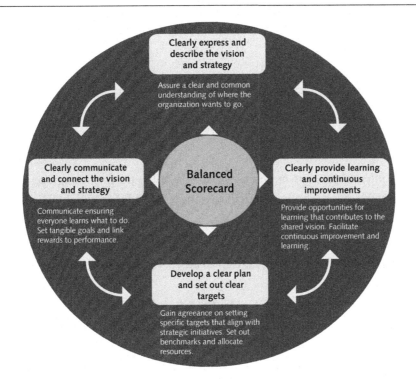

of the procedures can be used as an independent tool, but using them together can really enhance the success of an organization.

When an organization builds its management system around the balanced scorecard, it can align its long-term strategy more effectively. Therefore, the balanced scorecard becomes the foundation for managing organizations (Kaplan & Norton, 1996).

The balanced scorecard adheres to three broad guidelines:

1. Avoid the monopoly of solely utilizing financial performance measures;

2. Assume that anticipation is more important than reaction;

3. Recommend the selectivity of measures, aiming at avoiding surplus information. (Bourguignon, Malleret, & Nørreklit, 2001, p. 10)

As described in Chapter 2, the balanced scorecard translates the vision and strategy of a business unit into objectives and performance measures in four different areas: the financial, customer, internal business process, and learning and growth perspectives.

- *The financial perspective* identifies how the company wishes to be viewed by its shareholders.

- *The customer perspective* determines how the company wishes to be viewed by its customers.

- *The internal-business-process perspective* describes the business processes at which the company has to be particularly adept in order to satisfy its shareholders and customers.

- *The learning and growth perspective* analyzes the changes and improvements the company needs to realize if it is to make its vision come true.

These perspectives lead to the identification of the main process indicators that the company wants to control and that will be part of the balanced scorecard itself. Similarly, the organizational learning and growth perspective analyzes the changes and improvements that the company needs to realize if it is to make its vision come true (Kaplan & Norton, 1996, pp. 30–31). The identification of these key factors leads to the identification of key indicators.

Kaplan and Norton assume the causal relationships within the four perspectives of the balanced scorecard illustrated in Figure 3.2.

The performance metrics of the other three perspectives serve as guidelines for learning and growth. By developing focused learning initiatives, learning professionals ensure that objectives within the other perspectives are met. The performance metrics of organizational learning and growth therefore reflect how well the internal business processes perform. Even though learning and growth enables each of the other three perspectives, outcomes from the internal business processes and learning and growth support the outcomes of the customer perspective, driving toward improved financial results in the financial perspective.

Each strategic area should have both leading and lagging indicators, yielding two-directional cause-and-effect chains: lead and lag indicators apply horizontally within the areas and vertically between areas. This implies that strategy

Figure 3.2. Causal Relationship Within the Four Perspectives

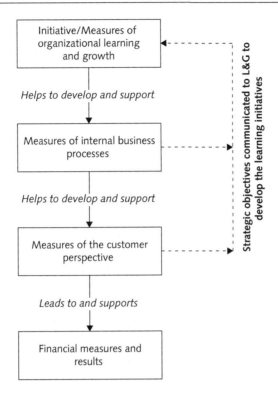

can be translated into a set of hypotheses about cause and effect (Kaplan & Norton, 1996).

Management views of the balanced scorecard are not just a strategic measurement system but also a strategic control system, which may be used to:

1. Clarify and gain consensus about strategy,

2. Align departmental and personal goals to strategy,

3. Link strategic objectives to long-term targets and annual budgets,

4. Identify and align strategic initiatives, and

5. Obtain feedback to learn about and improve strategy. (Kaplan & Norton, 1996, p. 19)

put it this way: What do you do when you decide to visit a foreign destination? You would most probably make an effort to integrate yourself in some way, whether learning some of the language, culture, or habits. Well, think of your organization as a foreign land—the foreign land of business. You now need to integrate your knowledge and expertise into this new land.

No longer is learning relegated to a simple functional role reacting to requests from operational units. It is being asked to adopt a more prominent role. But even though learning is gaining prominence, it does not automatically mean that everything learning delivers will be accepted—or even acknowledged. Those responsible and involved with workplace learning and performance must prove themselves.

Learning's contribution to the organization is primarily intangible. Managers can learn to value tangible outcomes and assets. They, however, view investments in learning as tangible and so expect tangible outcomes. As learning professionals, we must attempt to deliver tangible results, although this is often difficult. It is almost like proving that gravity exists. We all know it exists, but how can we tangibly show what gravity is? It is a similar situation for learning. When asked, most managers today would agree that learning is important and required for their people and for their competitive advantage. But when they are later asked about some type of organizational success, very few will give learning credit for its contribution to the achievement. This is the reality. It is not management's responsibility to recognize learning's role; it is the responsibility of the learning and performance group to demonstrate in some manner how their efforts contribute to the organization. Again, the proof must be relevant to management if you are to build credibility.

So we return to the point: in order to be relevant to management, one must understand how management views the organization. They are trying to successfully achieve specific business objectives. For example, let's say a production manager is responsible for the manufacturing of ABC Inc.'s widgets. These widgets are assembled into larger products called "doflickies." The production manager understands that ABC is in the business of marketing doflickies. He or she also understands the connections involved in developing the doflickies—the design of components such as the widget, the financial constraints, the acquisition of resources, and the customer need for doflickies. This helps the manager to better manufacture the required widgets.

The production manager thinks in the same way about those responsible for organizational learning. So learning professionals must transition from their current learning perspective to those of other organizational managers. To simplify the process of shifting your thinking from a learning-based approach to a systems approach, some basic questions need to be addressed:

- What is the purpose of your organization's existence?
- What are the products and/or services offered?
- What are the primary operational areas that directly contribute to its objectives?
- Who does the organization serve?

Now take some time to answer these questions in Exhibit 3.1. You may already know the answers, but before jumping to conclusions, speak to others in your organization and learn as much as you can to come up with complete answers.

The illustration in Exhibit 3.2 shows what happens in many meetings between learning professionals and senior (C-level) managers. How often has this type of

Exhibit 3.1. Critical Questions

What is the purpose of your organization's existence?

_____

_____

_____

What are the products and/or services offered?

_____

_____

_____

What are the primary operational areas that directly contribute to its objectives?

_____

_____

_____

Who does the organization serve?

_____

_____

_____

Exhibit 3.2. Thinking Like They Do

Think of a recent meeting with a senior manager. What was your focus during the meeting?

_____

_____

_____

In the discussions you have with senior management, what are the top five issues they are concerned with?

1. _____

_____

2. _____

_____

3. _____

_____

4. _____

_____

5. _____

_____

scenario happened to you? Most learning professionals we meet say it's common. Since we are exceptionally adept in our field, our bias is to demonstrate to others the value of our learning efforts. If both individuals in the illustration were learning professionals or involved in some way in employee development, then the conversation would be reciprocal. However, when one of the individuals is business oriented, or results-driven, communication fails. Most managers are focused on the end result. A manager is not all that interested in the details of how something was achieved, but rather on the outcomes. This is not to say that managers are oblivious to how things are done. Most will want to know the approach to a certain extent. But when trying to "pitch" your learning initiative to managers, be aware that they simply want to know that what you have to offer will get them to where they want to go.

Take some time to complete the questions in Exhibit 3.2. Revisit an occasion during which you proposed a learning solution to an operational or senior-level manager within your organization when you were relatively unsuccessful. Now respond to the first question. Ask yourself what you could have done to understand his or her needs better. What were some of the manager's concerns and preoccupations? Now respond to the second question.

The chapter from Gargiulo, Pangarkar, and Kirkwood (2008, Chapter 38) that begins on the next page provides you with a more in-depth understanding of how to develop a business approach to selling learning internally.

The types of discussions mentioned in the article occur frequently in organizations. It is not only your responsibility to conduct a needs assessment to determine the learning needs of a group, but you should also apply this skill to the needs of management. Conduct a needs assessment on the meeting you will have with a manager or managers. Research their concerns and objectives prior to the meeting, then develop your learning solutions and explain to them how the solutions will help them to resolve their concerns. There is an adage that we live by and suggest to internal learning professionals we work with, "Sell them what they want to buy, not what you want to sell."

Exhibit 3.3 will assist you in developing this skill. Take inventory of both your and your organization's concerns. First, reflect on the concerns and preoccupations for workplace learning and those responsible for workplace learning. These items can be things from an adequate assessment of learning needs to assessing Kirkpatrick

A Business Approach to Learning: Increasing Profits Through Marketing Methodologies

Training managers are challenged to "sell" the benefits of an intangible need to those wanting tangible results. External consultants understand this obstacle; however, when those responsible for training propose training solutions, they often encounter significant resistance. Senior managers recognize the importance for training but, with limited resources, they are also concerned with accountability and results. T&D is also challenged by other stakeholders, employees and management alike, to overcome indifference and skepticism of any proposed learning initiative.

The days when T&D managers were able to convince senior management that training could not be measured tangibly or financially are over. Managers of training departments must make a radical shift in their thinking to gain support for learning initiatives. As training budgets increase, senior managers expect to see some type of tangible return on their budget allocations, as they do from any other operational or functional activity. Increasingly, stakeholders at all levels want to see tangible outcomes as they relate to their function and environment.

The mistake T&D managers often make is attempting to position training as an essential need. Secret 1: Nothing is an absolute need to senior management. T&D believes they must convince senior management of the benefits and to actually invest funds to make proposed initiatives a reality. Doing this is a mistake and places T&D in a defensive position. Secret 2: Most senior managers are already

(continued)

sold on the need and the necessity for training. The buy-in is not whether they want to have training, it is about which training initiative presents the most benefits and tangible results to the organization at all levels.

T&D has grown up in the last few years; where once it sat at the "kiddie table," today it is invited to sit with the adults. When an organization commits to a seat at the executive table they are clearly stating to T&D, "Sell us on what training will do for the organization in business and strategic terms we understand." CLOs must prepare themselves with answers for questions such as:

- How does the learning strategy align with the organization's overall vision/direction?
- What are the expected and tangible outcomes/benefits of the learning strategy?
- How will it be marketed within the organization?
- How will we gain the buy-in from the affected departments/ individuals?
- How will T&D justify the cost and investment for the training?
- What metrics will we use to measure organizational impact?

This is not an exhaustive list of senior management questions, but it is a starting point for CLOs to demonstrate to their senior counterparts and stakeholders how T&D initiatives impact the organization through tangible business measures. It requires taking a "business" approach to proving T&D's worth.

1. Proving T&D's Worth

Management is primarily concerned with profitability. Every business unit is expected to be a profit center or, at the very least, demonstrate profitability in some way. For traditional cost centers such as T&D, this is a highly debated topic. The question often raised is, "How can T&D be profitable?" As much as we would like to provide you with a magic solution to this question, each approach is as unique as the organization itself.

In a recent *CLO* article, author Bob Zeinstra speaks about cost recovery as an alternative measure of T&D's profitability, stating, "... package the outcome to your stakeholders not as seeking profit, but as seeking cost recovery" (2004). Cost recovery is not a new concept but offers a "softer" approach to operational profitability. It does not make a corporate support division appear to be "making money" off of its employees.

Another method to profit center thinking is getting T&D to become an internal consulting group for the learning needs of other business units. This allows T&D to think through consultative approaches in terms of solutions, results, and meeting client (other business units) expectations the same way as if the organization sourced external consultants.

Positioning T&D as a consulting group helps it to:

- Answer the specific and targeted needs of business unit clients
- Deliver tangible business results
- Deliver focused solutions in line with organizational strategy

(continued)

- Be accountable to costing, pricing, and profitability
- Facilitate "buy-in" within the organization
- Develop effective solutions

Like every other business function, training's worth is determined by its contribution to helping the organization reach strategic objectives. But to do this, T&D must actually see itself as its own business and be fully accountable. This can be accomplished if T&D possesses a holistic approach to learning and performance, rather than simply focusing on the training function itself. This requires those responsible for training to possess not only expertise in training but also to have a basic comprehension of business and strategy.

This orientation positions training and development as a strategic partner helping stakeholders at all levels attain desired objectives and specific results. This is how T&D will facilitate "buy-in" of training initiatives throughout the organization.

2. Knowing Your Audience: Gaining Buy-In

As T&D managers develop their knowledge and understanding of organizational objectives in business terms, they increase their opportunity to deliver the right message to their customers—the organization and its business units. The greatest failure is not knowing, understanding, and clearly communicating what the customer wants. An effective marketing and communication strategy for T&D requires demonstrating tangible results to those expected to benefit from the training.

Marketing and selling your training internally is all about being prepared, involving the appropriate and affected individuals, and clearly understanding what executive management wants to hear. After all, we are basically talking about applying fundamental sales, marketing, and people skills. But to establish true credibility in the eyes of management, it is critical to demonstrate a clear relationship to business and strategic objectives. No matter how effective you are in developing a marketing strategy for training initiatives, there will always be critics trying to challenge your assumptions.

Marketing Mistake 1—Focusing on Features

The focus of any training must be on the benefits and not on the features. For example, if you are proposing a customer service program for front-line workers, one feature would be resolving client problems, and the benefit would be an increase in customer satisfaction or an increase in repeat sales. These are the tangible results senior managers want to see. Too many times we see organizations jump quickly on the "new business trend" bandwagon. This is another example of features taking precedence over benefits. Just because a topic is gaining popularity does not mean that it is appropriate for your staff or organization. Business decisions are based on deliverables in line with strategic objectives, not on appeal. Applying the feature/benefit principle will help prepare you to move your cause forward with those who are most resistant.

(continued)

Marketing Mistake 2—Focusing on One Level of Decision Making

Apart from only focusing on features, when seeking "buy-in" for training-related projects, training managers tend to focus on obtaining support from the highest level of decision-makers, senior management. There are only two outcomes from this approach. Either management approves or they reject the training project. If it is approved, then congratulations, but only one level of decision-makers are sold on the idea. At this point the proposed initiative, more often than not, is doomed to fail because those directly affected were not involved or consulted. Like wildfire, resistance spreads quickly, leading to non-acceptance of the training initiative, eventually jeopardizing and possibly killing the project. Management blames the training manager for the failure and lack of results, further propagating the belief that training is an expense and reinforcing to participants that training is a waste of time and money.

Marketing Mistake 3—Not Knowing Your "Buyers"

Training managers who successfully gain internal acceptance for training recognize early who they need to approach and quickly gain an appreciation for the concerns and needs of those directly or indirectly involved. These managers also have an understanding of the fundamental marketing philosophies: "know your audience" and "sell the buyer what they want to buy, not what you want to sell." Essentially, there are three groups to address: training participants (or employees); mid-level managers; and senior management.

Training participants will usually accept any training if it provides them with value-added resources and does not take time away from their immediate responsibilities. The training must be easy for them to absorb and incorporate into their daily activities if it is to change behavior. Changing behavior and attitudes of participants is at the core of how training will impact business results. It is important to balance the needs of the participant with the need for performance improvement. Effectively doing this aligns the participants' goals with the needs of business managers and broadens access to other possible alternatives.

When dealing with business unit managers, it is important to recognize their specific requirements. They are often challenged to leverage their employees' ability to achieve specific departmental or production objectives with the demands of senior management. At this level, managers are involved in budget planning and the allocation of funds directly affecting their environment. Being directly on the front lines of business, they are accountable to attain pre-set performance benchmarks on many levels, placing extensive demand on their resources. Taking these concerns into account, business managers have little patience or time for training solutions that do not produce immediate results and that take their employees away from their daily responsibilities.

Decision making at the senior level focuses on attaining strategic objectives, increasing profitability, and maximizing shareholder value. At this level, managers want to create an environment that increases sales and revenue through improving product quality and customer and employee satisfaction. Their objective is to optimize

(continued)

the return on their investment in every business-related activity, especially when investing in employees. In the knowledge economy, ideas, innovation, and synergy are critical to long-term success. Every training investment must ensure that the performance of the organization improves by developing a knowledgeable team of employees to effectively serve clients and to capitalize on new opportunities. It is usually at this level that many training managers pitch their proposals, often ignoring other levels of decision-making involvement.

Table 3.1 summarizes each of the target groups and their needs.

3. Answering the Seven Essential Questions

You will certainly encounter critics and individuals at every level of management. Being prepared for the "critical" questions is essential if you are to sell your solution. The following are some examples of questions often asked. These questions will help you face the challenges you may encounter when proposing learning solutions.

1. Is there really a need for training?

Training professionals often overestimate the value training can provide. If the perception of training is to change, then training managers need to be honest about its effectiveness. There are many instances in which a formal training solution is unnecessary. For example, your company has recently upgraded existing software. Is there a need for training or are employees capable of learning the software on their own? Maybe they only require coaching in some of the new features of the software.

Table 3.1. Defining Your Target Audience and Their Needs

Internal Target Audience Concerns	Internal Target Audience
Senior Management including: C-Level management Divisional Executives (presidents) Senior vice presidents Senior operational managers Senior functional managers	• Strategic alignment (balanced scorecard) • Budget requirements • Cost involvements • Financial outcomes/analysis • Tangible results • Intangible benefits • Business impact (level 4) • Return on investment (level 5) • Project justification to the board/ shareholders (major investments)
Mid-Level Management including: Business unit managers pOerational managers Functional area managers Divisional/operational coordinators Department/staff supervisors Controllers	• Attain business objectives/prescribed benchmarks • Meet budget allocations • Cost impact to budget • Staff time requirements • Alternative learning possibilities • Respect of current resources • Tangible business-unit results • Intangible business-unit benefits • Immediate application of skills (level 3) • Direct relationship to tasks/jobs
Training Participants including: Operational staff Functional staff Support staff Any training participant	• Correlation to their jobs/tasks • Benefits to their jobs/tasks • Time required/away from job • Contribution to personal growth • Contribution to professional development • Know what they need to know (pre-assessment and level 2 assessment) • Support to new skills acquisition (level 3) • Other available options to training • Personal financial benefits

(continued)

2. Do all employees need training?

Management believes the myth that all employees must pass through training if they are to maximize their investment. The impact of training is realized if the right individuals are involved. Focus your training efforts on the people with the need and those who will benefit most and clearly demonstrate to management the impact this focus will have on the organization. For example, if you are introducing a new product then the production team may require training in quality procedures, whereas customer service employees would require training on the use of the product.

3. What are the expected outcomes?

You will be asked this question. Training professionals often misdiagnose the problem the required training is attempting to solve. Training's primary goal is to improve on existing processes and outcomes. This leads back to the benefits mentioned earlier. When attempting to build a case for training, you must ensure the benefits answer the needs of your audience and the investment delivers on the actual expected returns.

4. How will the training move us closer to our goals?

Executives expect that every business decision will move them closer to a desired goal. Training investments are not exempt from this rule. Managers recognize that their people are the key to their success or failure. Even more importantly, they recognize that the investment they make in people is also unpredictable and volatile. Your responsibility is to assure and show management that the proposed training solution will lead them one step closer to their goals. Clearly show tangible links to operational and organizational strategic objectives.

5. Will this training meet management's expectations?

Each level of management has certain expectations from their investment. Clearly understanding what they are will help in your marketing efforts. Senior managers expect to see links between productivity and profitability. Setting up clear "benchmarks" against both internal and industry measures will certainly improve your case for training. Mid-managers want to see immediate outcomes and results. Work closely with them to develop an implementation plan that minimizes workplace disruption and equips their staff with the skills that will move them closer to their immediate objectives.

6. What resources will the training require?

All organizations are constrained by limited resources. Many managers also believe that there are more critical issues to resolve with these resources before they will commit to training. To avoid this objection, you need to know what resources are required. Do not underestimate your needs, and be prepared to justify your position. Then present this case to the decision-makers and those that are affected by the training.

7. What will the training cost?

Cost-benefit and profit-loss are terms that are not always familiar to training professionals. If not handled carefully, this question can be a trap. The key to selling your training internally is to speak in terms

(continued)

that management understands. Prove to them that training employees is an investment that will result in measurable and profitable outcomes. Clearly determine direct and unforeseen costs in relation to expected results. Remember, talk to them in business, not training, terms.

Your success depends on how you address the concerns at each level of decision-making and on whether the individuals affected participated in developing the proposed training solution. It requires an understanding of the benefits related to the needs of the employees and organization. Knowing your audience is essential to gaining support and the first step to selling training solutions internally.

The perception of training is changing and the need is growing. If real change is to take hold, training professionals must find effective ways to ensure true learning leads to results. Training is about developing abilities and knowledge that translate into sustained performance. Building organizational requirements and employee needs into the training solutions is essential to gain acceptance at every level. It is time for T&D to shift its thinking to business and strategic orientations focusing on performance and results to gain credibility and facilitate buy-in. Training and development must realize it is an integral component of the business, not an organizational footnote.

Level 3 (application of skills) and evaluating learning effectiveness. You know your role and organization the best, so list a maximum of five most important issues. Then, keeping in mind management's concerns from the previous worksheet, attempt to correlate how the concerns for learning relate to the needs and concerns for management. Always recognize that any learning initiative is only one component and method to helping managers achieve their objectives.

Exhibit 3.3. WLP Concerns

What are WLP's concerns about learning?

1. _____

   _____

2. _____

   _____

3. _____

   _____

4. _____

   _____

5. _____

   _____

How are management's concerns related to the list of WLP issues listed above?

1. _____

   _____

2. _____

   _____

3. _____

   _____

4. _____

   _____

5. _____

   _____

CLOSING THE COMMUNICATION GAP

Essentially, if we were to simplify the problem, we could say that there exists a large communication gap between those responsible for employee development and those responsible for operational management. Clear and effective communication is required for any relationship to be successful and should be the responsibility of both parties. In the relationship between workplace learning and management, the balanced scorecard provides a vehicle for both sides to leverage their strengths and link directly to organizational objectives. But surprisingly the communication gap remains. This is because each party speaks a different language.

Language of Management

Managers speak in the same way they think. Their approach to the organization is to view it as a system and then systematically break it down into objective-driven units. The objectives are also broken down into short-, mid-, and longer-term time frames, with a careful eye on the availability and use of organizational resources, which are essentially categorized in three silos: money, people, and time. Money, or financial resources, is placed first in this list because managers are conditioned to keep a watchful eye on how effectively they use the finances allocated and the results they derive to achieve their and the organization's objectives. This allows them to provide a tangible measure commonly referred to as return on investment or ROI.

Managers are not exclusively held to ROI measures but are also measured and scrutinized against many other financial measures. These measures are often compared and combined to tell a story of their performance. This is what managers would call a vertical analysis and ratio analysis. The performance for one period, however, is insufficient to provide any true value. As such, multiple periods are compared against a baseline or benchmark. The benchmark is usually established through forecasted financial performance and/or successful past performance periods. Managers must produce and quantify their results. When one area does not meet expectations, it affects the organizational system as a whole.

Managers must meet and, when possible, exceed their stakeholder needs and expectations. In publicly listed companies, stakeholders are traditionally seen as those who have invested their capital in return for growth and/or profitability. In recent years, most companies, even publicly traded ones, take a more holistic approach to stakeholders and often see them in four distinct groups: customers, employees, shareholders, and suppliers. Financially or otherwise, each of these groups has some vested interest in the organization.

The increased focus on strategy for management is more than simply helping their organizations to meet specific objectives. As a result of technology, globalization, and innovation, organizations are required to develop the ability to value and utilize the intangible "assets." Financial results, although still essential and relevant, are insufficient to provide managers with a complete picture of organizational performance. The economic factors have shifted significantly, and knowledge is now valued more than traditional fixed assets are. Whether they admit it or not, the "soft" assets within the organization are increasingly driving the value of the organization. These soft assets exist as knowledge and information within the organization, but the most challenging of them is people. As one CEO once stated to us, "Every night at 5 P.M. my 'assets' walk out the front door. And every night at 5 P.M. I hope they return the next day." C-level management thinking is on the topics listed here:

- Meet stakeholder needs
- Produce/quantify results
  - Increase revenue/market share
  - Return on all investments
  - Improve performance/ quality
  - Cost management
- Execute/align objectives
- Valuing intangibles/ knowledge

Language of Learning and Performance

Earlier we mentioned that learning within organizations is becoming increasingly relevant. It is also very important that we apply our abilities effectively in delivering learning solutions that adhere to proper learning methodologies and principles. This is the reason our role is necessary in every organization. The challenge is that we are often so focused on the learning context that we do not look to the true needs of the organization—such that our solutions can help in delivering tangible results.

Figure 3.3. The ADDIE Model

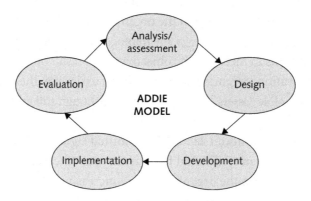

Traditionally our focus has been around learning itself and how we perceive outcomes. Learning professionals are taught to follow a systematic approach to learning development, frequently referred to as ADDIE (see Figure 3.3), which includes:

- Assessment/analysis of the need
- Design of the solution
- Development of the solution
- Implementation of the solution
- Evaluation of the solution

By following the ADDIE model, learning developers are able to create effective learning solutions. With the shift toward a knowledge-driven organization, learning's role is more important than ever. That being said, our focus still has not shifted sufficiently to the extent that we sell our solutions based on our learning concepts and models. Traditional WLP thinking follows this model:

- Learners' needs/styles
- Needs assessment/analysis
- Design and development
- Deployment and delivery

- Training on as-needed basis
- Focused on learning over strategy/outcomes (Levels 1 and 2)

How would we assess the knowledge-driven organization's overall business need? If you were to conduct a global needs assessment, it would come back saying to deliver results from investments. This is what is expected from every investment made by management in the organization. If we are to evaluate based on Kirkpatrick's model, then notice where management's actual need arises—at Level 3 (application of skills) and Level 4 (business impact). Although there is an effort on the part of learning to move toward delivering result-oriented solutions, our general preoccupation continues to be around Kirkpatrick's Level 1 (reaction) and Level 2 (retention/testing).

In Chapter 2 we introduced the external and internal perspectives of the balanced scorecard. The external perspectives are the financial perspectives and the customer perspective. For each, we must respond to one critical question applicable to the perspectives: "How do we look to our stakeholders?" and "How do our customers see us?" respectively. Each question helps to drive the performance measures, directly linking to the internal perspectives. Hence, the external perspectives are directing what is required internally for the organization to deliver on its external performance measures, therefore contributing to the organizational objectives. (As a reminder, review Figure 2.5, Summary of External Performance Perspectives.)

The internal perspectives, internal business processes and learning and growth, are essential to complete the cycle and to ensure that all of the performance measures deliver on what the organization expects to provide to its stakeholders. Management will naturally focus around the areas that directly contribute to the growth and profitability of the organization. These areas usually lie in the external perspectives. To deliver on these areas, however, the organization must develop and deliver its internal responsibilities. The key management concepts to be considered include operational effectiveness, quality assurance, innovation, and cost management. How these factors are managed will help to build a value-creating internal process that delivers the external results.

To understand and to begin to think like management, you have to learn their systems thinking perception. (As a reminder, review Figure 2.6, Summary of Internal Performance Perspectives.)

It is your turn to close the communication gap. We want you to explore your organization in the same detail that management understands the organization and within the context of the balanced scorecard. Exhibits 3.4 and 3.5 provide you with an opportunity to get into this management mindset.

Exhibit 3.4. External Perspectives

Financial Perspective: "How do we look to stakeholders?"

What are some of the financial objectives of the organization?

_____
_____
_____

What are the expectations/targets?

_____
_____
_____

Customer Perspective: "How do our customers see us?"

What is the organization's value proposition to customers?

_____
_____
_____

Who are your customers in the organization?

_____
_____
_____

How can you connect and help your customers in the organization?

_____
_____
_____

Exhibit 3.5. Internal Perspectives

Internal Business: "What must we excel at?"

What are the core measures valued by the organization?

_____

_____

_____

What are some of critical/strategic business processes to account for?

_____

_____

_____

What are some of the critical/strategic business processes identified by management?

_____

_____

_____

Learning Perspective: "How can we continue to improve and create value?"

Reviewing the three other perspectives, what are the areas that learning and performance can connect with?

_____

_____

_____

◆ ◆ ◆

ANSWERING MANAGEMENT'S QUESTIONS

For every business area, management asks specific questions related to organizational effectiveness and to alignment with strategic objectives. With an increased focus on intangible and knowledge assets, learning and performance is also considered a critical business area and expected to respond to management's questions and concerns. What are the questions asked? Many are quite familiar to business managers and considered second-nature; however, this is not necessarily

So how do you answer this question? The first step is to ensure that your learning strategy connects with each of the perspectives. Identify the critical areas of concern to the business unit and communicate your efforts in the way they expect to hear it.

A learning strategy would align with the financial perspective if it respects and maximizes the financial resources available to it and to the organization. This is also where management's concern over return on investment is demonstrated. As mentioned earlier, you will need to find a proper balance in respect to management's need for a return on their learning investment. Most C-level managers are not convinced about the ROI of intangible efforts such as learning. It is safer not to attempt to demonstrate or prove a "training" or "learning" ROI but to demonstrate the effectiveness of the learning strategy's efforts. At this level of decision making, return on investment, especially for intangible efforts, does not necessarily have to be in monetary form. Tangible improvements in business performance would be an acceptable form of ROI.

For the customer perspective, alignment is about understanding the needs of both the organization's customers and learning and performance's customers within the organization. To truly understand the value of your learning efforts, you need to first understand what the organization is trying to deliver to its marketplace. The value proposition should always be in the back of your mind as you work with various business units. Always know who your customers within the organization are and be aware of their needs and objectives. This may seem obvious, but surprisingly there still exists what we call the "functional mentality" of learning departments. They still see the organization as a whole as their customer and play a reactive role, waiting for the organization to come to them, rather than proactively acting like a business unit themselves. If learning expects to be taken seriously and demonstrate real value, it needs to begin acting like a business. We stress to learning professionals that it is essential to treat their department like their own business. This means viewing their organization as a market to develop and to segregate the various business units as internal customers. In this way the learning function can be proactive in building business and ensuring it meets the needs of its customer, hence, creating value for the organization.

Alignment with internal processes is an extension to the previous discussion on treating internal customer needs. In this instance, the internal customers of interest are the ones who focus on the internal processes to meet the needs of the external perspectives. The first question we ask is for learning to be aware of the core values and measures of the organization. As Stephen Covey said in *The Seven Habits of Highly Effective People* (1990), begin with the end in mind. Being aware of these important measures allows learning solutions to both be aligned with the needs of internal processes and to be more strategic. This leads to recognizing the critical and strategic business processes. If learning is to build any type of sustainable credibility, it will be by recognizing and developing solutions around these processes. Above all other activities in the organization, these are the core that account for the success or the failure of the organization. This is not discovered in isolation but rather by working in close collaboration with the internal process customer to learn about his or her critical core activities. The more critical the internal process is to the organization, the more attention it will receive from management. When learning is able to create results-driven initiatives contributing to the effectiveness of the specific process, management will more highly value its role. Although this may seem like common sense, it is too often overlooked when a needs assessment is conducted.

What Are the Expected Outcomes of the Learning Strategy?

One area of weakness for proposed learning initiatives in the past has been the omission of expected outcomes. For a time, management did not expect learning to be able to answer this question, except by saying that people would be trained. But because of increased accountability for functional business investments, the question of expected outcomes is asked more frequently. Additionally, learning has become much more sophisticated in the last ten to fifteen years, to the extent that learning outcomes are more targeted and focused on specific needs. The outcome of any learning initiative should be

- Clear with outcomes relevant to the needs assessment
- Connected to the business issue being addressed
- Capable of demonstrating a link between business results and initial expected outcomes

What Are the Tangible Benefits of the Learning Strategy?

The primary difference between this question and the last is that this is directly connected to the performance measures outlined in the various organizational scorecards. There are basically two types of learning strategies within the framework of the BSC: (1) the learning strategy as related to the overall organizational strategy (corporate or top-level balanced scorecard) and (2) the cascaded learning strategies corresponding to the business units (cascaded scorecards of the business areas). In both cases, when a learning strategy is developed around performance measures of the business and its corresponding initiatives critical to achieving the organization's objectives, learning begins to demonstrate tangible benefits through improved performance.

For example, let's assume that an organization's mission is to increase its market share by 25 percent in the next three years. In this instance, the driving perspective would be around the customer, which means that marketing and sales would require a scorecard that cascades down from and aligns with the corporate level mission. This marketing and sales balanced scorecard would have various objectives set forth, along with specific targets, performance metrics, and initiatives. They may or may not require support from learning, but this can only be discovered through regular meetings with the marketing and sales group to identify any gaps in employee skill development. Once a learning intervention is identified, learning has to develop solutions that not only align with their scorecard performance measures but also help the affected business area meet these measures. This is when learning interventions produce tangible results. This also validates learning and performance's value in delivering relevant and credible return on their investments.

How Will We Gain Buy-In from Affected Departments/Individuals?

We addressed this question in the article titled, "A Business Approach to Learning." Basically, as in the example above, the key is to always "partner" with the business units and connect with their scorecard performance measures. Doing this will certainly build credibility and value for learning interventions and also ensure buy-in, even from those most resistant.

These are just some of the many questions management may ask you, and remember that it is important to answer them in a way that is clearly understood and relevant to the business. Equip yourself to respond to their questions and to respond appropriately. You may already have a list of questions. If not,. Exhibit 3.6 provides you an opportunity to prepare.

Set some time aside to complete Exhibit 3.6 with your group. Once you have a complete list of questions, use Exhibit 3.7 to group them into categories. Many of the

Exhibit 3.6. What Is Management Asking You?

Question	Who Is Asking (Name/Title)
1.	
2.	
3.	
4.	
5.	
6.	
7.	
8.	

Exhibit 3.7. Responses to Management's Questions

Question	Response	Who (Name and Title)	Research Support	Impact on WLP	Response Date
1.					
2.					
3.					
4.					
5.					
6.					
7.					
8.					

USING BUSINESS DATA TO DEVELOP STRATEGIC LEARNING SOLUTIONS

Over the last few years, companies have been trying to make strategic use of the vast amounts of business data and information they acquire. Business data is now an essential part of strategic and tactical business management. In fact, Gartner (2006), an independent IT research firm, surveyed 1,400 CIOs and found that business intelligence is a priority for organizations as a strategic tool to help people lead, measure, optimize, discover, and innovate.

The ability to access, use, and share data and information in an efficient and relevant way helps improve business performance. Effectively utilizing business data can empower employees to:

- Align day-to-day operations with overall company strategy and objectives;
- Identify and understand the relationship between business processes and their impact on performance;
- Access information relevant to specific user roles and responsibilities;
- Gain contextual insight into business drivers; and
- Monitor the vital business indicators that are needed to move an organization forward such as:
  - Current status and trends of the company's financial performance
  - Organizational effectiveness and profitability
  - Critical operational metrics and key performance measures.

In short, every type of business data helps companies gain a comprehensive and integrated view of their business and facilitate better and more effective decision making. This is where learning professionals can use the available data to develop more focused learning strategies and initiatives.

The biggest challenge is that business is not usually thought of when you think about workplace learning and performance. Business managers often do not see the relevance of "training and development," which often takes a "back seat." Fortunately, this is changing, mainly due to the increasingly significant role of information and knowledge in a knowledge-based economy. Organizational leaders require their employees to act on the business data to gain an "edge" over the competition. The goal is to recognize, learn, solve, and act on the business intelligence at hand.

So what does this have to do with learning and performance? Business data is obtained through various sources. Without accurate data, the chances of making poor business decisions increase, leading to missed opportunities or, worse, eventual disasters. Identifying potential business opportunities such as how to increase profitability, cut costs, or calculate precisely where to spend resources for optimal impact are key issues for employees at all levels. Although the old adage states that knowledge is power, business knowledge is only useful (powerful) to an organization if it is relevant, learned, and applied. And learning plays a pivotal role as a catalyst in leveraging business data.

THE ROLE OF WORKPLACE LEARNING AND PERFORMANCE

Traditionally, those responsible for the learning needs of an organization focused on helping employees acquire and assimilate new skills and capabilities. Naturally, these are the core competencies of WLP professionals. However, the organization's leadership is concerned about and focused on business outcomes and improved performance. Closing the gap between what management wants to see and what learning can deliver will build value for those involved in WLP. Using the business data to develop learning solutions will deliver lasting and tangible business results for the organization.

Economic uncertainties and rapid market changes make planning and decision making much more difficult, but more critical than ever. The best protection against uncertainty is figuring out how to proactively use the information that is available. Learning and performance's revised role is to help managers to adapt quickly to new business scenarios and to work closely with business units to help employees react quickly to changing business conditions.

First, let's dispense with the idea that the business leadership of any organization will recognize the importance of learning. Their focus is solely on improved business performance, and learning and performance is one of many tools in their tool box to help get them to where they need to be. They will listen to and utilize any catalyst that helps them obtain results. Learning and performance must connect with management's world and link business data to performance oriented learning initiatives. Just as you would learn about the culture and language when visiting another country, in this case you are in management's country! Not only do you have to speak their language (business and performance), you also need to transform the information provided into learning solutions that will lead to desired business results.

Learning professionals must understand managers' decision-making processes and how they leverages business data to be able to develop effective learning solutions. Organizational decisions are one of three types:

- *Strategic decisions.* These are the major decisions that companies make in the interests of their corporate mission and objectives. These types of decisions are crucial to the success of the organization and often impact every part of an organization (for example, whether to acquire another company, enter a new market, or develop a new product). Although there are a limited number of these decisions to be made, their importance is great.

- *Tactical decisions.* These are usually the decisions that utilize business data the most and that can be implemented in a relatively short period of time. Tactical decisions help to achieve strategic goals by leveraging what is known. Examples include a product manager deciding what discount schedule to put in place, a pricing decision for a new product, or the marketing strategy required to build market presence and brand awareness.

- *Operational decisions.* These types of business decisions occur on a daily basis and, individually, may not carry much weight. When taken in aggregate, however, operational decisions can play a major role at the tactical and even the strategic level. These types of decisions are usually made by employees who are not knowledgeable about or too concerned with business data. There is an opportunity to bundle these types of decisions to drive improved business performance.

Every business decision can be categorized in one of these three areas. Arriving at a proper decision depends on the information available to the decision-maker, which in turn determines the outcome and the impact the decision will have on the organization. Business data not only facilitates the decision-making process, but often dictates what type of decision must be made.

Business data usually drives organizational leaders to make critical decisions. Business data incites change, and whenever change takes place, learning solutions are sure to follow. Managers may require the support of learning and performance to understand the data and arrive at appropriate decisions. This will add credibility and value for learning, providing for more targeted and result-driven learning solutions.

Let's look at how learning and performance can positively affect each type of decision based on business data.

Learning Based on Strategic Data

The business data available for this type of decision is usually more complex and involved. The data itself requires deciphering because it involves many factors, and the decision-making process is more intense, affecting the organization as a whole. Learning and performance solutions at this level are primarily informal and targeted. The learning solutions developed to support and help resolve the decision-making process are tied directly to the overall learning strategy and key performance indicators. This means that a proposed learning solution must cascade down through the organization and support the changes as they occur at the tactical and operational levels. For example, if some business data demonstrate that a primary competitor is finding success with a new feature on one of their products, then your organization needs to decide how to act on this critical information. Any change or modification in their business direction will impact your organization's strategy, and your learning strategy will have to address the requisite changes and new learning requirements at all levels. Simplifying this process for you is the value chain of the organization (refer to Chapter 5). If a change in strategy is required, then assessing the impact on the value chain will provide you with necessary information to revise your learning strategy. Furthermore, the outcomes of the learning initiatives you develop must be directly correlated to key performance indicators, usually through some type of strategic scorecard, such as the corporate level balanced scorecard and cascaded scorecards.

Learning Based on Tactical Data

Tactical decisions tend to utilize business data more of the time than strategic decisions do. Tactical data affects decisions that have direct implications on business and strategic objectives, especially in the short term. As such, learning solutions based on tactical data should demonstrate tangible results and be aligned to key performance measures cascaded down from the strategic level. For example, let's say one of your company's strategic goals is to be the most customer responsive and supportive organization in its market space. This would mean that the tactical business issues associated with this mission, such as customer service, employee product knowledge, and any other customer-oriented task, must be in line with the company mission. The tactical data obtained must be positive and be aligned with the strategic mission. If the tactical data, hopefully a leading indicator such as customer satisfaction measures, indicate any deviation from the mission, then learning and performance must act immediately. Preferably, as a learning professional, you would simulate scenarios for possible deviations before they happen and continually monitor the performance measures in place.

Learning Based on Operational Data

Even though this type of data does not normally indicate any immediate threats to the organization, it may, like a small crack in a dam, provide early indications of deviations that can lead to bigger business problems if not addressed early. A ship never sinks from the top down; it always begins with a leak in the hull. In the case of a company, a leak that begins at the bottom may grow bigger and work its way up. Learning initiatives at this level tend to address the maintenance and support of employee skills; the earlier you are able to read the operational data at this level, the more likely that you can keep employee skills at the appropriate level. Using our previous tactical example, introducing customer relationship management software would facilitate how a customer service representative (CSR) responds and addresses the needs of a customer. If the CSR, however, does not leverage the capabilities of the new system, then the "small leak" begins. Learning and performance should work in close partnership with other business units (or as we like to say, become the business unit's learning department) to learn what specific operational issues are affected and how to deliver effective learning solutions. Once again, this is best accomplished by reviewing the organization's value chain, determining specific needs, and developing continuous learning interventions that connect to performance measures. At this level, each learning strategy should be tailored to the needs of the business units and their specific operational requirements that cascade up to and align with the tactical and strategic concerns of the organization.

The impact of workplace learning and performance on organizational decision making at all three levels is shown in Figure 4.1.

Figure 4.1. WLP's Impact on Organizational Decision Making

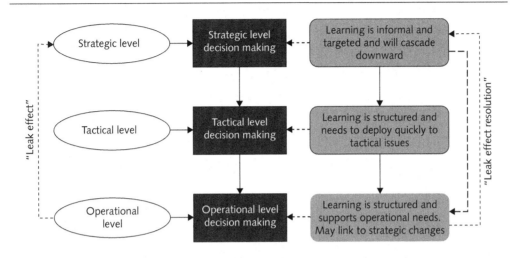

Exhibit 4.1 will assist you in framing the three levels of data with learning initiatives. Take the time to reconcile past, current, and future learning efforts with the needs of the organization. This will provide a starting point to develop your strategic knowledge and business understanding.

Exhibit 4.1. Learning Based on Strategic, Tactical, and Operational Data

Strategic Data

What is your organization's mission?

_____

_____

What are the key words/themes outlined in the mission?

_____

_____

Do you have a organizational learning strategy? Yes _____ No _____

If YES, what is your learning strategy?

_____

_____

If NO, in a few lines, develop a high-level learning strategy:

_____

_____

What business areas are most impacted by the organizational mission?

_____

_____

What business data is affected by this mission: Which performance metrics are measured?

_____

_____

Tactical Data

What is the business area being addressed?

_____

_____

What are the business objectives as it's aligned with the mission?

_____

_____

What business data affects this business area?

_____

_____

What does the business data indicate?

_____

_____

Which performance metrics is the business area accountable for?

_____

_____

What are the areas for improvement based on the business data and performance metrics?

_____

_____

What other information provided by the BU is helpful or required?

_____

_____

Operational Data

What are the operational issues of the business area being addressed?

_____

_____

Within each operational issue, what are the "leaks"?

_____

_____

Is the leak partially/completely resolvable with a learning intervention?
Yes _____ No _____

If YES, describe the problem/weakness/issue to address:

_____

_____

How does the problem/weakness/issue impact the tactical and strategic mission?

_____

_____

What action is required from learning to resolve the issue?

_____

_____

What action is required from the business area?

_____

_____

How will you know the intervention is successful?

_____

_____

Times have changed significantly for organizations of all sizes. Gaining an advantage in increasingly competitive environments is essential to simply survive, let alone thrive. Whether or not a company has access to relevant business data can mean the difference between real success and mediocre performance. Every piece of business data available provides companies with evidence and an early indication of how well the organization is meeting its business and strategic objectives. Companies that can exploit their own data and information to gain insight and make smarter decisions will have a clear competitive advantage over their competitors. This is where the role of learning and performance gains prominence, in translating the data into useable knowledge.

As business data plays a greater role and becomes a priority for senior management, companies will need flexible learning solutions that will address and help them act in the short term as well. As a company grows, the acquisition of more complex business data increases; learning and performance will no longer be relegated to the "back seat" but, like oil in an engine, will be viewed as an enabling force allowing companies to leverage the strategic usefulness of their business data.

NON-FINANCIAL PERFORMANCE MEASURES

In the previous section, we introduced the importance of interpreting the business data an organization produces. Traditionally, most of the business data obtained is financially driven and tangible. Although hard business data will always be available and necessary, it does not always provide a complete picture of a situation. In this age of knowledge and increasing competition, a more holistic approach is required to balance the measurements of past and future performance. This is the role of non-financial performance measures and data. The balanced scorecard is the one tool that is able to balance both within its framework, providing managers with a complete picture of the organization's performance and progress toward achieving its strategic objectives.

This Is Not Your Father's "Performance" Any More

Mention the word "performance" and many managers immediately shift their thinking to measures related to some type of financial result. Managers have been trained to believe that financial measures provide the most relevant and simplest way to demonstrate progress and productivity.

It is true that financial outcomes are tangible, immediate, and relevant, but their strength lies in measuring short-term objectives. In recent years, however, corporate America has had it share of downfalls relating to the manipulation of financial performance measures—so much so that shareholders and the public have sometimes demanded that performance measures be independent from financial outcomes and deliver a longer-term outlook. This outcry has led organizations to include more non-financially based measures.

The challenges with financial-based performance measures are two-fold. First, financial measures are often overused and too extensively relied on. Managers face a tremendous amount of pressure to perform and to demonstrate results quickly. The most convenient method to show results is through financial metrics. These measurements are fast and familiar. They also provide for a very narrow focus of the organization's impact in the marketplace. Second, financial-based measures do not reflect true performance drivers or intangible elements. For example, how does a manager quantify customer satisfaction or intellectual capacity in a financial context?

In recent years, many companies have found that a more inclusive and holistic approach to performance measurement is necessary. It is increasingly important that performance be directly linked to the strategic objectives of the organization. Financial performance metrics provide results related to short-term outcomes. But when dealing with organizational strategy, a long-term approach is required with a focus on non-financial performance measures.

Many non-financial factors have a lasting impact on a company's market value. Since these non-financial measures are more forward-looking and are linked to operational activities, they help to focus managers' efforts and can be used to better evaluate employee performance. These factors include employee knowledge, continuous process improvement, innovative capabilities, and intellectual capital.

The Growing Need for Non-Financial Accountability

Why are non-financial measures gaining prominence over financial metrics? It is because these measures provide a direct correlation to strategic objectives. Most financial measures focus on short-term accountabilities and leave out intangible factors that directly affect customers, suppliers, and employees. The same financial results lead to a narrow focus and set up adversarial environments based on irrelevant data. Financial measures can also be manipulated to meet the outcomes desired.

Numbers are not the most complete or appropriate measure to demonstrate organizational performance. Take for example a company expanding product research and development. This non-financial objective goes against traditional financial performance measures, negatively affecting financial indicators, increasing expenses, and reducing bottom-line results. But the company has a long-term objective of becoming a market leader, resulting in improved financial performance.

Integrating non-financial measures can help managers to communicate objectives, assist in the effective implementation of strategic plans, and provide incentives for management to address long-term strategy.

The use of non-financial factors is gaining ground in our knowledge-dependent environment. Critics of financial measures argue that the success drivers for many industries lie in intangible assets such as human capital and innovative capability. The real value of using non-financial measures is to show the firm's intangible assets and their relationship to quantitative results.

Many studies have examined the use of non-financial performance measures in U.S. companies. These studies commonly find that measures related to innovation, management capability, employee relations, quality, and brand recognition are major contributing factors to a company's overall value.

The evidence demonstrating non-financial based measures are better indicators of a company's financial performance is significant. Financial results traditionally do not take into account or capture long-term benefits. Under current laws, many expenses are declared in the period in which they are incurred, reflecting poor performance. But if the expenditures are justified, the benefits would be seen as a way of improving future profitability. For example, let's say you want to extensively develop your employee skills base and foster a more cohesive workplace. This would require a significant investment in training, coaching, and other methods of support. In the near term, the company would negatively affect its financial performance but the longer-term non-financial benefit would result in innovative ideas and products, leadership in market presence, increased productivity, and improved reputation through reduction in errors and defects. These intangible results will lead to many financial benefits—increased demand for and sales of products, increasing profit margins, and increasing future cash flow to name a few.

An additional benefit non-financial measures offer is their ability to balance factors both within and beyond your control. External factors, for example, are wild cards in performance measurement and often play havoc with forecasts. Non-financial measures are usually concerned with factors that are within the control of the organization, so when looking at non-financial results: (1) the company is less susceptible to external changes, (2) managers are able to direct their efforts on issues directly related to strategic objectives, and (3) both employees and managers can fairly evaluate and improve their performance as required.

Limitations to Non-Financial Performance Measures

Changing the rules on how one evaluates performance in an organization is a challenge. Financial-based measures are ingrained in most companies. New forms of performance evaluation are often met with skepticism, especially as organizations introduce "flavors of the month." The first hurdle when integrating non-financial-based measures is resistance from all levels of the organization.

Another major hurdle is the time and expense involved. Often the cost and time to develop a performance management system can exceed expected benefits. Excessive development and implementation time, incorrect selection and inconsistent application of measures, and the time involved in selling the solution to employees often leave performance-based measurement systems orphaned.

Consistency is key if any type of performance measurement system, financial or non-financial, is to be effective. Too often managers attempt to balance existing performance measures, usually financial, with new, unfamiliar non-financial based measures. This not only takes more time but also causes confusion among those using the measures. It is important to use the non-financial measures those in your organization are familiar with, answer to, and can be simply utilized and measured.

Performance measurement is linked to results, not constant evaluation. In theory, this makes complete sense, but you will find many organizations making any performance measurement process an exercise in futility, continually discussing, evaluating, and reporting performance results, rather than capitalizing on the results. With increasing competitive pressures and changing economic conditions, there is no time for extensive discussions of performance results. If your performance evaluation metrics, especially non-financial ones, require a significant amount of time, then it is time for you to rethink your performance criteria and how they are evaluated. Begin by reducing the indicators used, minimize reporting processes, and reduce meetings to discuss outcomes.

Another significant disadvantage of non-financial measures is the need to find a common base for measurement. As difficult as it may be, managers must ensure there is a common measure and a common understanding of the measurement. Because each organization is unique, each one will establish its own non-financial performance measures. Some develop measures in relation to strategic priorities and rank their importance through a weighted-average approach, whereas others arbitrarily assign subjective measures.

Your goal is to minimize the subjectivity of the measures, making them relevant to the employees and organization. Ensure that real and critical links are made to the non-financial measures you implement. Too often managers adopt a non-financial measure without demonstrating the relationship between the measure and a tangible indicator to performance such as shareholder value, market share, or earnings per share. A weak correlation to a tangible result could lead to a dead end.

Another mistake is attempting to implement too many indicators. In this case more is not necessarily better. Utilizing a multitude of performance indicators can lead to a dilution of the information and a loss of data integrity. Managers waste time trying to interpret irrelevant data. A large telecommunication company (see the following case study) developed a structured approach, clearly knowing its strategic objective and understanding that the business is built on customer experiences. Their performance strategy differentiates between internal and external factors and clearly defines relevant key performance indicators (KPI). The company's KPIs are directly linked backed to the strategic objective and deliver tangible results. When measuring the performance of call center representatives, for example, the company utilizes leading indicators such as revenue per person hour.

Performance in Action at a
Canadian Telecommunication Company

A large telecommunications firm is an industry leader in providing a multitude of communication solutions to millions of people and companies. The company continually remains on the leading edge of customer service and satisfaction and is recognized for its industry knowledge and solutions. They do this by aligning their strategic objective of placing customers first with specific performance and learning strategies.

According to the Marcus Daniels, director of organizational learning and effectiveness for their small medium business division (SMB), "It is not about complex strategies. Our success is simply based on the customer experience and satisfaction." Daniels continues to say, "Our business success and survival are solely based on our ability to meet our customers' needs, and we recognized this very early in the development of our strategy." Effective non-financial performance measurement is based on two basic criteria: (1) link to strategic objectives and (2) keep things simple.

The SMB learning team's performance measures strike a clear balance between the need for financial-based measures with a longer-term outlook on organization development through non-financial metrics. "We need to make sure that our long-term objectives and customer expectations are met, and this can't be done solely on financial outcomes," according to Daniels. "The numbers are the results we gain from focusing on the intangible issues that are at the heart of the company's success." Daniel's team breaks down their performance measures in a structured and systematic process. They have internal and external "lenses" that help them maintain their focus.

Looking Through Lenses

The SMB learning team views performance though a couple of lenses—an internal view that helps them manage capacity and

(continued)

productivity and outcome-based measures tied to the operations. In recruitment, for example, they measure cost per hire (internal) and a number of external measures (competency, psychometric, job simulation, interview results, etc.) to help choose the best candidates. They then measure on-the-job performance of new candidates coming out of induction training. Induction training targets certain KPI that are critical to the business.

From an organization development standpoint, the various components have been broken down and then benchmarked against industry standards. For example, knowledge management (publishing and authoring) and instructional design and delivery have specific performance targets. The learning team makes use of critical industry data and benchmarks. "We frequently measure and compare our performance against these benchmarks," states Daniels. "All of our projects and efforts have real-time reporting capabilities, so we can see exactly how we are performing against past performance and others in the industry." This internal benchmarking process helps the learning team to determine the resources available and the capacity required for any task. "Take our instructional design efforts. For example, if we want to deliver a four-hour course on a topic, we would need to ensure our design time is within or lower than industry standards. This helps us to develop efficiencies at all levels," he explains.

The SMB learning team's internal lens is an excellent example of structured performance measurement. "Knowledge management is focused on two areas: publishing and authoring. There are five types of documents that have been benchmarked, and actual publishing and authoring time is measured against the benchmark. From an instructional design standpoint, they are benchmarked against three types of interventions (regardless of modality, 'e' or classroom): simple, medium, and complex," states Daniels. Internally they manage capacity and productivity by measuring themselves against the benchmarks. With this data available in real time as well, Daniels is able to help identify issues and redeploy resources when needed.

In terms of external measures, learning interventions are aligned with the specific key performance indicators (KPIs) of the operations. According to Daniels, the KPIs "help to identify red flags in a time-sensitive way so we can be proactive in our efforts and address weak performance areas."

Daniels proudly states, "Our external recruitment process for the SMB call centers are focused on the three indicators and help it to bring in the right people, for the right job, in the right way." Key performance indicators are common in many organizations, but this company has worked to align operational KPIs with the learning team's targets. Daniels explains, "The KPIs bring together recruitment, the external lens, and our induction training, the internal lens. As an outcome of recruitment and induction training, we focus on three operational KPIs: first call resolution (a key component of customer satisfaction), revenue per person hour, and average call handle time." Daniels continues, "Our performance measures are our benchmarks and guide us in employee selection and development. We are so efficient that our cost of recruiting is less than half of agency fees. This is immediate proof of the effectiveness of our performance management process and how we impact tangible and intangible objectives."

(continued)

Another important non-financial performance indicator for the company is around learning/knowledge management. The SMB division leverages its knowledge tool and CRM system to ensure representatives are equipped to meet the company's "customer first" orientation. Daniels states, "It is important that we ensure our representatives obtain and apply their skills rather than just acquire knowledge. It is all about application of what is learned and leveraging the knowledge base we possess." The company does this effectively by providing new recruits a safe environment in which to learn and apply their new skills. During this simulation of real-life scenarios, management is capable of measuring the key performance indicators and how certain actions would affect the results. "This way we can realistically not only further develop our representatives but also test our performance measure before going live," explains Daniels.

The take-away Daniels leaves us with is: "Make sure your performance measures are clearly aligned with organizational objectives, integrate systematic performance indicators, and be able to link your intangible performance measures with tangible and relevant results."

SPECIFIC FACTORS THAT DRIVE PERFORMANCE

Developing effective performance measures begins with understanding objectives and values. These factors contribute to the overall success of the organization and help to translate strategic vision into specific actions.

Although this seems like common sense, managers still tend to miss the mark and develop measures that are irrelevant or overly complex. Developing non-financial-based indicators begins by understanding what you are attempting to address strategically. The telecommunication company in the case study, for example, does not link its performance to traditional industry measures but rather to customer experiences and satisfaction. Once you have identified the values, you are in an advantageous position to develop the performance drivers that directly link back to the overall objectives and, hence, link to tangible financial-based results.

Another way to develop performance measures is to identify key industry benchmarks. Competitors, suppliers, and industry clients possess a significant amount of reference data on current and past performance. This type of benchmarking can also lead to an internal comparison of historical performance. In either case, caution is required, since comparing performance measures, especially non-financial ones, can lead to significant discrepancies because objectives and cultures vary from one organization to another.

One of the most reliable methods of measuring non-financial performance is through the relationship of intangible measures to numerical data-driven performance. At the telecommunication company, the performance of call center representatives is tied to how they perform based on the customer experience; however, the results are based on average call handle time and first call resolution.

Figure 4.2 illustrates the flow to deriving the key performance indicators (KPIs) from the strategic objectives of the organization. Like the telecommunication company in the case study, it is essential to understand the direction the organization wants to take. In developing the strategic plan and balanced scorecard, management has clearly defined these objectives. The next step is to define the values of the organization. This is often based on the organizational culture, but is sometimes clearly defined within the organizational mission. The values often have the greatest influence on the strategic objectives of the organization. Defining the organizational strategic drivers is the next step in defining your key performance measures. These drivers will help the organization achieve its strategic objectives. Within a scorecard, the drivers are found in the financial, customer, and internal process perspectives. Within each strategic driver are strategic measures. The measures will assist you in developing the key performance measures for the learning and growth perspective and align your learning strategy. It is crucial that the key performance measures you define align with the other four steps of the process.

What are your key performance measures? In Exhibit 4.2, you'll define the KPIs within the learning area of your organization. You may need to do further investigation to determine the first four steps.

When considering key performance measures, first take inventory of the non-financial indicators currently used and identify those that are effective in their application. It is important to begin from the top (strategic orientation and objective) and work

Figure 4.2. The Flow of KPIs from Strategic Objectives

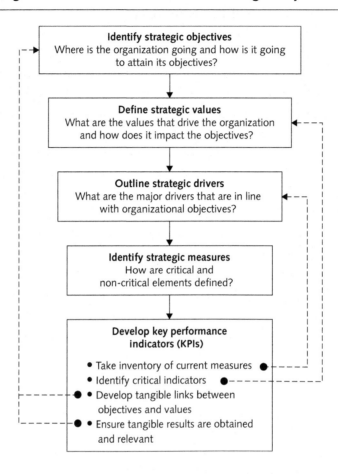

your way down to the value drivers of the organization. Discard all measures that do not deliver any value and develop new metrics addressing issues critical to advancing the organization toward its goals. Two things are important to remember: (1) not all performance indicators have to be identical for each task and (2) simplicity in your measures is usually most effective.

The next step is to integrate the measures through a transparent and easily accessible process that facilitates reporting and evaluation. The choice of performance measures should not be taken lightly, as they will impact all levels of the organization and employee performance.

Exhibit 4.2. Key Performance Measures

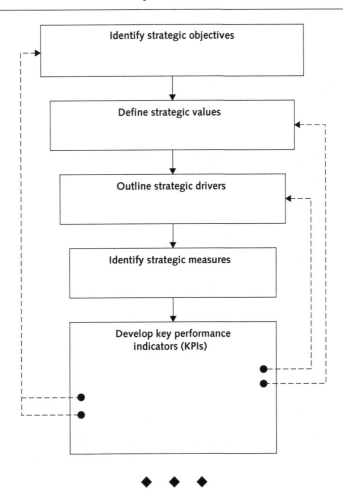

Each non-financial performance measure is as unique as each organization seeking to implement an effective performance management process. As direct and simple as financial performance measures can be, they do not reflect organizational strategy holistically. The true value of non-financial measures is dependent on the selection of appropriate objectives related directly to organizational strategy. But it is important to keep in mind that any performance management solution is a dynamic process and that choices made today may not reflect the direction taken tomorrow. Your performance management process must evolve with your organizational strategy and changes in the nature of the environment.

LAST THOUGHTS

Organizations of all types and sizes must be capable of remaining competitive in increasingly demanding times. With survival dependent on obtaining the right information, business data is crucial in helping organizations to make the right decisions. Only a few years ago, financially based business data was acceptable to decision-makers. The weakness lay in the timing of the information, as financial business data is based on past performance. With the need for real-time information and leading performance measures, lagging business data such as financial metrics are insufficient to support an organization for long-term growth.

For organizational leaders and managers, business data is at the forefront of their strategic development process. The decisions made will have a direct impact on people throughout the organization. Making proper decisions requires a comprehensive understanding of the types of business data available and the relevance of the data for the organization.

Business data provides an opportunity for learning professionals to contribute and add value through learning interventions. In a knowledge-driven economy, balancing financial and non-financial data is essential if the organization is to see a complete picture of what is required to achieve its objectives.

Learning and performance must be able to interpret business data to their advantage. This will empower them to develop more learning interventions and holistic learning strategies and to build an effective balanced scorecard.

Learning and performance's new role is to provide all areas of the organization at all levels with a way to adapt to new business realities and constant competitive changes. Learning must leverage business data while working closely with various business units, allowing employees to acquire new skills and knowledge to meet the needs of an evolving business. Companies must continually improve their ability to identify, organize, and analyze all the information available to them. Learning and performance must be actively involved in the process.

In this chapter you will discover how an organization creates value for its customers and its own long-term growth from its internal processes and how workplace learning and performance can deliver tangible value. By the end of this chapter you will have learned about:

- The organizational value chain: providing real value
- The value chain's proposition to the customer
- Deconstructing the value chain
- Building the learning and performance value chain

THE ORGANIZATIONAL VALUE CHAIN: PROVIDING REAL VALUE

In the current business environment, organizations can only survive if they are able to provide quality products or services at a reasonable and competitive price. To accomplish this, organizations must analyze and manage their cost structure while maintaining their strategy of long-term growth. Managing the various organizational aspects is accomplished by focusing on what Harvard economist and strategist Michael Porter (1985) describes as the "value chain." The value chain is important in understanding how an organization functions. The analysis of the value chain deconstructs the organization into strategically defined activities. This allows managers to devise effective strategies to develop and achieve their long-term mission.

The corporate value chain refers to the set of value-creating activities beginning with the raw material inputs, moving to the production and marketing of a product or service, and ending with how it is distributed to the final customer. The steps between are often referred to as value-added activities. Porter came up with this concept to help organizations to better analyze their cost structures and to better identify unique and value adding activities and strategies. According to Porter, "The value chain desegregates a firm into its strategically relevant activities in order to understand the behavior of costs and the existing and potential sources of differentiation. A firm gains competitive advantage by performing these activities more cheaply or better than its competitors" (Barnes, 2001, p. 50). An example of an organizational value chain is presented in Figure 5.1.

Management often divides the value chain into two primary segments. The supply inputs and manufacturing/production activities are regularly described as the upstream segment, whereas the marketing and distribution are referred to as the downstream activities. The value chain and the balanced scorecard are not mutually exclusive; rather, the value chain is essential to operational effectiveness of the organization and the balanced scorecard aligns performance measures within organizational groupings (the perspectives) encompassing the specific areas of the value chain. In the balanced scorecard, upstream segments are aligned with the "internal process" perspective, whereas downstream activities generally align with the "customer" perspective, as illustrated in Figure 5.2. This type of segmentation allows managers to identify the areas that are value-added or non-value-added, helping them to decide what to maintain in the process and what to eliminate.

A value-chain analysis essentially allows management to determine the full value of the organization's operations and provide an industry comparison. A value chain focuses on a set of value-creating activities from the beginning of the business process to the end. Monitoring and managing the value chain helps to

Figure 5.1. Organizational Value Chain

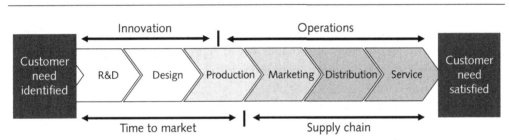

Figure 5.2. Value Chain Aligned with the BSC Perspectives

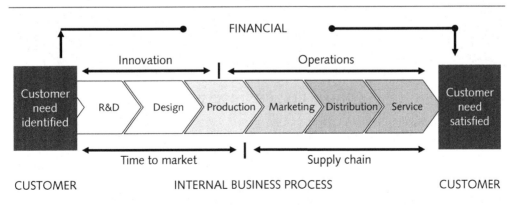

identify areas of improvement, including cost management, customer value, and innovation. It is important for workplace learning to understand the value chain in order to (1) discover areas where it can be part of the value creation activities and (2) develop appropriate learning solutions targeting these value creation activities (see Figure 5.3).

Once you define the organization's value chain, it is time to analyze the areas in which learning can add value and effectively contribute to the value chain's effectiveness. Managers will continually evaluate the value chain and seek efficiencies by performing a cost-benefit analysis for various activities in the value chain. Learning can influence the performance of some of these activities, ensuring the efficiencies of the value chain are enhanced. Figure 5.4 demonstrates how learning contributes to the value chain in the context of the balanced scorecard.

THE VALUE CHAIN'S PROPOSITION TO THE CUSTOMER

The value chain clearly illustrates how an organization is able to create value for long-term growth. This unique value is referred to as a value proposition, which develops out of a combination of an organization's core competencies and unique mix of product offerings. It provides a clear representation of specific organizational attributes through products and services that create customer loyalty and

Figure 5.3. Value Chain Aligned with the Learning and Growth Perspective

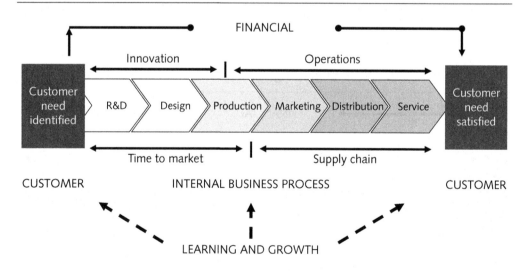

Figure 5.4. Deconstructing the Value Chain Around the BSC and Learning

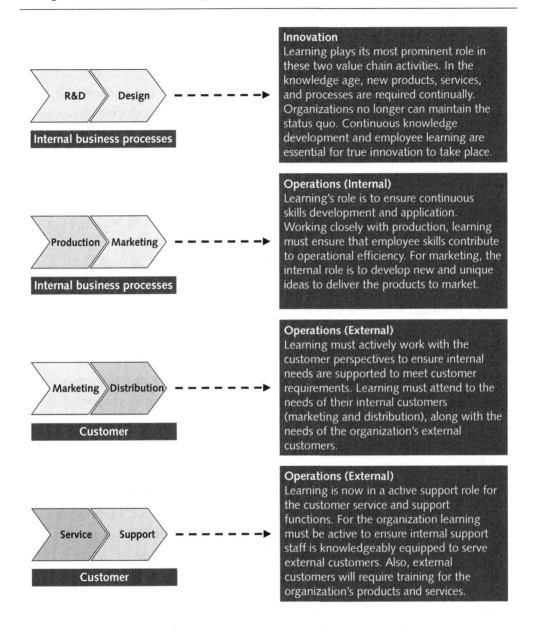

Innovation
Learning plays its most prominent role in these two value chain activities. In the knowledge age, new products, services, and processes are required continually. Organizations no longer can maintain the status quo. Continuous knowledge development and employee learning are essential for true innovation to take place.

Operations (Internal)
Learning's role is to ensure continuous skills development and application. Working closely with production, learning must ensure that employee skills contribute to operational efficiency. For marketing, the internal role is to develop new and unique ideas to deliver the products to market.

Operations (External)
Learning must actively work with the customer perspectives to ensure internal needs are supported to meet customer requirements. Learning must attend to the needs of their internal customers (marketing and distribution), along with the needs of the organization's external customers.

Operations (External)
Learning is now in a active support role for the customer service and support functions. For the organization learning must be active to ensure internal support staff is knowledgeably equipped to serve external customers. Also, external customers will require training for the organization's products and services.

R&D **Design**
Internal business processes

Production **Marketing**
Internal business processes

Marketing **Distribution**
Customer

Service **Support**
Customer

satisfaction. Within the value proposition some of the attributes are defined by the marketplace and competitive factors, while other distinguishable attributes differentiate the organization from its competitors. The value proposition is something against which to measure customer satisfaction and overall market share.

The organization's value proposition is a promise to deliver the products and services customers expect. Failure to deliver makes customers consider switching to alternative suppliers. Kaplan and Norton (1996, p. 73) describe the categories of the value proposition as follows:

- Products and services
  - Functionality—What will products/services promise to do for the customer?
  - Quality—Does the product/service deliver on the performance/output that is expected by the customer?
  - Price—Does the product/service provide value for the price the customer is willing to pay?
- Customer relationships
  - Knowledgeable people—Are the employees capable of meeting the needs and demands of the customers with the knowledge they possess?
  - Access to the product—Do the customers have access to the products/services they expect (delivery or access through known distribution channels)?
  - Responsiveness—Are the customers served and responded to in a timely manner and to their satisfaction?
- Reputation and image
  - Intangible factors—Many intangible factors attract specific customer groups to an organization. Items such as reputation, experience, and expertise are some of the many items that factor into a client's decision when selecting a product and/or an organization.

It is important to understand your organization's value proposition. This unique combination of attributes and factors is the basis of the organization's existence. The value proposition is the driver of the organization's value chain and directly influences what new products and services are offered, how they will be produced, where and how they will be distributed, and how they will be supported.

DECONSTRUCTING THE VALUE CHAIN

The first step for learning professionals when executing learning strategies is to have others in the organization share in the development of those learning initiatives to help them meet their business objectives. This will result in learning delivering value for internal customers so they can deliver value to their external customers and meet organizational objectives, as illustrated by Figure 5.5.

Management expects certain results from their business investments. Every dollar invested must demonstrate some type of tangible result. The more positive the result, the more value to the organization. Generally, this is considered to be return on investment, but it doesn't mean that all investments will return a monetary outcome greater than what was initially invested. Managers are held accountable for results, but as long as the results deliver value and connect to specific business objectives, then that is considered enough.

You may be able to measure ROI in monetary terms. However, management may not place much value on the result. They do, however, expect learning and performance to deliver a solution that will address operational concerns and demonstrate tangible business results.

WLP can exert influence by determining how its learning initiatives can contribute within the context of the balanced scorecard. Management sees the value chain in two parts—the internal customer value chain and the external customer value chain, as shown in Figure 5.6. The external customer value chain identifies the functions that impact the paying customer. If a function does not meet the needs of the customer, it will not deliver positive results.

Figure 5.5. Reconciling Business and Learning Needs

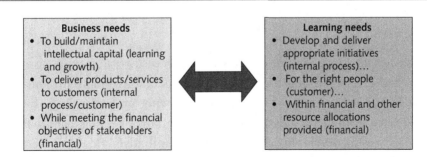

Business needs
- To build/maintain intellectual capital (learning and growth)
- To deliver products/services to customers (internal process/customer)
- While meeting the financial objectives of stakeholders (financial)

Learning needs
- Develop and deliver appropriate initiatives (internal process)...
- For the right people (customer)...
- Within financial and other resource allocations provided (financial)

Figure 5.6. Management's Perspective of the Value Chain

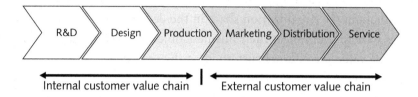

The internal customer value chain includes items that impact internal business units. Should the internal functions fail at any point in the value chain, the value proposition promise to the external customer will not be met.

When learning becomes an active partner in the value chain, it can help the business functions meet their performance measures outlined in the balanced scorecard. There are five steps for learning to take when becoming an active value chain partner:

1. *Get to know your value chain.* The first step is for you to learn about the organization's value chain and understand the connections and relationships that exist within it. Also, you must understand how both the internal and external components of the value chain function. It is critical to keep the external, paying customer in mind because the organization must meet his or her needs to survive and grow.

2. *Divide and conquer.* Now that you have an understanding of the value chain, it is time to break it down into its individual components. Each component may involve more than one business unit and it is essential to be aware of all connections. For example, the marketing component often includes and is responsible for sales.

3. *Partner up.* Once you have segregated each of the value chain components, approach each business unit to discuss its operations and needs. This informal needs assessment will provide you with a better understanding of what they expected from them. Clearly state your intention of helping them to meet their objectives by developing effective learning initiatives. Be transparent in your approach and make sure you are always focusing on their needs. The goal is

to demonstrate that the learning department wants to be proactive in helping them to meet their objectives.

4. *Go deep.* By striking a partnership with each business unit, the learning department will be in a strong position to help each unit develop effective learning solutions. Work with the business areas through a continuous time line rather than on an event-by-event basis. This will ensure continuity, meeting of performance benchmarks, and seamless connections to other parts of the value chain. Work closely with each unit not only to identify its specific needs but also to identify issues for the value chain as a whole. The goal is to develop learning solutions that align at all levels.

5. *Develop synergies.* As mentioned in step 4, you must assess the need for the value chain as a whole, since this directly correlates with the strategic direction of the organization and the performance measures in the balanced scorecard. Equally important if learning is to make a real impact and build lasting credibility is for learning professionals to understand and develop synergies across the value chain. By keeping a high-level context in mind, learning professionals can:

- Make learning a continuous and proactive process, not one based on reactions to isolated events
- Capitalize on synergies created by connecting initiatives in one area with those in others
- Measure and correlate the impact a learning intervention in one area will have on another area

Exhibits 5.1 and 5.2 will help you start to identify the value proposition, the components of the value chain, and the business areas that comprise each area of the value chain.

Now that you have defined the value chain and the business areas, it is time to align employees and skills. This is where learning should be able to really show off its worth. Within each business unit or function are job roles and responsibilities. Each of these job roles contributes to the operational effectiveness of the business unit. We can therefore conclude that, if we are to develop and/or improve the abilities of the employees, the effect would cascade throughout the value chain, ensuring that performance measures are attained and that strategic objectives are met.

Exhibit 5.1. Define Your Organization's Value Proposition

What is your organization's value proposition to the customer? (Example: BMW's message is "The Ultimate Driving Experience.")

_____

_____

_____

What specific areas of the value chain are instrumental in making the value proposition a reality? (Example: In the BMW example, R&D, design, and marketing would have the most influence.)

> R&D > Design > Production > Marketing > Distribution > Service

Internal customer value chain | External customer value chain

_____

_____

_____

Why are the components you listed above having the greatest influence on the value proposition?

_____

_____

_____

◆　◆　◆

Exhibit 5.2. Identifying Your Value Chain

R&D

Identify the business areas involved:

_____

_____

_____

What is the value of this role?

_____

_____

_____

Who should be involved in a discussion (name and title)?

_____

_____

_____

Design

Identify the business areas involved:

_____

_____

_____

What is the value of this role?

_____

_____

_____

Who should be involved in a discussion (name and title)?

_____

_____

_____

Production

Identify the business areas involved:

_____

_____

_____

What is the value of this role?

_____

_____

_____

Who should be involved in a discussion (name and title)?

_____

_____

_____

Marketing

Identify the business areas involved:

_____

_____

_____

What is the value of this role?

_____

_____

_____

Who should be involved in a discussion (name and title)?

_____

_____

_____

Distribution

Identify the business areas involved:

_____

_____

_____

What is the value of this role?

_____

_____

_____

Who should be involved in a discussion (name and title)?

_____

_____

_____

Service

Identify the business areas involved:

_____

_____

_____

What is the value of this role?

_____

_____

_____

Who should be involved in a discussion (name and title)?

_____

_____

_____

◆　◆　◆

The steps are simple and second-nature to most learning and HR professionals. They include the following:

1. Identify the job roles and responsibilities within each business function.

2. Take inventory and identify the essential skills and proficiencies required to be effective in this role and deliver value to the next step in the value chain.

3. Identify the BSC perspective and performance measure the job role corresponds to.

4. Identify the specific individual or individuals responsible for the job.

5. Take inventory of the individual(s) skills and proficiencies (see Figure 5.7).

6. Assess the individual's proficiency and skills essential in this role as specified in Step 3.

In Exhibit 5.3, you'll connect the value chain component to the employee and the required skills for effectiveness. Modify this form to meet your needs and spend the time to account for all of the key elements. When assessing the skills of

Figure 5.7. Relationship Between the Value Chain and Employee Skills

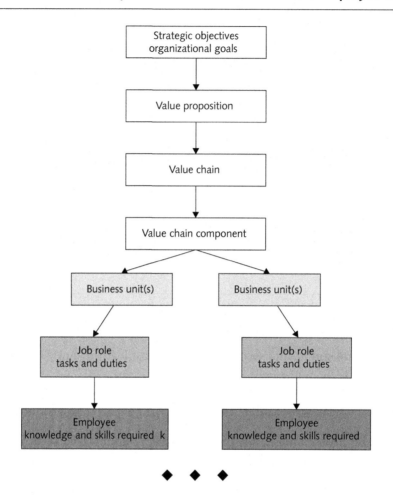

 Exhibit 5.3. Assessing Employee Skills and Knowledge

Value Chain Component: _____   Business Unit: _____

Employee Name: _____   Job Role: _____

Job responsibilities:

_____

_____

_____

_____

Essential skills and knowledge required:

_____

_____

_____

_____

Level: Literate _____ Fluent _____ Master _____

BSC perspective:

_____

_____

_____

_____

Identify performance measures for this job:

_____

_____

_____

_____

Employee skills and knowledge possessed:

_____

_____

_____

_____

Level: Literate _____ Fluent _____ Master _____

Employee skills and knowledge required:

_____

_____

_____

_____

Level: Literate _____ Fluent _____ Master _____

a job and employees, ensure that you account for proficiency levels required for each and assess employees against those requirements to help them to become more effective. Notice that the three levels of proficiency include being skills literate (the capacity to articulate knowledge); fluent (the capacity to perform a task); and master (to possess expertise in the skill).

Once you define the organization's value chain and analyze the areas in which learning can add value, the interventions you develop will certainly demonstrate significant results. In the same way that managers continually evaluate the value chain and seek efficiencies, you must continually evaluate the needs of your customers and develop new learning solutions. The opportunity for WLP lies in:

- Developing relevant learning opportunities in the chain
- Helping the organization meet performance measures
- Connecting directly to the business
- Contributing to achieving the organization's strategic objectives

Managers will seek cost or differentiation advantages by "reconfiguring" the value chain. This means actual structural changes, such as a new production process, new distribution channels, or a different sales approach. In addressing these changes, learning can take a strategic role.

BUILDING THE LEARNING AND PERFORMANCE VALUE CHAIN

Understanding the organizational value chain is the first step in building strong learning interventions. To enhance learning and performance's capabilities further and to deliver even stronger solutions, it is essential to develop a value chain for it as well, using a four-step process:

1. *Construct a value chain for learning and for the internal customers similar to the organizational value chain.* You want to create one that encompasses the flow of the learning department's process. This should extend to the organizational strategy and, when possible, its relationship to the critical business areas.

2. *Identify the unique drivers that add value to the WLP value chain.* Assess WLP's potential in adding value for its learning processes and proposals by examining

each step in the value chain. Identify the specific variables and actions through which WLP can add real value in relation to organizational needs.

3. *Select the most value-adding variables for WLP and the organization.* Among all of the drivers that may exist, select the ones that deliver the most relevant value for WLP, the organization, and each business unit. On the input or supply side, it is important to determine the core competencies of the department and what should be provided by external sources. For example, if the department is seeking to introduce an e-learning strategy for a decentralized organization, its core strengths may be in course development, but the technological and integration capabilities may be best left to an external e-learning provider.

4. *Identify the value linkages.* To determine how the value chain will actually create value for the internal customer, identify linkages within the customer's own value chain, such as reducing costs or increasing efficiencies. WLP's goal is to help their customers add value or differentiate themselves.

Figure 5.8 illustrates an example of the four-step value chain relationship process in greater detail.

On the left is a sample value chain created for a fictitious WLP department. On the right is a sample value chain obtained from a production business unit in the same organization.

In this example, the elements of the WLP value chain that add value and contribute to the growth of the organization are needs assessment, piloting and deployment, and rapid implementation of courses. However, designing and conducting assessments and application to the business needs are not listed as strengths.

We determined the unique value chain elements for WLP; but some will require the external expertise that will capitalize on WLP's strength in pre-selection of suppliers. The linkages in this example are as follows:

1. Needs assessment will assist order processing in discovering inefficiencies.

2. Rapid implementation and connection to the business need is required to help production increase their operational effectiveness.

3. Assessment and testing is essential to ensure consistency for quality control.

4. Measuring the impact on the business (Level 4) is important for allocation and distribution of orders since it impacts other business units' value chains.

Figure 5.8. Sample Value Chain for a Production Business Unit

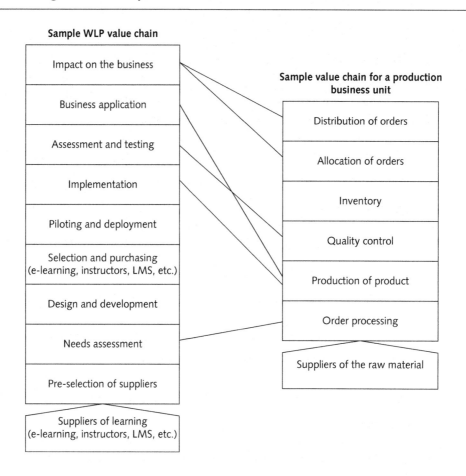

LAST THOUGHTS

Many opportunities exist for learning professionals to build value for the organization as well as credibility for learning's new role. An organization is highly dependent on the skills, abilities, knowledge, and experience of their employees. The link between the production value chain and these knowledge inputs is dependent on the types of interventions and strategies learning develops.

The organizational value chain begins with identifying a market or customer need and an output that satisfies this requirement. An organization must find a way to satisfy their clients' initial needs. The four perspectives of the balanced scorecard are helpful in this regard. Learning and performance must thoroughly analyze the areas in which it can add value. Managers must continually evaluate the value chain and seek efficiencies, and those responsible for learning efforts can ensure that the value chain is efficient.

The value chain is not the only consideration for learning and performance. Management expects tangible results from their investment in learning, "return on investment." Not all investments deliver monetary results, but there must be some type of tangible benefit to justify initial investments. Learning and performance can obtain these tangible results by connecting their efforts to the value chain.

The opportunity for WLP lies in:

- Developing relevant learning opportunities in the chain,
- Helping the organization meet performance measures,
- Connecting directly to the business, and
- Contributing to achieving the organization's strategic objectives.

Paying attention to these four main points will help WLP professionals to build significant credibility with management and enhance their reputation as operational business partners.

In this chapter you will learn:

- How management differentiates between investment and expense
- The value of an organization's financial statements
- How to tie financial statements to management objectives

HOW MANAGEMENT DIFFERENTIATES BETWEEN INVESTMENT AND EXPENSE

Management evaluates all business investments and expenses against financial statements. Management treats expenses and investments differently. Financially, investments are long term, whereas expenses are short term. This means they are also perceived differently when making decisions. When an item is seen as an expense, the item is used and disposed of quickly, usually within one year or less and is "expensed" during the same period. In periods of crisis or when seeking efficiencies, the first place managers look to reduce or eliminate costs are the organization's expenses. This is usually the case for learning initiatives, since they are often classified as direct expenses to the department. In contrast, investments are longer in duration and perceived as an integral part of the organization's development. Thus, learning must position itself as an investment by developing continuous learning strategies that contribute to strategic objectives, rather than periodic learning interventions that treat immediate needs.

THE VALUE OF AN ORGANIZATION'S FINANCIAL STATEMENTS

Every activity that occurs in an organization is reflected through financial statements for a specific period of time based on past performance or expected performance. Past financial performance is reported soon after the period in question and is provided to stakeholders. Future financial performance is based on many non-financial performance measures that drive the organization toward specific expectations. Eventually, this will be assessed, or benchmarked, against actual financial results. The financial statements, whether past or forecasted, are at the heart of a company's reporting process. Through an analysis of the financial data, you can gain an appreciation of how your efforts affect or contribute to organizational results. The financial statements and reporting mechanisms are the bases from which management evaluates all financial and non-financial decisions. The primary financial statements used to evaluate business results include the following:

- Income statement
- Balance sheet
- Cash flow statement

So what do managers look at when evaluating results? Their main considerations are

- Whether the value of the organization (shown on the balance sheet) increased through the use of internal resources
- Whether the organization's profits increased as a result of initiatives in place
- Ensuring that the organization has sufficient cash flow (liquidity) available for its short-term viability and differentiating between profits and cash
- Ensuring that proposed investments are aligned with the organization's strategic direction

HOW TO TIE FINANCIAL STATEMENTS TO MANAGEMENT OBJECTIVES

Each one of the considerations mentioned above drives management's handling of activities within the organization. Let's look at each one in more detail.

Management Performance Objective 1: Increase Organizational Value

Managers seek to continually increase their organizations' value over time. The balance sheet reflects this intention and demonstrates the financial strength of the organization or department represented (see Table 6.1). The value is reflected in both the increase in assets (what it owns) and the reduction of liabilities (what it owes). It also shows the funds invested and what is available for growth. Therefore,

Table 6.1. Structure of a Balance Statement

Assets	Liabilities and Stockholders' Equity
Current Assets. This includes cash, accounts receivables, and other assets that can be converted into cash relatively quickly.	**Current Liabilities.** This includes a company's liabilities that will come due within the next twelve months.
Property and Equipment. This is not exclusive to equipment and property and can be more accurately described as long-term operating assets (less appreciation on these assets).	**Long-Term Liabilities.** Debt not maturing in the next twelve months. A good example is outstanding bonds that don't mature for several years.
Other Assets. Includes anything that doesn't fit in the above categories	**Stockholders' Equity.** This reveals how the remainder of the company's assets are financed, including common and preferred stock, treasury stock, and retained earnings.

every investment made will affect one or both of these areas in some way directly or indirectly. This means that managers must quickly gain an understanding of what will help to add value to the balance sheet. The difficulty is that a balance sheet illustrates investments in tangible items. The challenge for managers is to demonstrate an increase in value for an intangible asset, such as a learning initiative that builds employee knowledge, and to justify it to stakeholders.

Although some organizations make an effort to recognize investments of intangible contributions on the balance sheet, not all managers are convinced. Learning professionals must be part of this effort. When they are developing learning strategies and learning initiatives, it is important to first acknowledge that it is an intangible investment. Second, they must back up their proposals by demonstrating tangible results. You may say, "That's easier said than done." However, it is crucial to demonstrate the results indirectly. Simply providing evidence of change when evaluating learning initiatives is sometimes sufficient to convince management of their effectiveness. The same principle applies here.

Keep in mind that the balance sheet reflects the overall value of the organization. This means that anything developed, purchased, and utilized will increase or decrease that organization's value. So you must provide the linkages to resolve management's concerns. For example, let's say that the balance sheet shows a significant increase in accounts receivables over a few periods. This may be a cue for you to work with the finance department to investigate what is causing the problem. It may be caused by a new financial system for which the staff is inadequately trained, or may be that the sales department has not been enforcing new payment terms. In either case, a learning solution would assist in alleviating this problem and thus future balance sheets would reflect a decreasing trend in accounts receivables, implying that the learning solution proved effective.

Obtain a copy of your organization's balance sheet. Compare it against the structure presented in Table 6.1. Take some time to review the balance sheet against past periods and forecasts. You should be able to discover areas of weakness and be able to propose improvements that the learning function can contribute. Follow these steps:

1. Obtain copies of past and forecast balance sheets.

2. Conduct a comparative analysis of the statements and forecast.

3. Identify areas of weakness and areas for improvement.

4. Limit your list to only two to three issues, list your assumptions, and describe the situation.

5. Approach the managers of these areas and begin a dialogue.

6. Assess whether WLP could play a role in resolving the situation.

7. If there is a role for WLP, work with the manager to develop a comprehensive solution that incorporates an appropriate learning intervention.

8. Support the effort after the solution has been implemented.

Utilize the form in Exhibit 6.1 as a template to begin documenting your efforts and mapping out the steps above.

Management Performance Objective 2: Increase Organizational Profitability

The most popular topic among managers is an organization's profitability, which refers to the effective use of resources during a specified period of time in comparison to what the organization earns. Essentially, the income statement summarizes the

Exhibit 6.1. Balance Sheet Value Creation

Have you obtained copies of the organization's balance sheets?

Yes _____ No _____

For what time periods (list the time periods):

_____

_____

_____

List the identified areas of weaknesses:

1. _____
2. _____
3. _____
4. _____

List the identified areas of proposed improvement (forecasted balance sheet):

1. _____
2. _____
3. _____
4. _____

List the affected/implicated department:

1. _____
2. _____
3. _____
4. _____

List the managers/leaders to approach:

1. _____
2. _____
3. _____
4. _____

Does learning and performance play a role?

Yes _____ No _____

    If YES, then answer the questions below for each department and situation.

Description of the situation:

_____

_____

_____

Description of the process:

_____

_____

_____

Estimated budget by the department:

_____

_____

_____

Estimated allocation to learning:

_____

_____

_____

Proposed learning intervention:

_____

_____

_____

Expected results:

_____

_____

_____

Proposed follow-up and support:

_____

_____

_____

Table 6.2. Structure of an Income Statement

Revenue. The proceeds that come from sales to customers.

Cost of Goods Sold. An expense that reflects the cost of the product or good that generates revenue. For example, if a loaf of bread costs 50 cents to make, then COGS is 50 cents.

Gross Margin. Also called gross profit, which is revenue minus COGS.

Operating Expenses. Any expense that doesn't fit under COGS such as administration and marketing expenses.

Net Income Before Interest and Tax. Net income before taking interest and income tax expenses into account.

Interest Expense. The payments made on the company's outstanding debt.

Income Tax Expense. The amount payable to the federal and state governments.

Net Income. The final profit after deducting all expenses from revenue.

operating activities of the organization. It shows all of the money the organization earns through its sales or revenues and what it has spent (costs and expenses) to reach its financial objectives. The difference between the two totals is net profits for the period. Like the balance sheet, the income statement is usually historical, showing past performance, but it is also developed to forecast future performance. Table 6.2 illustrates a typical layout of an income statement.

Learning departments must address two issues with the income statement. The first issue is to find a way for management not to perceive learning as an expense. If management expenses learning initiatives, it implies that learning is only a short-term fix. For accounting purposes, many learning initiatives will be expensed, but the overall learning strategy must be seen as an investment. The second issue is to determine how learning can contribute value within the context of the income statement. This will help learning efforts to become valued.

Managers look at an income statement in three sections. The first is the business's revenues that come from business activities. Managers will often refer to this as the "top line." Learning initiatives can be an indirect linkage to how revenue is generated and which departments are directly responsible. Learning solutions can significantly help to increase revenue. For example, the sales department is usually the first line of revenue generation. Learning could work closely with the sales team to make them more effective.

Within manufacturing environments, the top line also encompasses the costs of the products sold, including the production of goods. When sales begin to plateau, management will find ways to increase operational efficiencies and/or seek areas in which to reduce production costs. This is another key area for learning professionals to understand. They should also develop a relationship with the production department to assist it in achieving better results, even before management is involved. An example would be to develop continuous operational efficiency training programs for the production line and operators of equipment.

The difference between revenues and costs is referred to as gross profit or, when represented as a percentage, as gross margin (GM). Gross profit is constantly monitored as an indicator of the organization's health.

The second part of the income statement management looks closely at is the organization's operational activities. Commonly referred to as operating expenses, this section illustrates the expenses related to the operations and administration of the organization. As mentioned earlier, learning activities are listed in this area because there are specific accounting rules (not addressed in this text) on how to treat operating expenses and overhead. Operational expenses are items not directly linked to the core business of the organization, but required to ensure that an organization functions effectively. These operational expenses are often the first impacted by budget cutbacks and cost reductions. For example, marketing is an operational activity essential for every organization's long-term success. Working closely with marketing, investing in the development of specific result-driven learning initiatives can deliver solutions that help to increase the effectiveness of the marketing department that leads to increased customer inquiries and eventually to an increase in sales. This is the chain of cause-and-effect that learning can have within an organization. Investments in learning can be attributed in some way to the improved performance of the operational areas. In this way learning aligns itself with management's business and strategic goals.

The last component managers look at is the net income or the "bottom line," the amount of profit after all of expenses and costs are deducted from revenues. The challenge is to obtain increases year after year. If the net figure is stagnant or, worse, declining, it indicates poor performance internally. Monitoring this number provides an opportunity for learning to work with management to discover areas of improvement to reverse the trend.

Utilize the form in Exhibit 6.2 as a template to begin documenting your efforts and mapping out the steps above.

Management Performance Objective 3: Increase Organizational Liquidity

One of the most underestimated and ignored topics is the need for an organization to maintain liquidity. Liquidity refers to the amount of cash the organization has available to meet its short-term obligations. Often, inexperienced business-people do not differentiate between the organization's profitability and liquidity. An organization requires cash to survive. Take yourself for example. You may be earning an excellent salary and possibly have secured investments for retirement.

Exhibit 6.2. Income Statement Value Creation

Top line figure: $_____

List management's top objectives to increase the top line:

1. _____
2. _____
3. _____
4. _____

What is management's time frame to accomplish the top line objectives?

Objective	Time frame
1. _____	1. _____
2. _____	2. _____
3. _____	3. _____
4. _____	4. _____
5. _____	5. _____

Name the business areas directly affected:

Business area	How are they affected?
1. _____	1. _____
2. _____	2. _____

3. _____   3. _____
4. _____   4. _____
5. _____   5. _____

Complete a sheet for each business area:

Business area: _____ BSC perspective: _____

Manager: _____

Specify their performance objectives and targets:

Performance Objective   **Performance targets**

1. _____   1. _____
2. _____   2. _____
3. _____   3. _____
4. _____   4. _____

Description of the situation:

_____

_____

Description of the process:

_____

_____

Estimated budget: _____ Est. allocation to learning: _____

Proposed learning intervention:

_____

_____

Expected results:

_____

_____

Proposed follow-up and support:

_____

_____

Table 6.3. Structure of a Cash Flow Statement

Cash from Operations. This is cash generated from day-to-day business operations.

Cash from Investing. Cash used for investing in assets, as well as the proceeds from the sale of other businesses, equipment, or other long-term assets.

Cash from Financing. Cash paid or received from issuing and borrowing of funds. This section also includes dividends paid. (Although they are sometimes listed under cash from operations.)

Net Increase or Decrease in Cash. Increases in cash from previous year will be written normally, and decreases in cash are typically written in <brackets>.

To survive on a daily basis you still require money in your pocket to pay for food, shelter, and basic necessities. The same applies to all organizations. Table 6.3 illustrates a typical layout of a cash flow statement.

The primary purpose of the cash flow statement is to summarize the sources and uses of the organization's cash within a specified period of time. Essentially, it answers the questions, "Where does the cash come from?" and "Where did the cash go?" The cash flow statement is developed using information from both the income statement and the balance sheet. Managers not only monitor and manage the current cash flow requirements but, more importantly, forecast what their cash needs will be for the future. This is important for learning professionals, as many activities not initially budgeted in the operational forecast will be assessed against the importance of the need and the cash available to finance the initiative.

Management Performance Objective 4: Aligning Investment with Strategic Objectives

Many managers are still challenged trying to develop measures by which they can align their strategic objectives. Their comfort zone is around financial metrics, but there is no basis of measurement when it comes to driving the organization forward. What was once acceptable is insufficient to meet long-term strategic requirements. This is why the balanced scorecard is so necessary. As mentioned in Chapter 2, the word "balanced" emphasizes the balance between:

- Lagging performance measures (financial results) and leading performance metrics
- Financial results and non-financial performance measures
- Internal needs and external concerns

Managers are quickly embracing the balanced scorecard, as it helps them to move from a tactical or operational role toward a strategic management framework, and allowing them to work toward long-term objectives. They are using the scorecard to accomplish these critical management processes (Kaplan & Norton, 1996):

- Clarify and translate vision and strategy
- Communicate and link strategic objectives and measures
- Plan, set targets, and align strategic initiatives
- Enhance strategic feedback and learning

In our knowledge-driven world, developing and aligning an effective strategy is coming to the top of management's "to do" list. This alignment is required for economic survival and encompasses intangible factors such as skills, information, experience, and knowledge. This is why learning and growth have become drivers in the strategic context of the balanced scorecard.

LAST THOUGHTS

Management recognizes the current shift toward knowledge-driven factors to gain a competitive edge. This has led to the increasing inclusion of non-financial performance measures in financial statements. However, organizations are always going to be driven by financial motives, as stakeholders require financial results. This is the reality.

Rather than trying to work around the need for financial results, learning professionals should embrace it. This is an opportunity for workplace learning to learn to interpret financial data and communicate in financial terms. They can develop learning interventions that deliver tangible results. Through careful analysis of the organization's balance sheet, income statement, and cash flow statement, learning professionals can find business areas requiring attention and, hence, real possibilities for developmental learning interventions.

Progressive organizations must find a balance between the necessary financial reporting requirements and the need for leading, non-financial growth in performance. The balanced scorecard can be used to provide this strategic alignment. Learning and growth professionals must understand their role in this and deliver learning strategies that strike a balance between financial assessments and intangible performance. In this way, you will not only help the organization meet expected scorecard performance metrics but help the organization to meet its strategic objectives.

chapter, our focus is on developing the learning and growth perspective of the balanced scorecard and ensuring that these performance measures align with the other perspectives.

In this chapter you will learn about:

- Learning and growth perspectives
- Traditional performance thinking versus the balanced scorecard
- An organizational perspective of learning in the BSC
- Developing performance metrics for learning and growth
- Applying the learning and growth performance metrics

LEARNING AND GROWTH PERSPECTIVES

One of the most challenging aspects of organizational learning is attempting to measure and value its contribution to the organization. While it may be difficult to measure and manage, its value is demonstrated through how effective employees are on the job (Kirkpatrick Level 3), how effective organizational learning is for the organization (Kirkpatrick Level 4), and how it supports and contributes to the strategic objectives (Balanced Scorecard). The performance measures that focus around these factors will deliver results to decision-makers and your overall learning strategy.

To achieve the objectives set forth in the financial, customer, and internal processes perspectives requires the continuous development of people skills and capabilities. The measures and initiatives in the learning and growth perspective are the primary enablers ensuring the objectives in the other three perspectives are met. Essentially, the learning and growth perspective is the foundation the balanced scorecard is built upon. The learning and growth perspective encompasses the knowledge capacity and retention of the organization and, according to Kaplan and Norton (2004, p. 49), includes human knowledge, technological capabilities, and organizational capacity. Kaplan and Norton also emphasize that "learning" is more than just "training"; they note many other facets of how learning occurs including things like mentors, tutors, and the ease of communication among workers that allows them to readily get help on a problem when it is needed within the organization. Learning can play a prominent role in improving the effectiveness of these functions.

Recognizing the ability of an organization to effectively leverage all of its knowledge remains the focus of improvement as it relates to alignment of organizational strategy. People are essentially the primary resource of knowledge. More importantly, knowledge in a globalized and technology-driven world is not static. How these "knowledge workers" acquire and develop their knowledge is as important as how their knowledge is utilized. This requires that learning, the primary tool for knowledge acquisition, must be a continuous process. It is still impressive how many organizations claim that they are unable to find skilled workers to hire while either providing lip service to employee development or providing little if any training at all. One reason this is still happening is the lack of performance metrics to measure learning effectiveness. Metrics are necessary for an organization to focus its resources and funds where they can deliver the most value and to ensure measured performance. Those involved in the strategic planning process and scorecard development recognize that learning and growth is the foundation for the success not only of the organization but also for the development of their employees.

TRADITIONAL PERFORMANCE THINKING VERSUS THE BALANCED SCORECARD

It's important for you to have an understanding of the traditional performance thinking that still exists within the management framework in order to properly develop the metrics within the Learning and Growth perspective. The list below shows some of the differences in perspective.

Traditional Environment	BSC Environment
Evaluated based on short-term financial performance	Stresses the importance of investing for future periods
Makes it difficult to sustain/enhance capability of people	Hard investments require investment in people
People investment treated as period expenses in accounting	Reflects the shift in the roles employees play
Easy to cut back and produce incremental short-term earnings	Continuous process improvement and innovation
Long-term consequences don't show up	Past performance no longer an indicator of success
	Move from "reacting" to "proactively" anticipate needs

At the top of the list is how management views the performance of the organization. In the traditional context, performance is naturally based on financial results. These financial results are obtained in short-term periods and provide management with a short-term view of the organization's performance. This type of thinking is prevalent, especially in publicly trade companies. Shareholders review corporate performance in quarterly and yearly periods and compare past performance with the recently reported period. This is because they expect to see profitable returns on their monetary investments. Short-term financial performance is still relevant, but it must be in line with longer-term strategic goals. Management performing within a balanced scorecard context thinks in this way. They have the bigger picture in mind and are able to align long-term objectives with short-term expectations. These managers also recognize the importance of investing today to ensure for future outcomes. This is the basis of the structure of the scorecard and how performance outcome are attained.

In the traditional management thinking, people are not the focus of performance improvements. The second and third items in the list above show that investment in improving people is difficult. The focus for productivity improvement is through the organization's processes and assets. People are seen as an expense, implying that their contribution is not of value. In the scorecard environment, people are the most valued aspect of an organization's growth and success. Substantial investments are made in hiring, retention, and development of staff to ensure that the intellectual capital employees possess is utilized to the benefit of the organization. Employee skills are continually assessed, not to dismiss them, but rather to discover how to develop them.

Cost reductions and budget cutbacks are the norm in traditional performance environments. This is primarily because managers are rewarded on their short-term financial performance. This type of environment is not conducive to continuous improvement and innovation. When an organization focuses on achieving a mission, it uses a dynamic strategy where changes and improvements are frequent occurrences. Managers have no choice but to foster and nurture the strategy. This encourages thinking around continuous process improvements and innovation. This factor alone quickly separates the successful organizations from the dinosaurs.

Managers and novice scorecard architects will often lean toward more traditional aspects of performance measures rather than a balanced approach. This is a significant pitfall ensuring failure. Within a scorecard framework, financial performance is only one of many performance measures that, when brought together with other non-financial performance measures, determine success. The unique combination of performance measures also moves management and employees from reacting to concerns to proactively addressing them. When balanced, performance measures should prevent addressing key issues prior to them coming up in the actual execution of strategy. It is essential to consider these differences as you develop the performance metrics of the learning and growth perspective of the organization's balanced scorecard. Learning initiatives and associated performance metrics should provide a balanced approach and focus on helping all business areas meet their performance objectives.

AN ORGANIZATIONAL PERSPECTIVE OF LEARNING IN THE BSC

When an organization decides to put into place a balanced scorecard, it makes a conscious decision to execute its mission. This means that the mission, what the organization aspires to be, connects with all levels and business areas of the organization. This is a significant shift in thinking. It means that employees will need to take on new tasks and acquire new skills. The emphasis on strategy necessitates the development of employee skills and abilities in order for them to get the organization where it wants to be.

In their seminal book, *The Balanced Scorecard: Translating Strategy into Action*, Kaplan and Norton (1996) refer to this as organizational reskilling. Figure 7.1 illustrates the type of reskilling required based on skills gap and the percentage of workforce requiring reskilling. In periods of stability, organizations generally maintain employee skills by ensuring that regular learning initiatives are in place and usually do not require any special attention. (See the competency upgrade section of Figure 7.1.)

In the current economic conditions, skills development merits significant attention, but management and trainers must discriminate between strategic and tactical reskilling, as shown in Figure 7.1. When a mission is enforced and the strategy is executed, much of the workforce needs to develop skills in line with their current and expected job responsibilities. Even though learning is required across the workforce, each need is specific to a business function and responsibility.

Figure 7.1. Reskilling Matrix

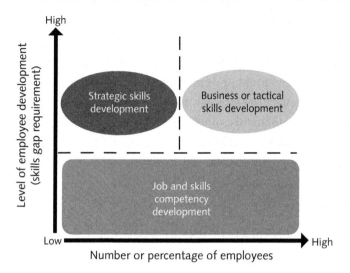

As learning becomes more strategic, it is also more focused on specific areas. The critical internal processes of an organization are defined, and these functions, at all levels, require very specific and precise learning interventions to ensure that the organization will meet its strategic goals.

Within the balanced scorecard framework, each perspective's critical processes are laid out with precise objectives and targets. The initiatives required to meet these objectives and targets are often the initiatives learning and growth will further investigate to assess the type and level of learning development required in relation to the reskilling matrix (Figure 7.1).

In a balanced scorecard environment, learning professionals must no longer simply react based on assumed needs. By shifting your paradigm to the reskilling mindset, you will be able to:

- Assess the learning requirement according to the level of organizational need;
- Prioritize learning initiatives in accordance with the reskilling matrix;
- Identify the strategically required learning needs for each initiative in each scorecard perspective; and
- Align the learning initiatives appropriately with each scorecard perspective's initiative.

Learning professionals must learn to harness the balanced scorecard environment. The ability to focus on the strategic concerns of the organization require you to:

- Identify how to embed learning into every internal client's strategically aligned efforts (refer to Chapter 3, Alignment with Management Expectations);
- Discern what is impeding the organization from achieving its objectives;
- Learn which short-term business goals contribute to strategic objectives; and
- Translate business conversations and business data into relevant learning solutions (refer to Chapter 4, Business Data and Performance Metrics).

When developing the learning growth perspective for your organization, recognize that management focuses on business areas that contribute to achieving the longer-term strategic objectives. This is also how they view learning's contribution. Referring to the reskilling matrix, always question the relevance and contribution every learning initiative will have on the organization's strategic objectives. It is important to prioritize the learning solutions according to how they contribute to the balanced scorecard initiatives in relation to the reskilling matrix.

Developing Performance Metrics for Learning and Growth

For every perspective in the BSC, there are four performance metrics to provide direction. Learning and growth is driven by the metrics within the other three balanced scorecard perspectives. This makes it more challenging for those responsible for learning to figure out which are the appropriate metrics to use. The purpose of learning and growth is to enable the needs of the organization's operations. This means that it is not possible to execute any type of strategy without proper support from the learning side. For a strategy to work, you need to have the right people with the right skills and knowledge doing the right things at the right time. This is what the learning and growth performance metrics are expected to do.

As do the other three scorecard perspectives, learning and growth has four primary performance metrics: the objectives, (performance) measures, (performance) targets, and initiatives. Let's see how they are developed within the learning and growth perspective.

Objectives for Learning and Growth

An objective is a clear statement of what needs to happen. Each one is derived initially from the scorecard perspective, driven by the organization's mission. This can become complicated because each objective within the other perspectives may require some type of learning support. Those responsible for the other scorecard perspectives may not even realize they require learning interventions. Whether or not others realize the need, it is still up to the learning professionals to discover the exact need and align the solution with the identified objective. The learning need may not be clearly evident at the corporate scorecard level; however, it will become apparent as you progress down through the cascaded scorecards. This will drive the development and direction of the learning and growth objectives.

For example, let's assume that at the corporate scorecard level one of the objectives for the customer perspective is to increase customer satisfaction in the next six months by 15 percent from current levels. Some learning professionals, especially those new to the scorecard environment, may decide to recommend a customer training course for the customer service group. This would be risky if the objective does not precisely describe the need or how to go about achieving the desired increase. This type of "knee-jerk" reaction helps to foster training's reputation as being ineffective and an unnecessary expense. Learning professionals must be diligent about identifying the learning need. Progressing down through the cascaded scorecards in this example, we might quickly discover that the managers of both operations and marketing have specific issues. In operations (internal process) there have been quality issues during the production of the products, causing an increase in product returns and warranty replacements. For marketing (customer), it appears that competitors have discovered our production problems and are capitalizing by selling to our current clients. At this point we could conclude that the initial corporate scorecard objective impacts the internal process of production and quality assurance and the increase is dependent on improvements in these business areas as well as additional support on a marketing and sales level. Learning professionals should work with the respective departments to ascertain the specific issues and then conduct a needs assessment to determine the specific learning requirements. This will drive the objectives for the learning and growth perspective. Then they would propose a learning initiative, develop the solution that ties into the cascaded targets, deliver the solution (Level 1), assess the learning taking place (Level 2), follow through on the implementation (Level 3), and finally assess the impact on the targets (Level 4).

It is important to keep things simple. However, you must ensure that the specific departmental scorecard objectives correspond with corporate-level objectives. Always begin at the top through an analysis of the corporate level scorecard, and don't get too bogged down on specific areas or perspectives. Review all of the perspectives' needs in the context of the organization's strategy. For learning to be effective, it must identify the strategic processes within the business. The goal is to ensure the people associated with or responsible for these roles are able to fulfill current requirements properly and are provided support to fulfill future needs associated with the strategy. Identifying the strategic processes internally (value chain process) will help learning and growth to:

- Develop focused objectives around the critical internal processes
- Enhance the value of the customer perspective
- Ensure financial perspective objectives are met

For example, let's say a company's mission is to be the leading provider of hand-held electronic products. Reviewing the value chain process, the strategic processes to achieve this goal would possibly be research and development, product design, production capability, and sales marketing initiatives. Identifying the critical roles in each of these four areas will help you to develop specific strategic-level objective statements for the learning and growth component and easily link these objectives to the other three scorecard perspectives. This would be visually represented through the organization's strategy map.

When developing objectives for the learning and growth perspective, keep the following in mind:

- *Do not jump to conclusions based on the objectives set forth at the corporate level.* This is risky and will affect your credibility if you are incorrect and miss addressing the real concern. Businesspeople are trained to use a systematic thinking process, develop possible alternatives to improve the situation, and finally arrive at a method to resolve the situation. Use a similar methodology and follow the thread of the objective from the corporate level down through the cascaded scorecards to arrive at a proper solution.

- *Learning and growth objectives are often closely related to the perspective objectives addressed.* Always keep in mind that learning and growth is an enabler within the balanced scorecard framework. Learning provides the essential support required. Not only will the corporate-level scorecard for learning and growth objectives support the objectives in the other corporate-level perspectives, but it will also cascade down to align with more specific objectives.

- *Keep the learning and growth objective focused on what is important.* The purpose of the balanced scorecard is to ensure that operational function and business-level strategies align with the longer-term strategic goals. The goal is to make sure the organization achieves its mission. When developing objectives for learning and growth, don't try to do it all. In the first place, you do not have the resources and, second, helping to address issues not linked to the strategic direction will not build value or credibility for learning. It is important to address what is important and not necessarily what is urgent. Focus on the perspective objectives identified as strategically aligned in both the short and longer term.

- *Work with the other perspectives, not in isolation.* Doing this allows others in the organization to see learning as a wasted expense since they are telling learning what they think is needed and then blaming learning when their solutions do not solve the problem. The balanced scorecard fosters interdependencies and interaction. The organization is a living system and what happens in one area affects other areas. Move out of the reactionary role and foster relationships across the organization and perspective groups. Become the "learning partner" to the strategically aligned areas within the scorecard. Learning's role has the capacity to be prominent because it is a vital resource for management in a knowledge-driven economy.

Measures for Learning and Growth

Performance measures indicate whether we are progressing toward or actually meeting our objectives and executing our strategy. As with the learning and growth objectives, selecting the most appropriate performance measures is highly dependent on the performance measures utilized in the other scorecard perspectives and the measures that reflect performance improvement. Developing the objectives allowed you to build relationships with those in the other perspectives and to clearly understand their needs. Communicating with these people will help you to discover the core competencies of affected business areas.

Two types of measures are derived from this process. First, determine the expected outcomes of each responsibility within the business and learn what measures are used to assess their performance. This is where you will work with the business unit manager and employees. Linking directly to these performance measures works toward modifying employee behavior (Kirkpatrick Level 3) and discovering how a learning solution improves business productivity (Kirkpatrick Level 4). Second, develop a core competency inventory of skills and have a basis of comparison to the competencies required to achieve the strategy objectives. Benchmarking current skills with required skills provides another performance measure of learning and growth's effectiveness.

Selecting the right performance measures is as critical as developing the measures in the first place. Having the right performance measures in place provides a point of reference for the organization and allows you and your business partners (internal business areas) to focus on the right areas. The following criteria will help you to select the most appropriate performance measures:

- *Connection to the strategy.* The purpose of having a scorecard is to ensure that the organization is effectively executing its strategy. Like a road map, the performance measurement tools you utilize will help you track strategic progress so that proposed solutions guide the organization in the right direction. If that doesn't happen, then the measures are inappropriate and misaligned with the strategy.

- *Objectivity through numbers.* Performance measures should be objective and as transparent as possible to ensure that the right decisions are made. Unfortunately, performance measures are often rated subjectively, allowing for each individual to interpret the results the way he or she wants. A quantitative approach alleviates the possibility of bias, minimizes the need for interpretation, and increases objectivity.

- *Use what you have available.* The balanced scorecard is simple to understand and use. The measures you use should also be simple, easily understood, and readily available. There is no need to create new methods of measurement, given the proliferation of measures probably already existing in your organization. Use performance measures that already exist to minimize cost and demand on resources. Those monitoring and managing the scorecard are already familiar with the existing measures, which will reduce the stress normally associated with having to accept new ones.

- *Be specific and clear.* Many measures can be misinterpreted by individuals. It is important that the measure you decide to use be clearly defined. For example, for a product quality measure, you must define what quality level is expected and how it is to be measured (e.g., Will it be based on number of product returns? On a reduction in product defects?).

Examples of Learning and Growth Measures

Absenteeism	Work-life balance
Staff turnover	Internal communication
Employee satisfaction	Productivity measures
Employee down time	Competency development
Workplace accidents	Work completion rates
Leadership development	Training time (employee or customer)

Let's revisit our example of wanting to increase customer satisfaction by 15 percent. In this example, we learned that specific quality issues with the product are causing an increase in product returns and higher warranty replacements. Competitors are trying to take clients away based on this information. The first step would be to determine which performance measurement tools production and marketing are using to monitor their performance. In this example, we could safely assume that production would refer to performance reports for product returns for the past few fiscal periods, equipment efficiency reports, and/or quality inspection reports, among many other performance measures. Production's performance would be based on benchmarking current levels of product returns or number of defects. Marketing's performance measurement tools could be client retention reports, sales reports of loyal customers, and/or call center complaint resolutions, among many other measures. Like production, marketing would also measure current performance based on an appropriate measure. For learning and growth, the measures will be the standards any proposed learning initiative will be held to, so it is important for learning professionals to discover how they can connect these with organizational needs.

Setting Targets for Learning and Growth

How do you eat an elephant? The answer is "one bite at a time." This silly question can be used to illustrate the point that, to achieve a stated objective, one must set an attainable target. In this example the objective is to eat an elephant, but our targets must be sufficiently realistic in the short term. Our long-term target is to eat the complete elephant, but we need to break this down into more manageable targets. The process is the same for setting your learning and growth targets. For learning and growth, the targets should relate to the performance measures, link to each objective, and be achievable for the business and individuals affected. For example, if you have an objective to increase sales effectiveness of the organization, and the performance measures are sales reports and a customer satisfaction index, a target may be a specified percentage increase in sales, say 10 percent, compared to the same period one year earlier. The type of learning intervention and its execution will be measured based on how well the sales team meets the target.

Setting appropriate targets is essential to achieve objectives, but how do you go about setting them? Targets will often already be set at the highest level of the balanced scorecard. Begin by analyzing the corporate level scorecard. You will certainly discover organizational targets aligned with the strategic objectives. If not, then you either do not have a complete scorecard or it was not done properly. If this is the case, speak with management. These are the decision-makers who are vested with the responsibility to ensure that strategic objectives are met. Conducting interviews with the senior executive group will move you in the right direction. Next, speak with other organizational stakeholders such as business unit managers, employees, and even customers and suppliers. Involving stakeholders in setting appropriate targets will help ensure that targets align with their expectations and help you to build strong relationships for achieving the organization's strategic goals. Targets may also be based on trends and industry benchmarks.

An analysis of the performance measurement tools will help you to discover what worked well and to set appropriate targets. Make sure your targets align with the business area's performance improvement needs. This will ensure that your learning solutions meet the needs.

In our example of increasing customer satisfaction, the high-level target set is a 15 percent increase over six months. After further discussions with the chief operations officer, production manager, quality assurance manager, and the vice president of marketing, the three-year target is set at a 40 percent compounded customer satisfaction increase, with 20 percent in the first year. Production and quality assurance determined that if product defects and warranty replacements decrease by 2 percent per month, they would be in line with the organization's targets. Marketing learned that a reduction of customer complaints by 1.5 percent per month and an increase of complaint resolution by 5 percent per month would align with the target as well.

Developing Initiatives for Learning and Growth

Once you have developed the learning and growth objectives, established performance measures, and set attainable targets, it is time to address how you will achieve these metrics. Initiatives are the actual learning interventions that will help you and the business areas involved to meet the first three performance metrics of the balanced scorecard.

This is learning and performance's opportunity to demonstrate its capability and expertise. It is crucial to work closely with the managers and individuals of the affected business units to select and define the initiatives that will have the greatest impact on the business objectives and align with the strategic objectives. You and your partners may come up with several interesting initiatives; however, select only the most strategically aligned and relevant ones.

Referring back to our customer satisfaction example, we learned that the primary corporate-level strategic objective for management was to increase customer satisfaction, which they believed would improve their financial performance. Those responsible for the customer perspective and those responsible for the internal processes determined the objectives they needed to attain to meet the corporate-level objective. The customer perspective, which encompasses the sales and customer service departments, was in line with the "increasing customer satisfaction" objectives, as this is within their direct control. The difficulty was in determining what led to the increasing customer dissatisfaction. After much analysis of customer satisfaction surveys, it was determined that customers were dissatisfied with the quality of the products. To summarize, the objectives of the customer and the internal process perspectives are

Customer perspective $\rightarrow$ increase customer satisfaction

Internal process perspective $\rightarrow$ improve product quality

From these two primary perspective objectives, performance measures and targets were set, as shown in Table 7.1.

After conducting a learning needs assessment for production (specifically manufacturing and quality assurance), marketing (primarily the sales team), and the customer support group, we disclosed our results with the respective business unit managers. Both managers agreed that these were the areas to address immediately and that would have the most significant impact on the scorecard objectives.

Table 7.1. Performance Measures and Targets

Corporate Level Scorecard	Objective	Performance Measures	Performance Targets
Customer Perspective	Increase customer satisfaction	Customer retention report	10 percent increase
		Repeat sales report	15 percent increase
		Customer satisfaction report (complaint resolution)	15 percent increase in three months
Internal Process Perspective	Improve product quality	Product return report	8 percent decrease in three months
		Production efficiency reports	10 percent increase
		Quality inspection reports	12 percent reduction in six months

Table 7.4. Performance Targets

Corporate Level

Scorecard	Objective	Performance Measures	Performance Targets
Customer perspective	Increase customer satisfaction	Customer retention report	10 percent increase
		Repeat sales report	15 percent increase
		Customer satisfaction report (complaint resolution)	15 percent increase in three months
Internal Process perspective	Improve product quality	Product return report	8 percent decrease in three months
		Production efficiency reports	10 percent increase
		Quality inspection reports	12 percent reduction in six months
Learning and Growth perspective	Develop customer service skills	Customer service performance measures	Develop 25 percent staff each month
			Increase service performance by 15 percent
	Develop business process improvements skills	Product quality metrics vs. productivity	Increase service performance by 15 percent
			Pre-assess all staff on quality skills
			Target top 30 percent of staff to develop process improvement skills

After determining the objectives and targets each department is expected to meet, we are in a position to work with them to develop specific initiatives, as shown below:

Customer Service Department

- Conduct customer retention skills training.
- Conduct mentor and coaching and coaching.
- Provide online tutorials and help desk tool to address customer needs.
- Conduct up-selling training sessions.
- Provide customer complaint resolution sessions and coach for performance on the job.

Product Manufacturing Department

- Work with equipment supplier to develop equipment training on quality verification features.
- Provide continuous operational procedural sessions and e-learning support for procedure applications.
- Conduct product quality testing sessions and assess application based on performance.
- Develop product testing course to assess all product test points.

Using a template can simplify the process. Exhibit 7.1 is a template you can use to select an initiative. Use this template when you are working with your initiative development team to list and describe the initiatives. The headings show the key success factors you need to define for each initiative. These five factors are the minimum requirements to define for each initiative, so add any other factors specific to your organization. Do not arrive at any conclusions or judgments from using this template; simply state the facts and requirements. Exhibit 7.2 provides a template for prioritizing initiatives and to score them against a specific rating scale. The example in Exhibit 7.3 demonstrates how initiatives 3 and 4 score the highest when weighted against the key factors. Once you have selected the most relevant initiatives, it is time to describe them in greater detail and lay out the specific requirements. The Initiative Description Template in Exhibit 7.4 provides a tool to document the initiative in detail so everyone involved is moving in the same direction.

Exhibit 7.1. Initiative Selection Template

BSC Perspective: _____ Business Area: _____

Specified Objective: _____

Strategic Linkage: _____

Initiative	Development Time	Required Funding	Resource Allocation	Time to Target	Strategic Alignment (Describe)
1.					
2.					
3.					
4.					
5.					
6.					

Exhibit 7.2. Initiative Prioritization Template

BSC Perspective: _____ Business Area: _____

Specified Objective: _____

Strategic Linkage: _____

SCALE: 1 = least important and 4 = most important

Criteria	Weighting %	Initiative 1	Initiative 2	Initiative 3	Initiative 4	Initiative . . . __
1. Development Time	___%					
2. Funding Requirements	___%					
3. Resource Allocation	___%					
4. Time to Target	___%					
5. _____						
6. _____						
TOTALS	**100%**					

◆   ◆   ◆

Exhibit 7.3. Sample Initiative Prioritization Template

BSC Perspective: _____ Business Area: _____

Specified Objective: _____

Strategic Linkage: _____

SCALE: 1 = least important and 4 = most important

Criteria	Weighting %	Initiative 1	Initiative 2	Initiative 3	Initiative 4	Initiative __
1 Development Time	30%	2	2	3	3	
2 Funding Requirements	20%	3	2	1	4	
3 Resource Allocation	35%	2	1	3	3	
4 Time to Target	15%	1	3	4	2	
5 _____						
6 _____						
TOTALS	**100%**	**2.05**	**1.80**	**2.75**	**2.70**	

Exhibit 7.4. Initiative Description Template

Date: _____

Initiator: Learning and Growth Owner: _____

Business Unit Affected: _____

Name of Initiative: _____

Initiative Developer Name: _____

Start Date: _____ End Date: _____

Description of Initiative:

_____

_____

Alignment with Strategy

BSC Perspective	Description	Priority
Financial		
Customer		
Internal Processes		

Resource Allocation

Time	Funding	People	Technology

What is the initiative dependent upon?

_____

_____

Specify the positions/jobs affected by the initiative:

_____

_____

Specify any specific needs/requirements/prerequisites for those involved in the initiative:

_____

_____

(continued)

of high-tech widgets in the next five years. In the following months they were successful in developing a balanced scorecard. During this process the senior managers discovered that the critical internal processes for ABC to achieve its mission were in the sales and custom widget design process. Ironically, the market is trending toward clients requiring custom-designed high-tech widgets. The senior managers responsible for sales and operations realized that the elements within the company existed; however, their staff was inadequately equipped with the skills to move toward the strategic objectives. After an initial meeting, they realized that the development of their employees' skills was required and approached the senior director for organizational learning to develop solutions to resolve their dilemma.

In a real-life application we would have a copy of the corporate balanced scorecard and possibly the cascaded scorecards from each business unit. In this example we are making the assumption that the analysis conducted by the senior management group is accurate. We will use the sales division to illustrate the process of building the learning and growth metrics requirements.

Here is how the learning department of ABC Inc. began.

Step 1: What Do We Want to Achieve?

Working with the senior sales director, we defined exactly what she needed to achieve. After an in-depth discussion with her and a preliminary needs assessment, it was clear that for ABC Inc. to become a market leader the sales department must focus on the development of the support teams' sales and customer service skills. We defined the objective for learning and growth for the sales division as: *Develop the sales effectiveness and customer service skills for the sales and customer support teams.*

Step 2: How Will We Measure the Results?

After another meeting with the senior sales director and the chief financial officer, it was determined that the key measures they wanted to impact were the sales numbers and the customer satisfaction index. It was agreed to utilize the existing sales and revenue reports and the customer satisfaction index reports that everyone in the company was familiar with. So the measures to use were: *Monthly sales and revenue reports and customer satisfaction index reports.*

Step 3: What Levels and Goals Are to Be Achieved?

During the meeting to decide the performance measures, the sales director and CFO also concluded that specific targets must be set. We quickly recognized the opportunity to refer to the recently developed sales and revenue forecasts and the recent trend analysis of the customer satisfaction index. We suggested that the company use the targets set in the sales forecasts and set a target based on the recent trending increase of customer satisfaction numbers. The targets set are: *Sales to increase 12 to 15 percent within the next six months; 15 percent increase in up-selling existing customers within four months; and increase customer satisfaction by 20 percent from last index measure.*

Step 4: What Are We Going to Do to Achieve the Objectives and Meet Our Targets?

This is where learning and performance earned their reputation. After a more comprehensive needs assessment, they met with the sales director to discuss the findings. It appeared that the salespeople's closing skills were inadequate to meet the proposed targets. Also, many of the members of the sales team were unfamiliar with many of the new high-tech widgets and the complementary products. The customer support team struggled with the timely resolution of customer complaints. The sales director agreed with the assessment and asked us to develop some initiatives. This is what we proposed:

- *Initiative 1:* Conduct a new product orientation program supported with an online tutorial to support client questions.

- *Initiative 2:* Source a sales training and coaching program that focuses on closing and up-selling skills. Ensure there is a continuous coaching process with skilled professionals and implement a sales mentoring process for new salespeople.

- *Initiative 3:* Work with the quality team to develop a client complaint resolution learning initiative to allow production and customer support to work together to resolve incoming complaints and ensure reduction of product defects.

Now it is your turn. Using Exhibit 7.5, identify a specific business issue within your organization. If possible, find a business issue that is relatively simple or use a recent request from one of the business units. Keep things simple and take some time to work through the steps as we did previously. Once you have completed the steps, try to map out the linkages as described in the strategy mapping section.

Exhibit 7.5. Improving and Creating Value

Learning and Growth

"How can we continue to improve and create value?"

Objectives: What do need to achieve?

_____

_____

Measures: What and how are you going to measure results?

_____

_____

Targets: What levels and goals are to be achieved?

_____

_____

Initiatives: What are you going to do to reach the objectives?

_____

_____

◆ ◆ ◆

LAST THOUGHTS

The learning and growth perspective of the balanced scorecard is the cornerstone of executing a successful strategy and achieving the organization's goals. Learning is the key to enabling the performance metrics of the other scorecard perspectives. Success, however, can be fleeting if your learning and growth strategy is not linked properly to the other perspectives of the scorecard. This requires attention not only to your performance metric but careful consideration of the performance metrics that drive the organization's strategy.

Experienced learning professionals must ascertain the level of learning to take place. The first step is to assess the learning that has to take place across the organization; second is to assess the percentage of employees requiring learning interventions. The first level of learning is reskilling required of all employees at any given time. The next level is focused on specific tasks for a narrower group of employees. The most focused level of learning is around the core competencies of the organization's value chain. At this level, the most critical processes to achieve the strategy are identified, along with those who are responsible in these areas.

An organization's strategy is also only as successful as the mindset of management. Traditional management thinking about increasing productivity through processes and assets is no longer valid in a knowledge-driven world. Organizations must now invest in the knowledge and skills development of employees. This also helps to position learning and growth in management's mind as more important long-term investment. This is not to say that financial outcomes are irrelevant. Any learning solution must still adhere to financial expectations, increase the organization's value, demonstrate an increase in profitability, and ensure adequate liquidity for short-term survival. Learning must position itself as an investment rather than an expense.

Once the learning strategy is properly positioned, learning can develop its own perspective by understanding the linkages within the organization, identifying the critical perspectives, enhancing the customer value proposition, and, as mentioned previously, ensuring that financial objectives are met.

As in all balanced scorecard perspectives, there are four performance metrics: objectives, measures, targets, and initiatives. The primary difference in how the learning and growth metrics differ from the other three perspectives is in how the learning and growth metrics relate to them. These objectives must align with each of the business area objectives being addressed. The performance measures are usually the tools available to and being utilized by the business area in question. The learning and growth targets are derived from both the objectives and the measurement process. The targets are the agreed-on benchmarks that the department is trying to meet. Finally, the learning initiatives are what those responsible for employee development will do to achieve the objectives.

These are the primary elements when beginning to develop the learning and growth perspective of the organizational balanced scorecard. The next step is to work through a simple example to assist you in your efforts, which we will do in the next chapter.

The effective execution of the learning and growth perspective of the balanced scorecard must not be overlooked.

In this chapter we will help you to utilize the elements required to execute a learning strategy within the learning and growth perspective. In this chapter you will learn about:

- Developing learning and growth perspectives
- Executing learning strategy
- Demonstrating results for learning
- Facilitating the development of learning and growth metrics

Using a sample company, we will focus on how to develop the learning and growth perspective based on the company's strategy map and balanced scorecard.

DEVELOPING LEARNING AND GROWTH PERSPECTIVES

In order to develop an effective learning strategy, you must clearly understand the organization's value proposition and mission. Learning professionals we meet often focus on the development of their learning strategy in isolation. We strongly advise you not to fall into this mindset, because the mission is the cornerstone of the organization's strategy. The degree to which an organization delivers on a differentiated value proposition to its customers dictates the level of financial performance it will attain. The mission and differentiated value proposition provide you with insight on the processes and competencies required. The value proposition should inspire you to develop a learning and growth value proposition that is aligned with the organization's needs.

The next important point when developing the learning and growth perspective is to understand how each business area is connected to the value proposition and mission. When developing the strategic plan, management consults with the various business areas/units and defines their roles and specifies their individual business missions as they relate to strategic objectives. Recognizing the connections and the relevance of the roles in each business area is crucial. Knowing the connections will help you to develop any proposed learning intervention.

Effectively communicating with other business areas, specifically your internal clients, is another area in which learning professionals must become more adept.

In previous chapters we emphasized the importance of communicating in terms that your clients comprehend. Recall that the balanced scorecard environment is driven by strategic linkages and performance outcomes. This requires you to translate your learning efforts, at whatever stage of development, into business-related and performance-driven terms. At the end of the day, management and business unit leaders are concerned about meeting objectives and achieving results. How they do so is irrelevant as long as it is within the capacity of allocated resources, delivers directly or indirectly to improved financial performance, and is timely. Keeping these criteria in mind and developing your business acumen will enhance your efforts significantly.

The ineffectiveness of strategy is usually a result of management's inability to connect the organization's long-term goals with what needs to be accomplished in the short term. The scorecard provides a link between the two and has the added benefit of aligning each business area and employee responsibility with the strategic objectives. Similarly, within the scorecard, learning and growth is aligned with the organization's strategic framework. Clear, concise learning strategies are only effective and derive significant value if the organization understands how your own actions are strategically aligned. In the same way that management utilizes the balanced scorecard to break down high-level objectives, your learning strategy must also cascade down through the organization and be executable at each level of the organization.

The final point is that you must have the ability to measure the strategic performance of any learning interventions. Don't use generic performance indicators such as customer satisfaction or quality that are open to interpretation by anyone looking at the results. Don't use lagging performance indicators. You must incorporate leading, non-financial performance measures because intangible assets are usually the essential elements for organizational learning and growth. Some examples of intangible elements include management effectiveness, process excellence, and application of employee skills and knowledge. Like financial measures, intangible measures do not provide a complete picture, so it is important to balance both. Management expects the learning and performance group to deliver on leading performance measures while respecting the need to deliver on financial performance. When developing performance measures for learning and growth, it is essential to strike a balance between these types of measures. These basic principles are summarized in Table 8.1.

Table 8.1. Summary of Basic Principles

Principle 1	Clearly understand the organization's mission and customer value proposition
Principle 2	Understand how each business area connects the mission and value proposition
Principle 3	Develop and nurture clear lines of communication directly with internal clients
Principle 4	Align all of the learning interventions in learning and growth with the objectives of the scorecard
Principle 5	Utilize a balance of leading and lagging performance indicators specific to the business issues addressed

EXECUTING LEARNING STRATEGY

A key first step when executing any successful learning strategy is the creation of a concise, but holistic, description of that strategy. Utilizing the balanced scorecard and a strategy map is one of the most effective ways for management to create a clear roadmap of an organization's strategic intent. Learning professionals must know all of the linkages that exist within the strategy map before reviewing the balanced scorecard. The strategy map clearly illustrates how an organization creates value and identifies the critical few objectives, measures, and initiatives required to drive performance. Remember that two of Kaplan and Norton's perspectives are externally focused and two are internally focused. The assumption is that the internally focused perspectives drive the outcomes in the external perspectives. Learning professionals must not become myopic and simply improve the performance of the internal issues. It is important to contribute to other areas of the organization—and this means monitoring the needs of the external perspectives.

Management's effective execution of strategy through the balanced scorecard is highly dependent on having all objectives link to the organization's mission. It is also essential that each of the driver perspectives (financial, customer, and internal processes) interconnect with the objectives of the others. The one perspective often ignored or undervalued is learning and growth. Even though knowledge is a sought-after asset in the current economic environment, it is not a perspective that is viewed as critical. Learning professionals must therefore demonstrate their ability to create value for the organization.

The following is a simple example of how the learning and growth perspective of a company implementing a new corporate strategy can be developed. Let's look at Widgets Inc., a fictitious widget manufacturing company. This simple case application will illustrate how learning and performance can link to the driver perspectives through understanding the impact of the strategic objectives.

1. Assess and Analyze the Strategy Map

Figure 8.1 is an example of a completed strategy map. One look at the strategy map and the company's strategic objective should be clear. In this example, the management of Widget Inc. wants to increase revenues in the coming years.

Figure 8.1. Sample Strategy Map for Widgets Inc.

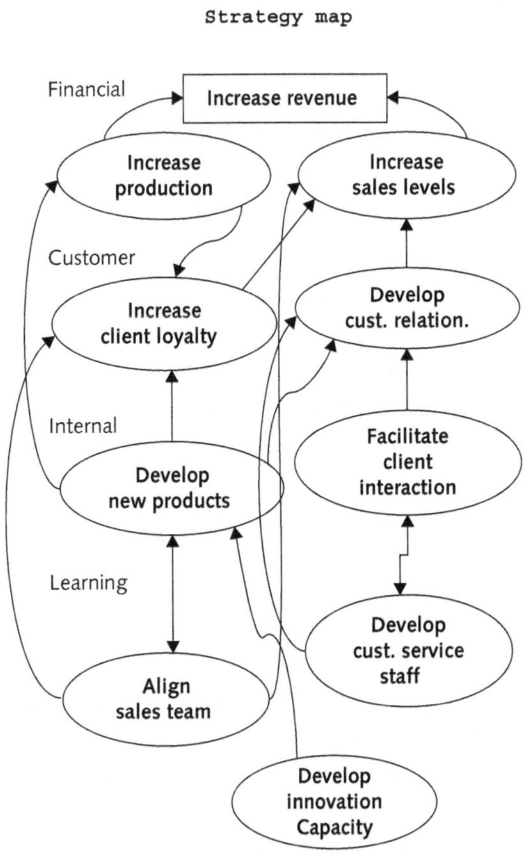

Figure 8.2 illustrates the strategy map alongside the completed balanced scorecard for Widget Inc. All of the perspectives with the exception of learning and growth include specific objectives derived from the strategy map, measures, targets, and the initiatives that ensure stated objectives are met.

Learning professionals must carefully and thoroughly analyze both the strategy map and the balanced scorecard to discover how they can strategically contribute to the objectives and properly align themselves with the initiatives outlined. The linkages within the strategy map are crucial for learning professionals to understand. They demonstrate the ripple effect any learning initiative has, how it affects the other business areas.

As mentioned earlier, management determined that Widget can meet its revenue growth objective if the sales team, customer service group, and product development group are equipped with the necessary skills and abilities to makes these individuals more effective in their roles. Looking at Figure 8.2, we can see that the objectives for learning and growth will be to:

- Develop/hire sales staff
- Develop/hire customer service staff
- Develop research and product development creativity

3. Determine the Performance Measurement Tools Utilized

The next step for the learning professionals of Widget Inc. is to determine which measures to use to evaluate their performance. By reviewing each perspective in detail we discover the following:

- For the customer perspective, the measures related to its objectives are to increase customer satisfaction levels, as measured by a survey, and to survey current customers.
- For the internal process perspective, the measures related to its objectives are the investment in R&D, market turnaround, and quicker customer response times.

We can then conclude that the measure the learning professionals should use to ensure their initiatives are working are:

- Monthly sales per client report and forecasts
- Monthly customer satisfaction reports

Figure 8.2. Sample Balanced Scorecard for Widget Inc.

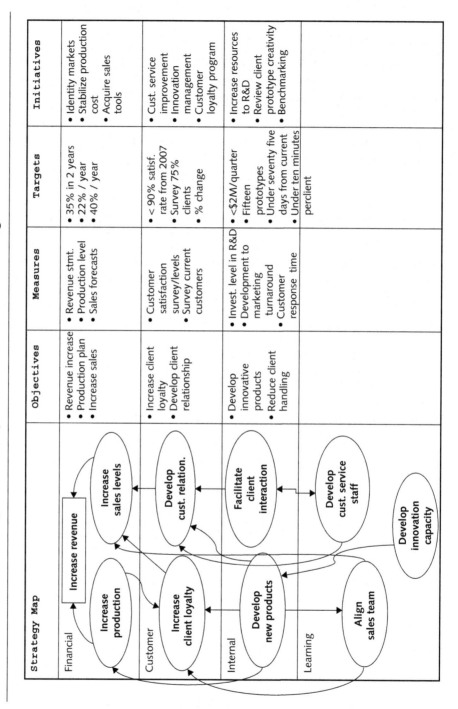

Strategy Map	Objectives	Measures	Targets	Initiatives
Financial	• Revenue increase • Production plan • Increase sales	• Revenue stmt. • Production level • Sales forecasts	• 35% in 2 years • 22% / year • 40% / year	• Identity markets • Stabilize production cost • Acquire sales tools
Customer	• Increase client loyalty • Develop client relationship	• Customer satisfaction survey/levels • Survey current customers	• < 90% satisf. rate from 2007 • Survey 75% clients • % change	• Cust. service improvement • Innovation management • Customer loyalty program
Internal	• Develop innovative products • Reduce client handling	• Invest. level in R&D • Development to marketing turnaround • Customer response time	• <$2M/quarter • Fifteen prototypes • Under seventy five days from current • Under ten minutes perclient	• Increase resources to R&D • Review client prototype creativity • Benchmarking
Learning				

Strategy Map elements:

Financial: Increase revenue — Increase sales levels — Increase production

Customer: Develop cust. relation. — Increase client loyalty

Internal: Facilitate client interaction — Develop new products

Learning: Develop cust. service staff — Develop innovation capacity — Align sales team

- Weekly customer retention statistics report
- Number of new prototypes

4. Determine the Performance Targets

We have now helped the learning professionals of Widget Inc. to list their objectives and to determine how their progress is measured. The next step is to align the effectiveness of any proposed learning initiative with the performance targets to which the other perspectives are being held accountable. The targets are usually aligned and matched with the performance measure used. In our example, one of the measures is monthly sales versus forecasted sales. Discussions with the sales team revealed that their performance is evaluated based on the number of new prospective leads with a percentage of closing new sales.

The performance targets any learning intervention must contribute to are as follows:

- For the customer perspective, a 50 percent increase in prospective sales leads, closing 10 percent of the leads, a 10 percent increase in customer satisfaction, and maintain current clients while increasing client retention by 15 percent per month.
- For the internal process perspective, product development should produce fifteen to twenty new product prototypes per year and reduce client handling time to under ten minutes per client.

5. Determine the Initiatives Affecting Learning

Within each perspective of every scorecard, initiatives exist to help those responsible for business areas in the perspectives achieve the objectives. These initiatives can be categorized as process-based, resource-based, or people-based. Learning professionals must recognize, however, that most initiatives have some "people" aspect. For example, under the financial perspective of Figure 8.2, one of the initiatives is to acquire new sales tools. This may be considered a process-based initiative, but it will indirectly affect the sales team, requiring them to learn how to utilize the new sales tools.

Among the initiatives for Widget Inc. (see Figure 8.2), we identified the ones that affect learning:

People-Based Initiatives
- Sales process improvements
- Customer service improvement
- Innovation management
- Prototype creation
- Research and development techniques

Process-Based Initiatives
- Identify of new market opportunities
- Stabilize and manage production costs
- Acquire sales tools
- Develop customer loyalty program
- Develop a benchmarking process

6. Determine the Learning Initiatives

Equipped with all of this relevant information, the learning professionals can now develop learning solutions that accommodate the performance metrics listed for learning and growth in the balanced scorecard. Figure 8.3 illustrates a completed sample balanced scorecard for Widget Inc.

Widget's learning professional and the learning team determined that the following learning solutions would be developed to address the strategic issues listed previously:

Sales Process Improvements
- Source a sales training program that would be adapted to address the needs of the sales team, including developing sales prospects and closing sales skills
- Train sales staff on the utilization of newly acquired sales tools
- Develop or source a session on more effectively identifying new market opportunities

Figure 8.3. Sample Completed Balanced Scorecard for Widget Inc.

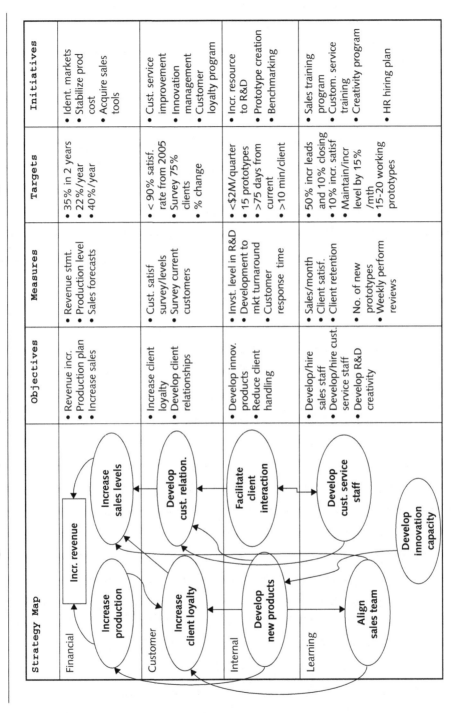

Strategy Map	Objectives	Measures	Targets	Initiatives
Financial — Incr. revenue, Increase sales levels, Increase production	• Revenue incr. • Production plan • Increase sales	• Revenue stmt. • Production level • Sales forecasts	• 35% in 2 years • 22%/year • 40%/year	• Ident. markets • Stabilize prod cost • Acquire sales tools
Customer — Develop cust. relation., Increase client loyalty	• Increase client loyalty • Develop client relationships	• Cust. satisf survey/levels • Survey current customers	• < 90% satisf. rate from 2005 • Survey 75% clients • % change	• Cust. service improvement • Innovation management • Customer loyalty program
Internal — Facilitate client interaction, Develop new products	• Develop innov. products • Reduce client handling	• Invst. level in R&D • Development to mkt turnaround • Customer response time	• <$2M/quarter • 15 prototypes • >75 days from current • >10 min/client	• Incr. resource to R&D • Prototype creation • Benchmarking
Learning — Develop cust. service staff, Develop innovation capacity, Align sales team	• Develop/hire sales staff • Develop/hire cust. service staff • Develop R&D creativity	• Sales/month • Client satisf. • Client retention • No. of new prototypes • Weekly perform reviews	• 50% incr leads and 10% closing • 10% incr. satisf • Maintain/incr level by 15% /mth • 15-20 working prototypes	• Sales training program • Custom. service training • Creativity program • HR hiring plan

An Application of the Learning and Growth Perspective

Customer Service Improvement

- Develop a customer service program that addresses how to build customer loyalty and develop skills to help client retention
- Develop a training session for the customer loyalty program

Research and Development Techniques

- Consult with a research and development specialist to create an internal program on effective research and product development techniques

Innovation Management

- Develop a creativity skills program to foster new idea creation

Prototype Creation

- Source a prototype development and management program to develop the product development team
- Develop a marketing focus group training program to ensure consistency in product evaluation and testing

Additional areas for employee skills development are expected, including:

- Training sessions and e-learning support for the new sales tools acquired by the sales department
- Work with the vendor of the new client processing systems to develop a focused training session aligned with the customer service and retention programs identified earlier
- Develop a learning session on the new customer loyalty program creating direct linkages with the customer retention program

The proposed learning initiatives listed are only some of the possible ways that the Widget learning team could develop to help the company achieve its objectives. Naturally, these and other proposed learning activities would be developed in greater detail and include learning tools and techniques most conducive to making sure they have the most impact on the areas of improvement.

The objective of the strategy map and scorecard analysis is to help you to assess exactly the strategic learning requirements for the organization. We stress the importance of completely understanding the relationships and the interdependencies existing within the organization and only identifying the areas in which learning can deliver measurable solutions.

The next issue is demonstrating how the proposed learning initiatives will contribute to achieving the specific targets. This is a challenging aspect for learning professionals, but this question is critical to building learning's credibility in the minds of management. The good news is that tools and techniques are available to learning professionals to demonstrate tangible contributions. The steps you will take are listed below:

- Step 1. Assess and Analyze the Strategy Map
- Step 2. Determine the Objectives
- Step 3. Determine the Performance Measurement Tools Utilized
- Step 4. Determine the Performance Targets
- Step 5. Determine the Initiatives Affecting Learning
- Step 6. Determine the Learning Initiatives

DEMONSTRATING RESULTS FOR LEARNING

Several methods can be used to demonstrate how learning contributes to the balanced scorecard targets. There is no need to invent new tools; simply utilize what the organization has available and what you are already familiar with and may currently have in place. Below is a non-exhaustive list of tools and techniques available. Each of these techniques on its own is not as effective as when combined with others.

Assessments (Kirkpatrick Level 2)

One simple and effective method to ensure individuals have acquired the skills to meet specific objectives is to assess how well the individual retains and applies the knowledge learned. Assessments are often viewed as ways to measure knowledge retention, not knowledge application, and unless the learner can demonstrate how to use or apply the skills, assessments are sometimes ineffective as a measure of performance. Assessments are usually more valuable and effective when combined with other more tangible means whereby the learner can prove that he or she is utilizing the new skills.

Simulations (Kirkpatrick Level 2 to 3)

Simulations can be used not only to assess how well learners retain knowledge but also to demonstrate how they apply new skills. Often used in more knowledge-intensive applications, simulations can be easily applied in a variety of workplace scenarios. Combined with other techniques, simulations can be very effective in measuring tangible results in a controlled measure.

Workplace Objectives (Kirkpatrick Level 3)

One way to measure learning effectiveness that is gaining popularity is linking workplace objectives with specific and focused learning objectives. The ability to design learning interventions with learning objectives that are directly correlated to what is expected on the job is a critical skill for learning professionals.

Control Groups (Kirkpatrick Level 3 to 4)

Setting up control groups is another way to demonstrate the effectiveness of a learning initiative in the workplace. Control groups can be used to compare the groups who received the training with those who have not. When used objectively, control groups can demonstrate the impact a learning intervention has on strategic objectives.

Coaching/Mentoring (Kirkpatrick Level 3)

Learning should not be limited to the learning environment, whether it is class-based or e-based. Many studies demonstrate that, when some form of support is provided, either through coaching or mentoring, learning retention increases significantly. This can take many forms, including the use of coaching teams and mentoring by immediate superiors.

On-Demand e-Learning (Kirkpatrick Level 3)

e-Learning has advanced significantly in the last few years. When used in a blended learning intervention, real-time e-learning tools can support learners when they need it, help to reinforce new skills, encourage application of new skills, and act as a virtual coach. This area can also provide for real learning—within budgetary restrictions.

Benchmarking (Kirkpatrick Level 3 to 4)

Benchmarking is the process of establishing a baseline of performance and comparing it with expected improved performance. This is probably the technique most familiar to management and one that provides the most evidence of meeting balanced scorecard targets. We would recommend that you utilize benchmarking whenever possible to build evidence of learning's contribution to scorecard and business targets.

Measuring the effectiveness of learning interventions is becoming of more interest to management. It is also an area that learning professionals struggle with regularly. Within the balanced scorecard framework. Many opportunities exist for learning to measure the performance of its initiatives. Learning professionals should not necessarily take total responsibility for achieving the performance targets it is involved with, but it should devise methods to demonstrate how it contributes to the organization's overall goals.

FACILITATING THE DEVELOPMENT OF LEARNING AND GROWTH METRICS

As seen in the Widget Inc. example presented earlier, learning professionals should ensure that they obtain the necessary information to begin developing and establishing specific performance metrics for the learning and growth perspective. To do so, it is necessary to obtain a copy of the organization's or a specific department's strategy map and balanced scorecard.

Exhibits 8.1 through 8.9 (also included on the website) correspond with the steps to developing the learning and growth perspective. Table 8.2 provides a cross-reference for the steps for developing the learning and growth perspective and the exhibits in the rest of this chapter.

LAST THOUGHTS

Completing the learning and growth perspective of the balanced scorecard is the culmination of enabling the perspectives that drive strategy to accomplish their specific objectives. More than simply making quick assumptions, developing the performance metrics for learning and growth should be a systematic process beginning with a thorough analysis of the organization's strategy map and scorecard.

For learning and growth to demonstrate relevance to management and build credibility, it is essential for learning professionals to utilize what management has defined and expects to achieve. This requires the ability to understand and properly identify the strategically critical processes defined in the strategy map.

Once the critical areas are identified, it is necessary to determine the scorecard initiatives for which learning can contribute the most value. For each of the leading perspectives, initiatives are briefly outlined. For each of the initiatives required to achieve a business objective, there are possible learning opportunities. The initiatives are either resource-, process-, or people-based. Those that are people-based present learning and growth with opportunities to deliver tangible results to the organization's scorecard.

Table 8.2. Steps with Corresponding Exhibits

Step	Description	Template
Step 1	Analyze the Strategy Map	Exhibit 8.1. Identifying Strategically Critical Areas
		Exhibit 8.2. Strategic Linkages Analysis
Step 2	Determine the Objectives	Exhibit 8.3. Identifying Objectives
Step 3	Determine the Performance Measurement Tools Utilized	Exhibit 8.4. Customer Perspective Performance Measures
		Exhibit 8.5. Internal Process Perspective Performance Measures
		Exhibit 8.6. Financial Perspective Performance Measures
Step 4	Determine the Performance Targets	Exhibits 8.4, 8.5, and 8.6
Step 5	Determine the Initiatives Affecting Learning	Exhibit 8.7. Balanced Scorecard Initiatives
		Exhibit 8.8. Balanced Scorecard Initiatives and Learning Initiatives
Step 6	Determine the Learning Initiatives	Exhibit 8.9. Balanced Scorecard Learning Initiatives and Performance Metrics

Aligning learning initiatives with the initiatives and objectives in each business area helps to build synergies and to ensure the business objectives will be met successfully. Alignment is more than simply addressing business initiatives. Alignment is also about utilizing existing tools and resources that are readily available to you and familiar to management. The performance metrics assigned to the perspectives are also the same metrics that learning's proposed initiatives will help achieve.

Through proper analysis, systematic thinking, and leveraging the opportunities within the scorecard, you will be able to effectively develop the learning and growth perspective, deliver focused learning interventions, and help to deliver the tangible results sought by management through the balanced scorecard.

Exhibit 8.1. Identifying Strategically Critical Areas

Identify the areas that have the most impact on the organizational strategy and determine the factors impacting the identified areas.

What are the business areas most critical to achieving the strategic objectives?

_____

_____

How do these business areas impact other business areas in the organization?

_____

_____

What are the specific objectives for these critical business areas in question?

_____

_____

What are management's expectations of the business area managers?

_____

_____

Exhibit 8.2. Strategic Linkages Analysis

State the linkages and connections between the perspective objectives and clearly explain the relationships.

State the strategic linkages to Financial perspective objectives:

_____

_____

State the strategic linkages to/from the Customer perspective objectives:

_____

_____

State the strategic linkages to/from the Internal Process perspective objectives:

_____

_____

State any other linkages and connections that are relevant to achieving the objectives:

_____

◆ ◆ ◆

Exhibit 8.3. Identifying Objectives

Obtain a copy of your organization's or department's strategy map and conduct an analysis by answering the questions below.

Define the strategic objective of the organization:

_____

State the objectives of the Financial perspective:

_____

_____

State the objectives of the Customer perspective:

_____

_____

State the objectives of the Internal Process perspective:

_____

_____

Exhibit 8.4. Customer Perspective Performance Measures

What are the performance measures used for the Customer perspective?

_____

_____

What are the reports or tools used to evaluate the performance measures?

_____

_____

What are the performance targets for the Customer perspective?

_____

_____

What are the initiatives for the Customer perspective that affect learning?

_____

_____

◆ ◆ ◆

Exhibit 8.5. Internal Process Perspective Performance Measures

What is the performance measures used for the Internal Process perspective?

_____

_____

What are the reports or tools used to evaluate the performance measures?

_____

_____

What are the performance targets for the Internal Process perspective?

_____

_____

What are the initiatives for the Internal Process perspective affecting learning?

_____

_____

Exhibit 8.6. Financial Perspective Performance Measures

What is the performance measures used for the Financial perspective?

_____

_____

What are the reports or tools used to evaluate the performance measures?

_____

_____

What are the performance targets for the Financial perspective?

_____

_____

What are the initiatives for the Financial perspective affecting learning?

_____

_____

Exhibit 8.7. Balanced Scorecard Initiatives

What are the initiatives for the Financial perspective?

People-Based Initiatives

1. _____
2. _____
3. _____
4. _____
5. _____

Process-Based Initiatives

1. _____
2. _____
3. _____
4. _____
5. _____

What are the initiatives for the Internal Process perspective?

People-Based Initiatives

1. _____
2. _____
3. _____
4. _____
5. _____

Process-Based Initiatives

1. _____
2. _____
3. _____
4. _____
5. _____

Exhibit 8.8. Balanced Scorecard Initiatives and Learning Initiatives

Categorize the initiatives according to the business area and propose learning initiatives (at least one for each perspective).

Balanced Scorecard Level Addressed:

Perspective:

Item	Business Area	Initiative	Learning Initiative
_____	_____	_____	_____
_____	_____	_____	_____
_____	_____	_____	_____
_____	_____	_____	_____
_____	_____	_____	_____
_____	_____	_____	_____
_____	_____	_____	_____

◆   ◆   ◆

Exhibit 8.9. Balanced Scorecard Learning Initiatives and Performance Metrics

List the learning initiatives and the corresponding objectives, measures, and targets (one for each perspective).

Balanced Scorecard Level Addressed:

Perspective:

Item	Learning Initiative	Performance Objective	Performance Measure	Performance Targets
____	_____	_____	_____	_____
____	_____	_____	_____	_____
____	_____	_____	_____	_____
____	_____	_____	_____	_____
____	_____	_____	_____	_____
____	_____	_____	_____	_____
____	_____	_____	_____	_____

These five principles should always be part of your strategic thinking process when you are working through the balanced scorecard and developing the performance metrics for the learning and growth perspective. Table 9.1 lists the five principles with the corresponding tools (some from Chapter 8) that we will utilize to develop Sky Air's learning and growth perspective:

Let's begin the exercise to help Bruce Anderson, one of Sky Air's co-founders, and Sky Air's management team to complete the learning and growth perspective of the company's recently developed strategy map and balanced scorecard.

CASE APPLICATION: SKY AIR LIMITED

Sky Air Limited (SAL) is a passenger airline company started five years ago. The company has seen rapid growth in a very competitive market environment, the passenger airline business. Although the market is highly competitive, SAL capitalized on the lack of a low-cost, quality air carrier. The industry is populated with major airlines that are continually reducing services while increasing prices. The founders of SAL, Bruce Anderson and Landon Sykes, are both former airline executives with over fifty years of combined experience.

Dismayed with their efforts trying to convince their former employer about the low-cost market opportunity, Bruce and Landon decided to take advantage of it themselves and start Sky Air. After sourcing many major initial investors, including their former employer, who invested 25 percent in the new airline, the company was able to lease a fleet of planes and set up the airline's organizational infrastructure. They were also successful in hiring very competent and experienced staff, who demonstrate dedication in their work.

From the start, SAL has been very popular among travelers of all types. The combination of low cost with quality service and proven on-time reliability challenged competitors to keep up and revolutionized how people see air travel. Both Bruce and Landon believe that low cost does not mean travelers have to also sacrifice their needs. Every element of the company that affects the customer is focused on, ensuring their complete satisfaction.

Bruce and Landon agreed that Bruce would become CEO. Both realized that brand recognition and creative advertising are the keys to success in the airline business. Bruce quickly implemented an aggressive marketing campaign to make the traveling public aware of the airline's existence and its unique low-cost offering.

During the formative start-up years of the airline, its marketing efforts were so successful that demand for its service grew rapidly. Sales grew very quickly and steadily, requiring the company to lease more planes and to hire more staff, resulting in higher operating costs. Bruce and Landon were not concerned, as their intent was to focus on growing revenue and establishing the SAL brand, even though other major airlines were filing for creditor protection. Their efforts signaled to their customers and the industry their success and established their presence as a serious competitor.

SAL's growth, however, came at the expense of its profitability. During the first three years, Bruce, management, and the board of directors committed to a market growth strategy, allowing the company to steadily increase revenue (top line) while experiencing break-even financial scenarios. In the last two years, Sky Air has experienced financial losses (bottom line), having its profit decrease and losses grow steadily. Fortunately, the losses have not placed the company in financial jeopardy; however, if the strategy is not changed, losses will continue to mount, placing Sky Air in a precarious position.

At a strategy planning meeting with an ad hoc team composed of Bruce, Landon, senior level (C-level) managers, and some members of the board, a decision was made to change the company's strategy. The decision was to move from a market growth strategy to one where SAL can build stability and increasing profitability. Bruce and Landon understood that the new profitability strategy must realize results quickly if the company was to survive.

Bruce, as CEO, realized the biggest challenge with the new strategy would be to integrate it throughout the organization, link it to departmental objectives, and have it understood by all employees. Bruce heard about the success of the balanced scorecard and strategy map among other competitors and its use in the industry and decided that this would be the tool of choice for Sky Air to implement its new strategic direction.

Bruce and the senior management group, representing the major business units, met over several weeks to plan and develop the strategy map and balanced scorecard for SAL. Bruce stressed the importance of their mission to remain intact while they shift from a revenue growth strategy to one of profitability. Over three years, profitability would increase by 25 percent per year from the last fiscal year results. Management concurred and ensured that what made the company successful to date would remain as its core values. The core elements customers expect are quality, courteous service, on-time flights, and affordable fares. The mission statement of the company remained the same:

Sky Air will be the traveler's affordable choice, delivering on-time quality service without compromise within the North American airspace.

Bruce called a meeting of his senior-level staff. He wanted to congratulate them on a job well done in translating the company's three-year strategic plan to the new balanced scorecard initiative. "It was a long process, with months of focus and determination, but we are seeing the end and will be deploying the BSC in the coming months," declared Anderson.

One issue concerned Bruce—the skills and competency development of the staff. Bruce understands that Sky Air is successful partially as a result of its employees, but being more of a traditional manager, he also believes that the company's processes and planes are equally valuable. He does value learning in the organization, but is not always convinced it is required. He knows Sky Air has a qualified team of employees but wants to make sure the employees possess the skills required to attain the BSC objectives. After all the work senior management put into developing the strategy map and scorecard, they overlooked the learning and growth component, and they did not include a member of their learning and performance department in the development stage. They included only objective of "training staff."

Bruce recognized the oversight and realized the error of not completing the learning and growth perspective. He needs to make sure that the staff competencies are developed and aligned with the new strategy. To help complete the learning and growth perspective, he has invited you, as Learning and Performance Director, and your team to resolve this need. Bruce presents the completed BSC to you (see Figure 9.1) and asks for your help in completing the learning and growth component. The senior management team wants to have the learning and growth perspective align with the strategy map and have the scorecard include specific objectives, measures, targets, and initiatives at the corporate level showing how it contributes to achieving the other objectives and ultimately making Sky Air profitable in the next three years. Bruce and Landon would also like you to focus on the needs of the two primary areas that directly affect profitability and customer needs as described in the mission.

THE STEPS FOR RESOLVING THE CASE

Step1A: Assess and Analyze the Strategy Map

Our first step is to obtain a copy of Sky Air's strategy map. Bruce Anderson was able to provide us with the strategy map presented in Figure 9.2. From the strategy map

Figure 9.1. Incomplete Sky Air Strategy Map and Balanced Scorecard

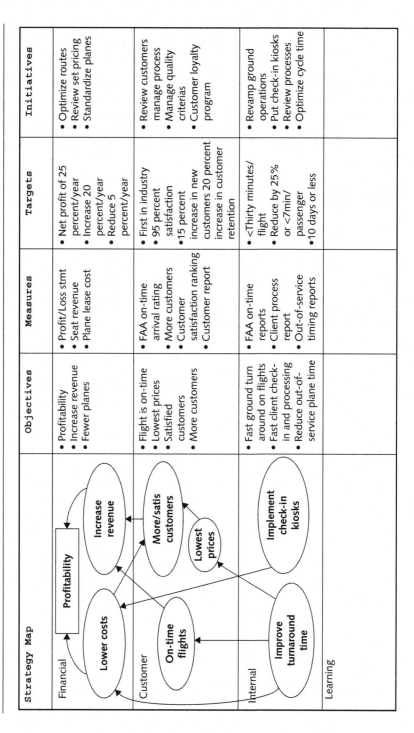

Strategy Map	Objectives	Measures	Targets	Initiatives
Financial	• Profitability • Increase revenue • Fewer planes	• Profit/Loss stmt • Seat revenue • Plane lease cost	• Net profit of 25 percent/year • Increase 20 percent/year • Reduce 5 percent/year	• Optimize routes • Review set pricing • Standardize planes
Customer	• Flight is on-time • Lowest prices • Satisfied customers • More customers	• FAA on-time arrival rating • More customers • Customer satisfaction ranking • Customer report	• First in industry • 95 percent satisfaction • 15 percent increase in new customers 20 percent increase in customer retention	• Review customers manage process • Manage quality criterias • Customer loyalty program
Internal	• Fast ground turn around on flights • Fast client check-in and processing • Reduce out-of-service plane time	• FAA on-time reports • Client process report • Out-of-service timing reports	• <Thirty minutes/flight • Reduce by 25% or <7min/passenger •10 days or less	• Revamp ground operations • Put check-in kiosks • Review processes • Optimize cycle time
Learning				

Figure 9.2. Sky Air Strategy Map

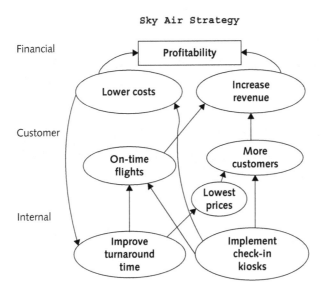

we can clearly see that Sky Air's new objective is focused on making the company profitable. Therefore, objectives in the financial, customer, and internal process must align with this strategic objective.

Step 1A requires you to complete Exhibit 9.1 to identify the strategically critical areas outlined in the strategy map.

Our Response to Step 1A: Assess and Analyze the Strategy Map

Now it is our turn. We have completed Exhibit 9.1, and we encourage you to compare our results with yours.

What Are the Business Areas Most Critical to Achieving the Strategic Objectives?

The simplicity of the case could lead one to assume that all of the objectives in the strategy map are critical strategic areas the company must focus on. If you made this assumption, it would be incorrect. You may also arrive at the same conclusion by analyzing your organization's strategy map. The reason we stress that you seek out the truly critical areas is to simplify your assessment of the learning

Exhibit 9.1. Identifying Strategically Critical Areas

Identify the areas that have the most impact on the organizational strategy and determine the factors impacting the identified areas.

What are the business areas most critical to achieving the strategic objectives?

_____

_____

How do these business areas impact other business areas in the organization?

_____

_____

What are the specific objectives for these critical business areas?

_____

_____

What are management's expectations of the business area managers?

_____

_____

◆ ◆ ◆

requirements for the organization. If you assume all of the areas are critical, you will be faced with some specific challenges such as:

- Not all of the areas require learning intervention and thus do not need to be included in the performance metrics of learning and growth. As mentioned in Chapter 8, it is essential to look at each objective in detail and to assess whether it is people-, process-, or resource-based. The first two are the areas on which learning would focus, because learning is not typically concerned with obtaining resources for the organization.

- Improving learning and performance's credibility in making this type of assumption. Being focused will demonstrate to management your ability to address the _right_ issues, not all of the issues.

- Not having sufficient time or available resources (people and money) to address what it is learning can actually address effectively. The goal is to develop interventions having the greatest impact on the business objectives.

In the Sky Air example, the areas in which learning can be influential when helping to achieve the strategic objective of profitability are:

- Maintaining/increasing on-time flights
- Improve turn-around time of flights
- Facilitate customer processing (implementing check-in kiosks)

How Do These Business Areas Impact Other Business Areas in the Organization?

Answering this question requires that those responsible for learning have a proper understanding of all of the areas of the business. This is where learning professionals must shift their paradigm from reacting to requests to becoming proactive partners in the strategic development of the organization.

The business areas directly affected include:

- Flight ground operations
- Flight on-board operations
- Flight ticketing processes
- Flight boarding process
- Airplane maintenance operations
- The flight ground crew

These all require well-trained and motivated employees, the province of learning and performance.

What Are the Specific Objectives for These Critical Business Areas?

The question here is what these business areas, within their respective perspectives, are expected to accomplish so that Sky Air can achieve its long-term strategic objective. In an actual application, you would want to speak with those responsible for the areas to learn more specifically what they need to respond to. In our example, we will assume the director of learning has spoken with all of the area managers to gain further insight into Sky Air's needs. Let's look at each one in more detail, identifying the perspectives with which each business area is associated.

- Flight ground operations: This business area falls under the internal process perspective and its objectives are to:
  - Improve the turnaround time of flights
  - Reduce the time planes spend at the gate
- Flight on-board operations: This business area also falls under the internal process perspective and relates to the customer perspective. Its objectives are to:
  - Improve the turnaround time of flights
  - Improve quality of on-board maintenance
- Flight ticketing processes: This business area falls under the customer perspective, but is directly related to the internal processes. Its objectives are to:
  - Implement check-in kiosks
  - Improve client processing
  - Reduce customer wait times
  - Increase customer satisfaction
- Flight boarding process: This business area also falls under the customer perspective, but is directly related to the internal processes. Many of the objectives are the same as for the ticketing process, because the same department and manager are responsible for its effectiveness. Its objectives are to:
  - Implement check-in kiosks
  - Improve client processing process
  - Reduce customer wait times
  - Reduce time to settle passengers once they are on the plane
- Airplane maintenance operations: This business area also falls under the internal process perspective and its objectives are to:
  - Increase efficiencies in the maintenance process
  - Reduce time planes are out of service for scheduled maintenance

What Are Management's Expectations of the Business Area Managers?

This is a fundamental question asked regularly within organizations. Objectives are always in place; however, they mean very little if there is little accountability or no type of measurement process connected to them. This is where the balanced scorecard provides accountability. Targets, or the goals that each objective must achieve, correspond to management expectations. The targets are predefined in strategic meetings with the various department managers. Many targets are represented by some numerical measure, but there are also qualitative expectations that may or may not be represented in the scorecard.

For Sky Air, the expectations are as follows:

- Flight ground operations:
  - Improve the turnaround time of flights
    - Maximum flight turnaround time of thirty minutes or
    - 25 percent reduction from the previous year turnaround time
  - Reduce the time planes spend at the gate
    - Maximum of forty-five minutes per flight
- Flight on-board operations:
  - Improve the turnaround time of flights
    - Maximum flight turnaround time of thirty minutes
  - Improve quality of on-board cleaning process and maintenance
    - Ensure 100 percent quality levels for all processes
- Flight ticketing processes:
  - Implement check-in kiosks
    - Implement kiosks in all airports where Sky Air is represented
    - Develop two partnerships with competitor airlines to utilize kiosks for check-in
  - Improve client processing process
    - Processing client time to reduce by 25 percent or to fewer than seven minutes per customer on average
  - Reduce customer wait times
    - Reduce client waiting time by 50 percent and ensure 25 percent of passengers utilize kiosks in the first year
  - Increase customer satisfaction

- Based on previous year's survey, increase customer satisfaction level by 35 percent this year and achieve 85 percent satisfaction within three years
- Flight boarding process:
  - Implement check-in kiosks (see flight ticketing process)
  - Improve client processing process (see flight ticketing process)
  - Reduce customer wait times (see flight ticketing process)
  - Reduce boarding-on-plane time once passengers are on the plane
  - Get passengers settled and seated within eight minutes of boarding the plane
- Airplane maintenance operations:
  - Increase efficiencies in the maintenance process
  - Reduce time planes are out of service for scheduled maintenance
    - Implement a critical processes checklist
    - Reduce out-of-service time by 20 percent from previous year
    - Attain a ten day or less out-of-service time within two years

Step 1B: Strategic Linkages Analysis

The next step in our analysis is to *identify the strategic linkages* within the strategy map and scorecard framework. This is a necessary step in our effort to understand how a learning intervention applied to one area affects or impacts other areas connected to it. There are some linkages for Sky Air. The initial step will require careful analysis of the strategy map. In your organization, an actual application will require that you go beyond the strategy map and scorecard. Other interactions and informal connections may exist, and you need to be aware of these. Disrupting these interactions may have further negative affects and negate the expected benefits from your efforts.

Proceed with the analysis for Sky Air by completing the strategic link analysis in Exhibit 9.2 with the information you are provided. Making justifiable assumptions is acceptable.

Our Response to Step 1B: Strategic Linkages Analysis

How did we answer? As in the previous exercise, your responses may be different from ours. Take some time to compare the differences and ask yourself why you provided the answers you did.

Exhibit 9.2. Strategic Linkages Analysis

State the linkages and connections among the perspective objectives and clearly explain the relationships.

State the strategic linkages to the Financial perspective objectives:

_____

_____

State the strategic linkages to/from the Customer perspective objectives:

_____

_____

State the strategic linkages to/from the Internal Process perspective objectives:

_____

_____

State any other linkages and connections that are relevant to achieving the objectives:

_____

_____

◆　◆　◆

The purpose of a strategy map is to illustrate the strategic linkages; however, this exercise is to show you the areas that require learning and performance's attention. So let's begin our analysis:

State the Strategic Linkages to the Financial Perspective Objectives

The strategic focus for Sky Air is to increase its profitability and stabilize its growth. Business people will often look at the obvious first, and in this case that is lowering costs rather than increasing revenues. This means that improving turnaround time will be the basis of increasing efficiencies leading to profitability. Learning initiatives directed toward improving turnaround times (operational efficiencies) will begin a cascading process of benefits to other areas of the company.

State the Strategic Linkages to/from the Customer Perspective Objectives

The improvement of the operations by turning around flights quicker and boarding more passengers in any given period is the basis of our assumption. Looking at the customer perspective, the linkages that are also important to passengers are on-time flights and lower prices. If we wanted to carry our assumption further, we may say that there is an indirect relationship between the passengers' need for on-time flights and the ease and simplicity of the boarding process. From this, we can infer that the check-in kiosks and ticketing process may require specific attention. These are some strategic areas that learning could address to help the organization meet customer expectations.

State the Strategic Linkages to/from the Internal Process Perspective Objectives

We determined the linkages earlier for the financial perspective, and it appears that the internal processes are the primary drivers to improving profitability. What we do not see in the strategy map is the detail of what it will take to improve the turn-around time of the planes. We can discover some of the critical areas through the objectives, but will need to further investigate for any other operational improvements. At this point we can safely assume that improving the ground crew performance and boarding process will positively impact the performance of the organization.

State Any Other Linkages and Connections That Are Relevant to Achieving the Objectives

In the Sky Air example we have not discovered any other prominent areas relevant to improving the company's profitability. However, there is an underlying aspect of Sky Air that, if addressed, could improve the organization's effectiveness. Significant performance improvement would come through more effective cross-functional teamwork. This would mean cross-training the ground crew, boarding team, and ticketing agents, allowing these groups to work more effectively together and understand others' processes. Developing a learning initiative for this process would help the company's operational processes work more coherently.

Step 2: Determine the Objectives

In Exhibit 9.1, Identifying Strategically Critical Areas, we were able to determine specific objectives for Sky Air. These are listed under our Response to Step 1A above.

In reality, an organization's strategic framework is more involved than what the Sky Air case presents. In the Sky Air example, the critical objectives are synonymous with the organization's objective. In your organization, it is essential to discern between critical objectives and all of the other stated objectives presented in the scorecard. Exhibit 8.3, Identifying Objectives, is a tool for you to take inventory and determine your objectives. Take the time to complete this template to assist you in your effort to maintain focus on what the organization is required to accomplish.

Step 3: Determine the Performance Measurement Tools Utilized

The next step in developing the learning and growth perspective is being aware of how the perspectives are measured and what measurement tools are utilized. The measures and tools usually correspond with how the targets are set. The targets are benchmarked against a base from the measurement tool used.

For Sky Air, answer the questions in Exhibits 9.3 and 9.4, making reasonable assumptions as to why you are using or selecting specific measures and measurement tools.

When deciding on the performance measures to utilize, it is best to use reports and tools that are selected in the scorecard and/or that are already in frequent use. This is helpful in that you will be using tools with which management is familiar and will be speaking in the language they understand best.

Exhibit 9.3. Customer Perspective Performance Measures

Answer the questions below for the Customer performance measures.

What are the performance measures used for the Customer perspective?

_____

_____

What are the reports or tools used to evaluate the performance measures?

_____

_____

HINT: Refer to Question 4 in Exhibit 9.1, Identifying Strategically Critical Areas, and only the business areas involved with the Customer perspective.

Exhibit 9.4. Internal Process Perspective Performance Measures

Answer the questions below for the Internal Process performance measures.

What performance measures are used for the Internal Process perspective?

_____

_____

What are the reports or tools used to evaluate the performance measures?

_____

_____

◆ ◆ ◆

Our Response to Step 3: Determine the Performance Measurement Tools Utilized

To respond to the Sky Air case, we provided a hint on what you should look at with respect to each perspective. In the first question in Exhibit 9.3, Customer Perspective Performance Measures, the areas to focus on are shown in Table 9.2.

For Sky Air's internal process perspective, we also provided a similar hint on what you should look at with respect to the internal processes. In the first question in Exhibit 9.4, Internal Process Perspective Performance Measures, the areas to focus on are shown in Table 9.3.

We are now in a position to proceed to Step 4, Determine the Performance Targets. In the Sky Air case, we were able to determine the performance targets for the critical areas through our analysis of the balanced scorecard and conversations with the respective business unit managers. In some instances, this will be the case for you, but it is still essential for you to complete Step 4 by developing a comprehensive learning and growth perspective.

Step 4: Determine the Performance Targets

Because we have already determined from the scorecard the expected performance targets, in this case Step 4 will be a benchmarking process. This is acceptable, and we encourage you to develop a comparative process to see how any learning intervention will help to contribute to or resolve the specific business issues. For this exercise, we are providing a partially completed matrix for you to complete.

Table 9.2. Customer Perspective

Processes	Sub-Process Objective	Performance Measure
Flight Ticketing Processes		
Implement check-in kiosks	Implement kiosks in all airports Sky Air is represented	IT implementation report
	Develop two partnerships with competitor airlines to utilize kiosks for check-in	Senior leadership metric
Improve client processing process	Processing client time to reduce by 25 percent or less than seven minutes per customer on average	Client processing report based on time
Reduce customer wait times	Reduce client waiting time by 50 percent and ensure 25 percent of passengers utilize kiosks in the first year	Passenger ticketing reports and online booking reports
Increase customer satisfaction	Based on previous year survey increase customer satisfaction level by 35 percent this year and achieve 85 percent satisfaction within three years	Customer satisfaction reports and customer complaint levels
Flight Boarding Process		
Reduce boarding-on-plane time once passengers are on the plane	Get passengers settled and seated within eight minutes of boarding the plane	Boarding time reports and gate timing reports

There is some latitude as to how you arrive at your performance targets. After further meetings with the senior directors of customer service, airline maintenance, ground crew operations, and flight staff, we compiled Tables 9.4 and 9.5, which show Sky Air's past performance in the client and internal process perspectives, respectively.

Utilizing both the customer and internal process perspective past performance matrices, complete Step 4 by matching the current performance targets with the past performance results and arriving at the required improvements target differences, which can be entered in Tables 9.6 and 9.7.

Table 9.4. Customer Perspective Past Performance Matrix

Processes	Sub-Process Past Performance
Flight Ticketing Processes	
Implement check-in kiosks	Five airports across the country currently market testing check-in kiosks
	Currently two strategic alliances with regional air carriers
Improve client processing process	Client processing currently at ten to twelve minutes per client
Reduce customer wait times	Customer wait times are based on the processing time, currently at fifteen to eighteen minutes per client
Increase customer satisfaction	Prices: 65 percent approval; Service: 58 percent approval; Cleanliness: 76 percent approval; Timeliness: 83 percent approval
Flight Boarding Process	
Reduce boarding-on-plane time once passengers are on the plane	Currently it takes on-board staff fourteen minutes to board and settle on the plane

Table 9.5. Internal Process Perspective Past Performance Matrix

Processes	Sub-Process Past Performance
Flight Ground Operations	
Improve the turnaround time of flights	Flights turnaround time in the last two years averaged forty to sixty minutes
Reduce the time planes spend at the gate	Currently planes spend sixty minutes at the gate
Flight On-Board Operations	
Improve the turnaround time of flights	Flight turnaround time in the last two years averaged forty to sixty minutes
Improve quality of on-board cleaning process and maintenance	Prices: 65 percent approval; Service: 58 percent approval; Cleanliness: 76 percent approval; Timeliness: 83 percent approval
Airplane Maintenance Operations	
Increase efficiencies in the maintenance process	Currently utilizing FFA maintenance checklist
Reduce time planes are out of service for scheduled maintenance	Out-of-service time averages fifteen days

Table 9.6. Customer Perspective Performance Target Improvements

Processes	Sub-Process Past Performance	Sub-Process Objective (See Tables 9.2 and 9.4)	Target Difference
Flight Ticketing Processes			
Implement check-in kiosks	Five airports across the country currently market testing check-in kiosks	Implement kiosks in all airports Sky Air is represented	
	Currently two strategic alliances with regional air carriers	Develop two partnerships with competitor airlines to utilize kiosks for check-in	
Improve client processing process	Client processing currently at ten to twelve minutes per client	Processing client time to reduce by 25 percent or less than seven minutes per customer on average	
Reduce customer wait times	Customer wait times are based on the processing time, currently at fifteen to eighteen minutes per client	Reduce client waiting time to by 50 percent and ensure 25 percent of passengers utilize kiosks in the first year	
Increase customer satisfaction	Prices: 65 percent approval; Service: 58 percent approval; Cleanliness: 76 percent approval; Timeliness: 83 percent approval	Based on previous year survey, increase customer satisfaction level by 35 percent this year and achieve 85 percent satisfaction within three years	
Flight Boarding Process			
Reduce boarding-on-plane time once passengers are on the plane	Currently it takes on-board staff fourteen minutes to board and settle on the plane	Get passengers settled and seated within eight minutes of boarding the plane	

Table 9.7. Internal Process Perspective Performance Target Improvements

Processes	Sub-Process Past Performance	Sub-Process Objective (See Tables 9.3 and 9.5)	Target Difference
Flight Ground Operations			
Improve the turnaround time of flights	Flights turnaround time in the last two years averaged forty to sixty minutes	Maximum flight turnaround time of thirty minutes or 25 percent reduction from the previous year's turnaround time	
Reduce the time planes spend at the gate	Currently planes spend sixty minutes at the gate	Maximum of forty-five minutes per flight	
Flight On-Board Operations			
Improve the turnaround time of flights	Flight turnaround time in the last two years averaged forty to sixty minutes	Maximum flight turnaround time of thirty minutes	
Improve quality of on-board cleaning process and maintenance	Prices: 65 percent approval; Service: 58 percent approval; Cleanliness: 76 percent approval; Timeliness: 83 percent approval	Ensure 100 percent quality levels for all processes	
Airplane Maintenance Operations			
Increase efficiencies in the maintenance process	Currently utilizing FFA maintenance checklist	See below	
Reduce time planes are out of service for scheduled maintenance		Implement a critical processes checklist	
	Out-of-service time averages fifteen days	Reduce out-of-service time by 20 percent from previous year	
	Out-of-service time averages fifteen days	Attain a ten day or less out-of-service time within two years	

Tables 9.8 and 9.9 show the performance target differences we found for Sky Air's critical business processes. This analysis of the performance target differences can assist you in developing more focused and tangible learning interventions.

Compare your results to what we provided in Tables 9.8 and 9.9.

Step 5: Determine the Initiatives Affecting Learning

Step 5 is the transition from our analysis of the issues and requirements of the organization to recognizing which specific initiatives require learning initiatives. In Chapter 8, we discussed how initiatives can be categorized in one of three areas:

- People-based initiatives
- Process-based initiatives
- Resource-based initiatives

Learning interventions that provide results always focus first on people-based initiatives and second on the process-based initiatives, since these initiatives indirectly impact employees.

Using Tables 9.10, 9.11, and 9.12, begin assessing the initiatives and determine in which category they fall, focusing only on the ones that are people- or process-based.

Our Response to Step 5: Determine the Initiatives Affecting Learning

This step is relatively straight-forward. It is important, however, to be diligent in your assessment by asking specific questions in ascertaining whether learning interventions would have any type of impact on improving or resolving the process or initiative in question. Some initiatives may have a well-hidden people aspect to them that, if overlooked, could limit the results any learning initiative would provide. It is important to be thorough and not hurry through this step. It is this step that will help you to complete Step 6 to develop the appropriate learning initiatives and performance metrics for the learning and growth perspective. Review and compare our responses (see Tables 9.13, 9.14, and 9.15) with yours.

In any actual scenario that you will encounter, it is important to detail, as specifically as possible, the reasons why you believe an initiative is people-, process-, or

Table 9.8. Customer Perspective Performance Target Improvements

Processes	Sub-Process Past Performance	Sub-Process Objective (See Tables 9.2 and 9.4)	Target Difference
Flight Ticketing Processes			
Implement check-in kiosks	Five airports across the country currently market testing check-inkiosks	Implement kiosks in all airports Sky Air is represented	Remaining forty airports to implement kiosks
	Currently two strategic alliances with regional air carriers	Develop two partnerships with competitor airlines to utilize kiosks for check-in	Still require two additional alliances with major air carriers
Improve client processing process	Client processing currently at ten to twelve minutes per client	Processing client time to reduce by 25 percent or less than seven minutes per customer on average	A reduction of three to five minutes required in client processing
Reduce customer wait times	Customer wait times are based on the processing time, currently at fifteen to eighteen minutes per client	Reduce client waiting time to by 50 percent and ensure 25 percent of passengers utilize kiosks in the first year	
Increase customer satisfaction	Prices: 65 percent approval; Service: 58 percent approval; Cleanliness: 76 percent approval; Timeliness: 83 percent approval	Based on previous year survey, increase customer satisfaction level by 35 percent this year and achieve 85 percent satisfaction within three years	Prices: increase of 23 percent approval; Service: increase of 20 percent approval; Cleanliness: increase of 24 percent approval; Timeliness: increase of 17 percent approval; three-year average satisfaction of 91 percent
Flight Boarding Process			
Reduce boarding-on-plane time once passengers are on the plane	Currently it takes on-board staff fourteen minutes to board and settle on the plane	Get passengers settled and seated within eight minutes of boarding the plane	A reduction of six minutes on settling and seating passengers

Table 9.10. Financial Perspective Initiative Type

Processes	Initiative Type		
Profitability and Stability			
Profitability improvement	People ☐	Process ☐	Resource ☐
Manage and lower costs	People ☐	Process ☐	Resource ☐
Increase revenues	People ☐	Process ☐	Resource ☐
Reduce fleet size	People ☐	Process ☐	Resource ☐

Table 9.11. Customer Perspective Initiative Type

Processes	Initiative Type		
Flight Ticketing Processes			
Implement check-in kiosks	People ☐	Process ☐	Resource ☐
Improve client processing process	People ☐	Process ☐	Resource ☐
Reduce customer wait times	People ☐	Process ☐	Resource ☐
Increase customer satisfaction	People ☐	Process ☐	Resource ☐
Flight Boarding Process			
Reduce boarding-on-plane time once passengers are on the plane	People ☐	Process ☐	Resource ☐

Table 9.12. Internal Process Perspective Initiative Type

Processes	Initiative Type		
Flight Ground Operations			
Improve the turnaround time of flights	People ☐	Process ☐	Resource ☐
Reduce the time planes spend at the gate	People ☐	Process ☐	Resource ☐
Flight On-Board Operations			
Improve the turnaround time of flights	People ☐	Process ☐	Resource ☐
Improve quality of on-board cleaning process and maintenance	People ☐	Process ☐	Resource ☐
Airplane Maintenance Operations			
Increase efficiencies in the maintenance process	People ☐	Process ☐	Resource ☐
Reduce time planes are out of service for scheduled maintenance	People ☐	Process ☐	Resource ☐

Table 9.13. Financial Perspective Initiative Type

Processes	Initiative Type	Reasoning
Profitability and Stability		
Profitability improvement	Process ☐	Management is overseeing this process through the cascading interventions within the scorecard. Learning role will primarily be in the cascaded areas.
Manage and lower costs	Process ☐	Management is overseeing this process through the cascading interventions within the scorecard. Learning role will primarily be in the cascaded areas.
Increase revenues	Resource ☐	Management is responsible for developing this aspect with the resources available to the company.
Reduce fleet size	Resource ☐	Management is responsible for developing this aspect with the resources available to the company.

Table 9.14. Customer Perspective Initiative Type

Processes	Initiative Type	Reasoning
Flight Ticketing Processes		
Implement check-in kiosks	Resource ☐	Implementing kiosks is a resource-based activity, as it is about installing new equipment.
Improve client processing process	People ☐	All the processes are in place and it has been determined that the staff do not have the appropriate skills.
Reduce customer wait times	People ☐	All the processes are in place and it has been determined that the staff do not have the appropriate skills.
Increase customer satisfaction	People ☐	All the processes are in place and it is known that the staff do not have the appropriate skills.
Flight Boarding Process		
Reduce boarding-on-plane time once passengers are on the plane	People ☐ and Process ☐	New processes are implemented and the staff does not have the appropriate skills to manage them.

Table 9.15. Internal Process Perspective Initiative Type

Processes	Initiative Type	Reasoning
Flight Ground Operations		
Improve the turnaround time of flights	People ☐	All the processes are in place and it has been shown that the staff do not have the appropriate skills.
Reduce the time planes spend at the gate	People ☐ and Process ☐	New processes are implemented and the staff does not have the appropriate skills to manage the new processes.
Flight On-Board Operations		
Improve the turnaround time of flights	People ☐ and Process ☐	New processes are implemented and the staff does not have the appropriate skills to manage the new processes.
Improve quality of on-board cleaning process and maintenance	People ☐	All the processes are in place and it has been determined that the staff do not have the appropriate skills.
Airplane Maintenance Operations		
Increase efficiencies in the maintenance process	People ☐ and Process ☐	New processes are implemented and the staff does not have the appropriate skills to manage the new processes.
Reduce time planes are out of service for scheduled maintenance	People ☐	All the processes are in place and it has been shown that the staff do not have the appropriate skills.

resource-based. Developing this evidence will allow you to develop Step 6, Determine the Learning Initiatives, in more detail and provide you with support in the event that management requires justification.

Step 6: Determine the Learning Initiatives

This step is the culmination of your diligent effort throughout the strategy map and scorecard analysis. This is the step that capitalizes on your expertise in developing and implementing targeted and focused learning initiatives. It is also the step that will determine how you are able to incorporate your learning efforts into the organization's balanced scorecard framework.

Utilizing Exercises 8.8 and 8.9 from Chapter 8, we will begin to bring together all of our analysis and assessment of Sky Air and complete the learning and growth performance metrics. Step 6 will require some investment of time to complete. In our example, we will walk you through three parts. When completing Exhibit 9.5 for Sky Air, please make reasonable assumptions and do not limit your responses based on the number of lines provided for answers.

◆　◆　◆

Exhibit 9.5. Sky Air Learning and Growth Analysis

What is the strategic objective of Sky Air's scorecard?

_____

_____

_____

Identify specific employee groups that would have the most impact on the BSC.

A. _____

_____

B. _____

_____

C. _____

_____

Identify Sky Air's learning and growth *objectives* for the employee groups.

A. _____

_____

B. _____

_____

C. _____

_____

D. _____

_____

Identify the *measures* specific to Sky Air's learning and growth objectives.

A. _____

_____

B. _____

_____

C. _____

_____

D. _____

_____

Set tangible *targets* specific to Sky Air's objectives and measures (realistic assumptions allowed).

A. _____

_____

B. _____

_____

C. _____

_____

D. _____

_____

◆　◆　◆

Our Response to Step 6, Part 1

What Is the Strategic Objective of Sky Air's Scorecard?

As mentioned earlier and as is illustrated by its strategy map, Sky Air's strategic objective is to build profitability and foster stable growth within the coming years. The reason we ask the question repeatedly is because it is essential to see the big picture and to align with management's focus. The strategic objective is the driver of all the activities that take place in the organization.

Identify Specific Employee Groups That Would Have the Most Impact on the BSC

Reviewing the analysis from Steps 1 through 5, it is clear that our employee group focus is as follows:

- The flight crew and maintenance staff (ground crew)
- The boarding staff and ticketing agents (boarding staff)
- The flight staff (flight crew and flight attendants)

For Sky Air, these groups will have the greatest impact if they are directed and developed appropriately. Many of our learning initiatives will focus primarily on these groups.

Table 9.17. Internal Process Perspective

Employee Groups	Processes	Learning Objectives
Flight Ground Operations		
The flight ground crew and maintenance staff (ground crew)	Improve the turnaround time of flights	Align and develop ground crew and maintenance staff to improve turnaround times
The flight ground crew and maintenance staff (ground crew)	Reduce the time planes spend at the gate	Align and develop ground crew and maintenance staff to improve turnaround times
Flight On-Board Operations		
The maintenance staff (ground crew)	Improve quality of on-board cleaning process and maintenance	Develop maintenance skills and align with more efficient processes

Table 9.18. Customer Perspective

Employee Groups	Learning Objectives	Performance Measure
The boarding staff and ticketing agents (boarding staff)	Align and develop boarding staff and ticketing agents to process clients more effectively	Client processing report based on time
The ticketing agents	Align and develop ticketing agents to reduce wait times	Passenger ticketing reports and online booking reports
The boarding staff and ticketing agents (boarding staff)	Develop staff in contact with passengers with proactive customer service techniques	Customer satisfaction reports and customer complaint levels
The boarding staff	Align and develop boarding staff to board and accommodate passengers on the plane	Boarding time reports and gate timing reports

differences from Step 4. Sky Air is a case with tangible targets; to be even more effective, the learning director would attempt to determine what amount the learning initiative would help to contribute to the forecasted targets. You would do the same in your efforts. There will be many targets presented to you, and you will have to ascertain which targets are relevant to your learning efforts and how much you will be able to contribute to helping attain the targets. This latter point will require

Table 9.19. Internal Process Perspective

Employee Groups	Learning Objectives	Performance Measure
The flight ground crew and maintenance staff (ground crew)	Align and develop ground crew and maintenance staff to improve turnaround times	Arrival and departure time reports and FAA gate rating and reports
The flight ground crew and maintenance staff (ground crew)	Align and develop ground crew and maintenance staff to improve turnaround times	FAA On Time Departure Rating and reports
The maintenance staff (ground crew)	Develop maintenance skills and align with more efficient processes	Maintenance reports, cleaning performance reports, respective FAA quality-assurance benchmarks

some investigation on your part through analysis of the business issues and meeting with those responsible for the respective areas.

Tables 9.20 and 9.21 summarize the conclusions of Sky Air's learning director.

Our Response to Step 6, Part 2

Part 2 of Step 6 relates to listing the proposed initiatives in relation to the objectives and performance targets. It is at this stage that you will develop initial learning initiatives according to each perspective and business area. This may require additional work on your part, as it requires the development of learning interventions that would work well with the business issue and help resolve the specific objective. You will want to draw on your own and your team's assessment and design skills to outline some specific initiatives.

In our Sky Air example, we provided a possible response template in Exhibit 8.9. Exhibit 9.6 is a template completed by Sky Air's learning director and the learning team.

The last step is the conclusion of the process of completing the performance metric of the learning and growth perspective. At this stage you want to go back to the organization's strategy map and the balanced scorecard.

You may have a strategy map and scorecard more or less similar to what is presented in this chapter. In whatever way it is presented within your organization, you will now literally draw the components of the learning and growth

Table 9.20. Customer Perspective

Employee Groups	Learning Objectives	Measures	Targets
The boarding staff and ticketing agents (boarding staff)	Align and develop boarding staff and ticketing agents to process clients more effectively	Client processing report based on time	A reduction of three to five minutes required in client processing
The ticketing agents	Align and develop ticketing agents to reduce wait times	Passenger ticketing reports and online booking reports	A target of seven to eleven minutes waiting time.
The boarding staff and ticketing agents (boarding staff)	Develop staff in contact with passengers with proactive customer service techniques	Customer satisfaction reports and customer complaint levels	Prices: increase of 23 percent approval; Service: increase of 20 percent approval; Cleanliness: increase of 24 percent approval; Timeliness: increase of 17 percent approval; and three-year average satisfaction of 91 percent
The boarding staff	Align and develop boarding staff to board and accommodate passengers on the plane	Boarding time reports and gate timing reports	A reduction of six minutes on settling and seating passengers

perspective (the learning and growth objectives) on the strategy map. Once you have done this, the next step is to make the appropriate strategic linkages to the other perspectives.

Complete the Sky Air example as a way to practice this aspect and better understand how to do this for your organization's requirements. Exhibit 9.7 presents the Sky Air strategy map and scorecard with three blank areas in the map. The first step in your responsibility as Sky Air's learning director is to fill in the three areas of the strategy map and make the appropriate strategic linkages. One hint: the three areas are the objectives of the primary audience that have the most strategic impact on Sky Air's strategic objective.

Table 9.21. Internal Process Perspective

Employee Groups	Learning Objectives	Measures	Targets
The flight ground crew and maintenance staff (ground crew)	Align and develop ground crew and maintenance staff to improve turnaround times	FAA On Time Departure Rating and reports	A reduction of ten to thirty minutes in flight turnaround
The flight ground crew and maintenance staff (ground crew)	Align and develop ground crew and maintenance staff to improve turnaround times	FAA Gate Rating and reports	A reduction of fifteen minutes on the gate time
The maintenance staff (ground crew)	Develop maintenance skills and align with more efficient processes	Maintenance reports and cleaning performance reports, plus respective FAA quality assurance benchmarks	Prices: internal improvement of 45 percent; Service: internal improvement of 62 percent; Cleanliness: internal improvement of 24 percent; Timeliness: internal improvement of 17 percent

Once you have made the linkages, the second step is to complete the performance metrics for Sky Air's learning and growth perspective. Ensure that the linkages help you to discover the appropriate metrics developed earlier in this exercise.

Our Response to Step 6, Part 3

Much of the hard work required to complete Sky Air's learning and growth perspective was accomplished in the previous steps. Being systematic in your analysis and process discovery is crucial for you to arrive at this point. At the end of this section, you will find our completed balanced scorecard for Sky Air (Figure 9.3).

A properly developed and effective scorecard follows the general rule of four; that is, four perspectives, four performance metrics, and four points to each metric.

Exhibit 9.6. Sample Completed Balanced Scorecard Learning Initiatives and Performance Metrics: Customer

List the learning initiatives and the corresponding objectives, measures, and targets (one for each perspective).

Balanced Scorecard Level Addressed: Corporate level

Perspective: Customer

Item	Learning Initiative	Performance Objective	Performance Measure	Performance Targets
	Develop a blended learning program to address new client processes and to develop skills in efficient client processing	Align and develop boarding staff and ticketing agents to process clients more effectively	Client processing report based on time	A reduction of three to five minutes required in client processing
	Review ticketing process and conduct a needs assessment	Develop a learning session and e-learning tutorial to support efficient ticketing processes.		
	Develop a learning program for the utilization of the implementation kiosks	Align and develop ticketing agents to reduce wait times	Passenger ticketing reports	A target of seven to eleven minutes waiting time
	Source and customize customer service program for airlines. Identify areas of client dissatisfaction and address these issues in a learning program	Develop staff in contact with passengers with proactive customer service techniques	Customer satisfaction reports and customer complaint levels	Three-year average satisfaction 91 percent in four areas
	Review boarding process and address areas for more effective boarding techniques. Develop brief learning solutions to reduce boarding issues.	Align and develop boarding staff to board and accommodate passengers on the plane	Boarding time reports and gate timing reports	A reduction of six minutes on settling and seating passengers

Exhibit 9.7. Completing Sky Air's Learning and Growth Perspective

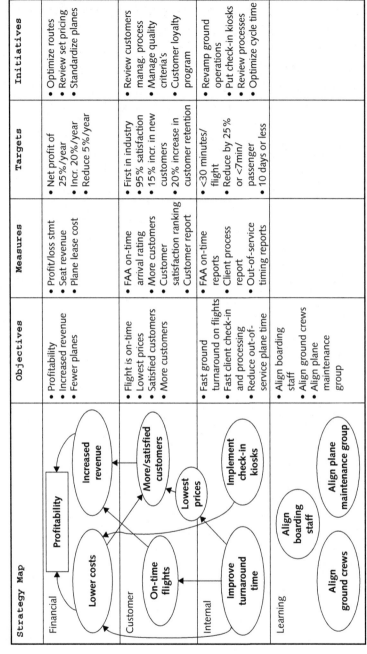

Strategy Map		Objectives	Measures	Targets	Initiatives
Financial		• Profitability • Increased revenue • Fewer planes	• Profit/loss stmt • Seat revenue • Plane lease cost	• Net profit of 25%/year • Incr. 20%/year • Reduce 5%/year	• Optimize routes • Review set pricing • Standardize planes
Customer		• Flight is on-time • Lowest prices • Satisfied customers • More customers	• FAA on-time arrival rating • More customers • Customer satisfaction ranking • Customer report	• First in industry • 95% satisfaction • 15% incr. in new customers • 20% increase in customer retention	• Review customers manag. process • Manage quality criteria's • Customer loyalty program
Internal		• Fast ground turnaround on flights • Fast client check-in and processing • Reduce out-of-service plane time	• FAA on-time reports • Client process report • Out-of-service timing reports	• <30 minutes/ flight • Reduce by 25% or <7min/ passenger • 10 days or less	• Revamp ground operations • Put check-in kiosks • Review processes • Optimize cycle time
Learning		• Align boarding staff • Align ground crews • Align plane maintenance group			

Figure 9.3. Sample Completed Sky Air Balanced Scorecard and Strategy Map

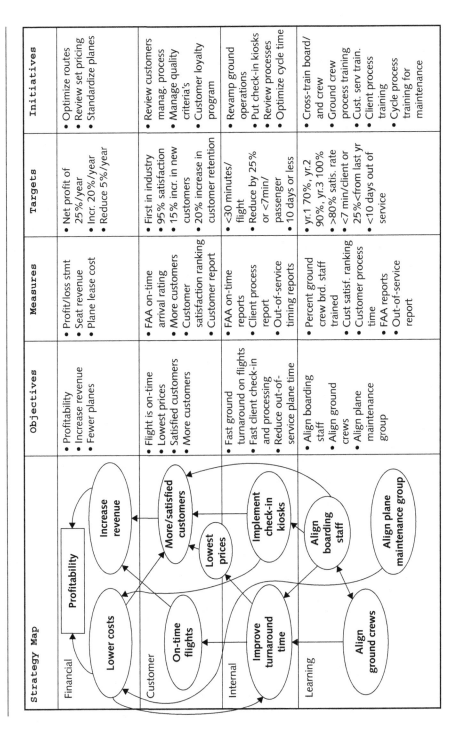

Strategy Map	Objectives	Measures	Targets	Initiatives
Financial	• Profitability • Increase revenue • Fewer planes	• Profit/loss stmt • Seat revenue • Plane lease cost	• Net profit of 25%/year • Incr. 20%/year • Reduce 5%/year	• Optimize routes • Review set pricing • Standardize planes
Customer	• Flight is on-time • Lowest prices • Satisfied customers • More customers	• FAA on-time arrival rating • More customers • Customer satisfaction ranking • Customer report	• First in industry • 95% satisfaction • 15% incr. in new customers • 20% increase in customer retention	• Review customers manag. process • Manage quality criteria's • Customer loyalty program
Internal	• Fast ground turnaround on flights • Fast client check-in and processing • Reduce out-of-service plane time	• FAA on-time reports • Client process report • Out-of-service timing reports	• <30 minutes/ flight • Reduce by 25% or <7min/ passenger • 10 days or less	• Revamp ground operations • Put check-in kiosks • Review processes • Optimize cycle time
Learning	• Align boarding staff • Align ground crews • Align plane maintenance group	• Percent ground crew brd. staff trained • Cust satisf. ranking • Customer process time • FAA reports • Out-of-service report	• yr.1 70%, yr.2 90%, yr.3 100% • >80% satis. rate • <7 min/client or 25%<from last yr • <10 days out of service	• Cross-train board/ and crew • Ground crew process training • Cust. serv train. • Client process training • Cycle process training for maintenance

—

supporting and enabling them through a well-aligned learning strategy tied to the learning and growth perspective.

This top-down approach continues through each level of the organization, progressing down to personal scorecards. Those at the lower levels provide feedback about whether they will be able to align with the strategy, the resources they require, and what they need to do to achieve their objectives. Every department scorecard must connect so that every part of the organization is moving in the same direction. Figure 10.1 illustrates both the top-down and the bottom-up approach that must be used.

The "business" departments of every organization are used to providing answers to senior-level accountability questions. So when it comes to developing a sub-level scorecard for their department, these managers are often in line with corporate-level needs. For many of the "softer" departments such as learning and performance, this is not necessarily the case and they may not be able to respond in a way that management expects.

Traditionally treated as an expense and a "necessary evil," learning and performance has moved very quickly from obscurity to full strategic prominence. Learning is now treated as a strategic asset, especially now that it is an integral component of the balanced scorecard and the organization's strategic planning process.

Figure 10.1. Cascading Scorecard Development Process

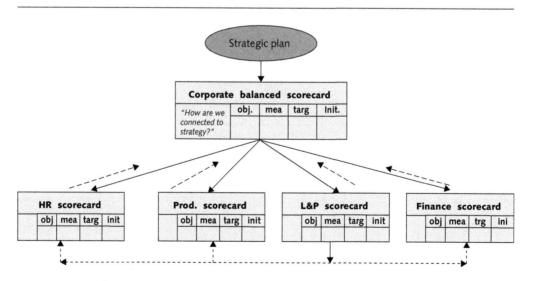

In the same way that senior management develops the corporate balanced scorecard, the learning department must now develop a scorecard for their department. Within this scorecard you will address the financial objectives of the department, meet internal customer needs, develop specific processes to meet these needs, and build a professional development strategy for the learning team.

Questions to Ask

Before you begin to develop the learning department's scorecard, it is important to address certain questions that may be asked of you by management. The answers to these questions will help you to position the department's scorecard within the organization's framework and will also help you to discover more about management's thought process.

One of the first questions to ask management is: "Where does learning fit in the corporate strategy?" Too often senior management makes overtures about following certain business trends, but does not follow through. For example, one recent trend is building a knowledge organization. Asking where learning fits in will reveal how serious management is about leveraging the knowledge capital of their people. Asking this question may force management to consider how to strategically align their learning efforts with their strategic objectives. Even though learning is expected to become more "business-oriented," the reality is that most senior managers are unaware of how to actually incorporate learning into their strategic plans. Learning professionals can play an important role in helping management to think critically about learning's role.

The next question to ask strategy decision-makers is: "As we develop our scorecard, what corporate strategies should we consider?" Also ask: "What corporate-level themes do we need to incorporate?" The answers to these questions will reveal the direction management is taking. If you have not noticed already, senior managers are not always clear about their intentions or about how they intend to execute their strategy. The balanced scorecard can help to alleviate this problem, but the problem is still likely to exist. Even though it should be senior management's responsibility to communicate strategic intent, you must take the initiative to ask for it.

The final question is: "Are there specific links or integration with other business units that we should be aware of as we develop our business strategy and performance measures?" This is similar to what we discussed in previous chapters about partnering with business units to determine their needs. The difference is that the needs of a business unit may not be aligned with management's expectations for that business unit. Asking this question will also uncover which business units management consider critical to the successful execution of the organization's strategy.

It is essential to develop strong investigative skills. The information you are able to uncover from the decision-makers will help you to develop a learning department scorecard and more effectively address the primary learning requirements of the organization. The questions to ask are listed below:

- Where do we fit within the corporate-level strategy?
- As we develop our strategy, our map, and our scorecard, what corporate strategies should we consider?
- Which corporate-level themes should we be sure to incorporate?
- Are there links or integration with other business units that we should be aware of as we develop our strategy and performance measures?

THE LEARNING DEPARTMENT BSC: A DIFFERENT PERSPECTIVE

The process of completing the learning department scorecard is not much different from the process of creating the corporate-level scorecard. Working through this process will help you to understand the process senior management goes through. There are, however, some differences considering that, in the bigger picture, learning and growth is an enabling function of the three perspectives in the corporate scorecard.

All of the elements of the learning department scorecard are the same as for every other scorecard in your organization. We will continue to use Kaplan and Norton's model, using the four perspectives of financial, customer, internal processes, and learning and growth. Note that if your organization's scorecard utilizes different labels, then make your learning department scorecard consistent with the corporate-level labels. It is also acceptable if your organization customizes a scorecard to their specific strategic orientation.

The next may be that your organization uses different performance metrics. In a typical balanced scorecard, the performance metrics for the primary business

Figure 10.2. Sample Balanced Scorecard Performance Metrics

Financial	Customer	Internal Process	Learning and Growth
Revenue/sales	Client satisfaction	Production rate	Employee satisfaction
Return on capital	Client retention	Productivity effectiveness	Employee retention
Net income/profit	Client loyalty	Inventory levels and turnover	Employee productivity
Return on investment	Lead generation	New product development/release	Quality of work environment
Cash flow	Sales wins		
Receivable turnover	Net income/profit	Order cycle time	Information dissemination
Direct costs	Complaint resolution	Quality and accuracy	System and process support
Variable costs	Price competition	Asset utilization	
Comparative expenses	Perceived market value	Innovation	Ethics and safety
	Market share	Post-sale support	Motivation and empowerment
	Client profitability	Break-even levels	Skills alignment
	Image and rep	Process cost management	

perspectives are naturally business driven. Figure 10.2 is a non-exhaustive list of performance metrics typically used in the balanced scorecard.

A learning scorecard may use some of the corporate performance metrics listed in Figure 10.2; however, typically the performance metrics used must accommodate how a learning department performs and how it measures its performance. If learning is expected to deliver results for the business, then it must also be allowed the latitude to benchmark itself against performance metrics influenced by learning evaluation methodologies such as Kirkpatrick's or other credible methodologies. Figure 10.3 lists examples of performance metrics influenced by learning's specific performance evaluation requirements.

The last difference in perspective is that learning professionals may want to reposition learning as a business-oriented department. As we have said, the best way to modify management's perception is to treat learning as a profit-driven function, even though management sees it as a cost center. Switching your mindset will

Figure 10.3. Sample Learning Scorecard Performance Metrics

Financial	Customer	Internal Process	Learning and Growth
Adherence to budgets and forecasts	Internal client satisfaction (Kirkpatrick Level 1)	Internal process metrics (such as production rate)	Leadership development
Training as percent of revenue	Contribution to function ratio in $$ (such as reduction in defects)	Productivity effectiveness	Succession planning
Average learning invest./employee		Internal compliance	Career development
	Internal client loyalty	Training evaluation (Level 2)	Training completions
Contribution to function ratio in $$ (such as reduction in defects)	Client results	Training integration and support (Level 3)	Training plans
			Compliance (Kirkpatrick Level 2)
Return on capital invested (Level 4)		Error rates	Application (Kirkpatrick Level 3)
		Average training per employee	Strategic skills alignment
			Motivation and empowerment

help you to see that the department's survival is dependent on results and on the satisfaction of your customer—your organization. Looking at things in a new way helps you to complete a "corporate" scorecard for the department and gives you the ability to develop results-based performance metrics. Remember that the department's scorecard must always align with the strategic orientation of the corporate scorecard. Basically, the learning department's strategic objective is a strategic objective for the organization, not just for the department. Let's look at each of the perspectives individually in the context of developing a learning department scorecard.

Financial Perspective: "How Do We Look to Our Stakeholders?"

Considering that the learning department is not truly a profit-driven area of the business, the financial objectives and metrics will not be based on any revenue-related activities. That being said, many of the functional supportive business areas such as learning are asked to set themselves up as profit centers. This can be done by having the learning department charge any business unit requesting a service a "transfer" price. Transfer prices are predetermined by adding a percentage to the cost of the product or service provided.

Financial objectives for the learning department are typically cost-driven and would include financial metrics such as:

- Adherence to budgets and forecasts
- Training as a percentage of revenue
- Average learning investment per employee
- Contribution to function ratio in dollars (for example, training leading to a reduction in production defects)
- Return on capital invested (Level 4) (for example, how well training assisted in making the capital invested work for the organization)
- Return on sales (how well learning contributes to learning effectiveness)

If the learning department has profit-driven objectives, then the following metrics might also be used:

- Profit-and-loss measure (utilizing financial statements to demonstrate profitability such as income and cash flow statements)
- Return on assets (how well training assisted in the maximum use of fixed assets such as production equipment)
- Balance sheet improvement of the department (increase in value of the department through their efforts)
- Return on investment of both learning efforts and the investment of other business units

Both of these lists are far from complete. Every organization will use some form of these metrics but will also have financial measures specifically designed to its needs. Your objective is to determine which organization-specific metrics are applicable to your needs.

Exhibit 10.1 asks the essential questions to help you properly complete the financial perspective for the learning department's scorecard.

Exhibit 10.1. Financial Perspective: "How Do We Look to Our Stakeholders?"

Answer the following questions for your department.

Who are your stakeholders?

_____   _____

_____   _____

_____   _____

_____   _____

What do your stakeholders expect from you?

_____

_____

_____

_____

What are your departmental financial objectives?

_____

_____

_____

_____

What are some of the financial measures you have to account for?

_____

_____

_____

_____

How do you/will you measure your return on capital?

_____

_____

_____

_____

Customer Perspective: "How Do Our Customers See Us?"

The learning department's customers are all the business units within the organization. More precisely, within the scorecard framework, the customers are the business units under each balanced scorecard perspective, especially those identified as strategically significant to the organization's achieving its objectives. In the article in Chapter 3, we addressed a business approach to learning. The premise was that learning professionals should treat internal customers, the other business units within the organization, as actual customers. Remember that you need to address the internal customers as if you were a consulting firm hired to resolve their concerns. The needs of your internal customers are highlighted in the customer perspective of the department's scorecard. Unlike a consulting firm, which would treat the needs of their customers equally, you must address these needs in order of strategic importance and management priority. In Chapter 9 we identified the most strategic issues for Sky Air as part of developing the learning and growth perspective of the corporate scorecard. The internal customers responsible for strategic issues are the primary customers in the learning department scorecard. Metrics to measure customer satisfaction might include the following:

- Internal client satisfaction (Kirkpatrick Level 1)
- Contribution to function ratio in $$ (such as reduction in defects)
- Internal client loyalty
- Attention to specific client results
- Client buy-in/retention
- Number of issues resolved
- Client profitability
- Adherence to strategic objectives
- Adherence to business objectives
- Meeting client budget requirements

Exhibit 10.2 asks some of the primary questions to help you understand your internal customers. As shown in the Sky Air case, it is necessary to define customers' critical business issues by referring to their departmental scorecards and tying them to the corporate-level scorecard. It is important to begin by addressing those

Exhibit 10.2. Customer Perspective: "How Do Our Customers See Us?"

Answer the following questions for your department.

Who are your customers?

_____

_____

_____

_____

What are your customers' critical issues/concerns (refer to their departments' BSCs)?

Customer

_____

_____

Issues

_____

_____

_____

_____

How are their objectives related to the corporate strategy/BSC?

_____

_____

_____

_____

What are you doing to satisfy your customers' expectations?

_____

_____

_____

_____

How are you developing your relationships with your customers?

_____

_____

_____

_____

customers with strategic-driven issues prior to resolving the non-strategic but critical issues of other internal customers.

The strength of the learning scorecard comes first from building strategic relationships with internal customers and then from identifying the strategic issues impeding these customers from effectively achieving the organization's strategic objectives.

Internal Process Perspective: "What Must Learning Excel At?"

At the corporate scorecard level, internal processes are the core business processes of the organization. Learning professionals address these core processes when developing a learning strategy for learning and growth. The internal processes are the core business processes required for the learning department to function effectively.

The internal processes are the foundation of developing solutions that meet your customer needs. Often those responsible for learning are not fully aware of those internal processes within the strategic framework of a balanced scorecard. It is crucial to fully understand how learning solutions are assessed, designed, developed, and delivered. Left out of the analysis are the inputs or the resources required. Working through the entire process not only helps you to clearly understand the learning process but also helps you to discover areas of potential efficiencies. Some of the areas measured in this perspective include:

- Internal process metrics (such as, production rate)
- Productivity effectiveness
- Internal compliance
- Training evaluation (Level 2)
- Training integration and support (Level 3)
- Error rates
- Average training per employee
- Productivity effectiveness
- New training development
- Training design cycle time
- Quality and accuracy

- Innovation
- Break-even levels
- Process cost management

Do not take this area lightly, as we often see those involved with the learning function do. Take the time to walk through every detail of the learning department's developmental and functional process. The strength of your scorecard will come from the internal process perspective. Exhibit 10.3 will help you to consider the major questions in this area.

Learning and Growth Perspective: "How Can Learning Continue to Improve and Create Value?"

The learning and growth perspective is about maintaining and developing the skills of the learning team. Essentially, it is about professional development; the expectation for the learning staff to be abreast of the most current knowledge and employee development skills and techniques available to assist the organization in its efforts should be high. Surprisingly, this is often not the case. Continuous development of the learning staff's skills should be at the top of the learning director's list.

When we bring this point up to learning professionals, they quickly agree, but professional development is still found at the bottom of the "to do" list. With your organization concerned about building a learning organization and being able to effectively leverage the knowledge available to them, there is little tolerance from management for not developing the learning staff.

Following are some examples of the areas covered in the learning and growth perspective of the department's scorecard:

- Leadership development
- Succession planning
- Career development
- Training completions
- Personal and staff training plans
- Application of skills
- Strategic skills alignment

Exhibit 10.3. Internal Process Perspective: "What Must Learning Excel At?"

Answer the following questions for your department.

What do you do for the organization?

_____

_____

_____

_____

What must you excel at?

_____

_____

_____

_____

Which areas must you improve?

_____

_____

_____

_____

What are some of critical/strategic business processes you have to account for?

_____

_____

_____

_____

How do you fit in the business value chain and what do you contribute to it?

_____

_____

_____

_____

- Industry certifications
- Industry conference attendance and participation
- Motivation and empowerment
- Employee satisfaction
- Employee retention
- Employee productivity
- Quality of work environment
- Information dissemination
- System and process support
- Ethics and safety
- Skills alignment

Rather than trying to address every item on this list (which is far from exhaustive), decide which are critical to your department's and organization's needs. Essentially, you are conducting a skills needs assessment for the learning department and for the needs of your internal clients. Second only to the internal process perspective, learning and growth determines how effective the core processes you implement and utilize will be for the department. Any weaknesses or lack of skills on the learning team will result in failure to execute strategy effectively. The learning department staff must develop the perspectives and performance metrics for their departmental scorecard.

Complete Exhibit 10.4 to begin your assessment of your specific needs. This is the first step in developing a continuous learning plan for the learning team that will help the department to improve and create lasting value.

A RAPID DEVELOPMENT PROCESS FOR THE LEARNING SCORECARD

Developing a balanced scorecard is an intensive and detailed process, and it can be intimidating for learning professionals to develop one for their department. We encourage you to invest the appropriate amount of time and resources to develop a thorough departmental scorecard. To help facilitate the process and get started, we will walk you through a rapid development process to establishing a learning department scorecard.

Exhibit 10.4. Learning and Growth Perspective: "How Can Learning Continue to Improve and Create Value?"

Answer the following questions for your department.

What do you do well?

_____

_____

_____

_____

What are your weaknesses?

_____

_____

_____

_____

What can you do to continue to improve/add strategic value to learning and performance?

_____

_____

_____

_____

What skills/knowledge do you require to help your customers?

_____

_____

_____

_____

What is the leadership and succession plan for learning and performance?

_____

_____

_____

_____

Step 1: Completing the Financial Perspective

For rapid development, you should ask and answer at most a handful of key questions:

- What are your department's financial objectives?
- How will you measure your return on the capital employed (ROCE)?
- What does the C-suite (and any other critical stakeholder) expect financially and in terms of results from learning and performance?

The first question ("What are your department's financial objectives?") is a question all departments must ask themselves. For the learning department, profitability is not usually the expected outcome, so you would focus on the department's budget allocation. Answers to the second question might include "adherence to budget allocation" or "return on the capital employed" (ROCE). The ROCE is a financial ratio measuring the efficiency and profitability of an organization's capital investments. The learning department's ROCE is very similar, but more a measure of how well it is utilizing the capital (budget) allocated to it to produce the results management expects. For example, management may allocate a budget amount to the learning department to produce effective learning solutions. To answer the third question, the learning team must evaluate which methods and delivery mechanisms will bring the expected results while maximizing the funds available.

Step 2: Completing the Customer Perspective

If the corporate and business unit scorecards are completed properly, then this step should be relatively simple. The development of all of the organizational scorecards will point out the needs of all the business units. We reiterate, however, that priority should be given to internal customers with critical strategic issues. From your analysis of the organization's scorecard, the questions to answer include:

- Who are your internal customers?
- What are their critical issues?
- How do their issues contribute to the corporate BSC?

The answers for these questions are either apparent or will be clearly communicated by management to the learning department.

Step 3: Completing the Internal Process Perspective

In its scorecard, management focused on the critical issues affecting the internal processes of the organization. The learning team should look at the learning department's internal processes in the same way. Remember that the internal processes of an organization or department are the cornerstone of its eventual success. This is no different for learning and development. The questions the learning team must ask itself include:

- Which L&P internal processes require intervention (that is, what are the critical issues)?
- What can be improved with a learning intervention?
- What are the essential organizational issues requiring attention?
- What is the average budgeted amount per employee for training?

The learning team must be able to identify critical areas within the organization that require immediate attention. These internal process areas need learning solutions to meet their objectives and thereby to contribute to the execution of the corporate strategy. For example, let's say a company is about to introduce a new product. Management expects that customers will be able to easily use the new product and approaches the learning team for solutions. The learning team should be able to assess the need and develop learning solutions that will facilitate the product introduction.

Step 4: Completing the Learning and Growth Perspective

This is an area that learning professionals must understand well beyond all of the other perspectives. Because this perspective is about professional and skills development, every member of the learning team must possess the most relevant professional knowledge and skills to understand and communicate with other members of the business. To address these needs, the questions you must answer include:

- What are the training plans for learning and performance?
- What is the leadership and succession plan for learning and performance?

Table 10.1. Sample Learning Department Balanced Scorecard

Strategy Map	Objectives	Measures	Targets	Initiatives
Financial	Meet expected budget allocations	L+P budget percentage measured against income statement	15 percent of Year 1 revenue to learning initiatives	Conduct needs assessment of department's financial need
Customer	Identify top three strategic learnings required for strategically aligned internal customers	Customer survey responses and interviews		
	Corporate BSC issue identification	Sample 25 percent of each department		
	Identify top three issues at corporate level	Learning plans and strategy for initiatives		
Internal	Assess internal department needs	Inventory of staff skills and tools		
	Ensure competency of 50 percent of staff in six months, all by end of year	Develop personal development plans, acquire tools		
Learning	Ensure compliance and certification of L+P	Department needs assessment and staff survey of priorities	100 percent compliance in eight months; 100 percent certification in eighteen months	Pre-exam, then post-exam; source certification courses

LAST THOUGHTS

The success of every organization using a balanced scorecard is from the careful and detailed implementation of the business unit scorecards. The process of cascading the performance metrics from the corporate level all the way down to every business unit provides management with the ability to execute the organization's strategy.

The results come when the business units function well and meet their objectives. These objectives, however, may depend on employee abilities and skills that they do not currently possess or have not adequately mastered. In a constantly evolving strategic environment, all levels of an organization require timely support from the learning area. The learning department must develop its own cascaded scorecard. With learning's growing strategic role, the necessity of a proactive and aligned learning scorecard is more important than ever. After years of being relegated to the back office, learning is now front and center.

Developing a scorecard presents a significant challenge for many learning professionals, especially with the pressure of meeting and supporting the organization's strategic demands. But the process of developing the scorecard may help the learning team to focus better on its internal customers' strategic issues. But the end results are only as strong as learning's internal process, that is, how the learning team assesses, identifies, designs, and develops learning solutions for the rest of the organization.

Like other business units, the learning department requires skills and knowledge. The department's internal process depends solely on the learning team members' intellectual capital. The learning and growth perspective of the scorecard ensures that the internal processes are relevant, leading to support for customer requirements, which helps management meet its strategic objectives.

By asking the right questions for each of the department's balanced scorecard perspectives, the learning team can start to develop an aligned and proactive learning scorecard. Do not underestimate the intricacies and interdependencies of the learning department's scorecard. Learning professionals will discover that the learning scorecard is one of the key underpinnings of the corporate-level scorecard and increasingly a significant part of the success of an organization's strategy.

For years business leaders were challenged to find the "answer" for addressing these new market factors. They discovered that their people were the key.

This is excellent news for learning professionals, but it also presents new and significant challenges because the people preoccupied with learning's role, business leaders, do not view learning the same way we do. This book was written to help learning professionals learn to communicate in a business and strategic mindset. In this last chapter, we want to provide tell you about some of the strategic-oriented influences on workplace learning we foresee in the future.

With the exception of management gurus, who many times influence the direction of business trends, nobody can really predict how the workplace of the future will take shape. Unlike the first half of the 20th century, where changes were periodic and stability commonplace, the knowledge age is the opposite. The once sacred cows and taboos of the business world are now fair game. Start-up entrepreneurs continually challenge the status quo, globalization increases competition, innovation becomes a necessity not a luxury, customer loyalty declines, and demand for knowledgeable and skilled people increases at a staggering rate. For those corporations that thrive on stability, the business environment today is rocking them to their foundations. In today's business environment, there are too many variables to clearly predict how business and the marketplace will evolve. Even the once regular business cycles (economic cycles, product life cycles, and career-life cycles) are irregular and unpredictable.

We are not going to make any bold predictions. The only accurate prediction that we can make is that change will continue. In this chapter we will address some of the primary business issues and areas we believe are affecting most organizations' strategy and learning environment:

- The new variables: technology, workers, and the world
- Expectation of return on workplace investment
- Managing learning for a generational workforce
- Developing the entrepreneurial employee
- Developing specialists, not generalists
- Increasing trend for customer intimacy
- Managing knowledge for maximum benefit

THE NEW VARIABLES: TECHNOLOGY, WORKERS, AND THE WORLD

In recent years the world has witnessed a significant shift in how business is conducted. Just fifty years ago the United States accounted for about 53 percent of the world's GDP. The demand for American goods at home and abroad was so great that almost any product could find a market. Today, the U.S. share of the world GDP is approximately 25 percent (2007 International Monetary Fund List) and decreasing. Business leaders struggle with how to manage this shift, and thought leaders struggle to keep up with the constant changes. The impetus for the economic shift is partly accessibility and constant evolution of technology, the need for knowledge workers, and the growth of emerging markets. Many of these factors are moving targets for an organization's strategic planners. Trying to predict the changes that will occur is challenging.

The last couple of decades ushered in a technological revolution in how work is accomplished. Technology's considerable impact on business has been both a blessing and at times a curse. Technology is intended to facilitate processes, create efficiencies, and essentially make our lives simpler. These are the same issues business leaders seek to integrate into their efforts to gain a competitive advantage. At the same time, technology has been an "equalizer" for small, large, and geographically distant organizations. Technology has also introduced new challenges both internally and externally, bringing the world closer and making it move faster.

Technology facilitates globalization, greatly increasing competition from areas of the world not thought of as threats in the past. It enabled the most remote and unfavorable regions to gain knowledge and the tools to challenge the developed world.

As simple as technology has become, it still requires specific skills not only to use it effectively but also to harness its capabilities. It also requires continuous learning, since technology is constantly changing and evolving. Creating new technologies requires new skills as well as the ability for people to innovate. This brings us back full circle, requiring people to continuously learn new technological solutions.

Managing the new types of change requires a plan, more specifically, a battle plan or the effective execution of a strategic plan so that an organization can achieve its goals. The balanced scorecard and other scorecarding tools provide a simple framework to link the critical factors together.

EXPECTATION OF RETURN ON WORKPLACE INVESTMENT

Learning has grown significantly since the days when it was known simply as "training." It has also struggled in the last few years trying to find how it fits into its new business paradigm. Workplace learning experts and gurus have been attempting to force-fit a variety of business terms into learning application contexts. One of the most popular terms is "return on investment" (ROI). It is very important to know the ROI of investments in learning and good results gives credibility to the work of the learning department. The standard ROI formula is shown in Figure 11.1.

The ROI calculation can be applied to many scenarios. In a typical business environment, returns are the results gained from tangible investments. Therein lies the problem. Learning is not a tangible investment. This is why business leaders have a difficult time accepting learning's ROI in the traditional sense. And learning professionals add to the problem, and damage their own credibility, by presenting their results in the traditional way.

When businesspeople conduct an ROI analysis, it is based on reasonable assumptions and tangible aspects. This usually leads to reasonable results. When a calculation is conducted on a learning investment, the results may seem unreasonable from a business perspective. This is not because the ROI is negative—quite the opposite—the result is too positive. Presenting financial ROI measures that are "too good to be true" will be seen in a negative light. This does not mean that the ROI calculation is incorrect; however, it will not be seen as credible. The result must be realistic, comparable to other possible options, and, most importantly, tangible.

When presenting an ROI calculation to decision-makers, remember to give tangible data. The same decision-makers rightly expect that any investment made in a business initiative will demonstrate some form of return that benefits the organization. Because a financial ROI model is not appropriate for measuring the impact of an intangible business investment such as a workplace learning initiative, you must use indirect measures and find ways to make them tangible.

Figure 11.1. ROI

$$ROI = \frac{(\text{Gain from Investment} - \text{Cost of Investment})}{\text{Cost of Investment}}$$

First, determine what end result is expected. Then show the connection between what you have done and the strategic objectives on the organization's balanced scorecard. Doing this reinforces the importance of learning and the cascading effect that a learning initiative has on the bottom line. Examples of business objectives you can connect your results to are listed below.

- Conflict resolution
- Cost reduction
- Customer complaints
- Customer loyalty
- Customer retention
- Customer satisfaction
- Effective cost management
- Effective time management
- Employee morale
- Faster client response time
- Improved communication
- Improved work safety
- Increased innovation
- Increased productivity

- Increased profitability
- Increased team cohesion
- Job satisfaction
- New customers
- New product prototypes
- Order processing efficiencies
- Product defects
- Reduced absenteeism
- Reduced duplication/ redundancy
- Reduced maintenance costs
- Reduced recruitment costs
- Reduction waste
- Sales growth

The way to assess which business ROI measure to use is to do the following:

- Ask the business manager requesting the learning, "What is the objective/issue you want to achieve/resolve?"
- Obtain the objectives for the business area that the learning initiative is to address (a copy of the business unit scorecard will help).
- With the business manager, determine which business metrics the learning initiative will affect.
- Establish benchmarks (baseline) measures for the selected business metrics.
- Determine what other factors connect to and affect the business metrics.

- Uncover any other initiatives in place that address the same issue.
- Assign a weight or percentage for the level of improvement learning is responsible for.
- Develop a learning plan and strategy.
- Build a budget to show the learning investment required.
- Develop a cost-benefit scenario to show the relationship between the investment and the expected benefits based on the selected business ROI metrics.
- Obtain commitment and "buy-in" from the business manager.
- Follow through on the learning initiative to ensure behavioral change has taken place.

You may not complete all of these steps, but the main point is to manage the investment of the learning initiative in relation to the expected benefit. The benefit is not simply financial return, but a business objective relevant to the business manager.

Moving to the Next Levels

We have said this before, but remember that workplace learning lives in a different world from the rest of the organization, which sees learning interventions differently. If learning professionals are to add real value and derive specific benefits from their learning interventions, then it is time to move from the current way that they evaluate learning to new ways more relevant for the rest of the organization.

Learning professionals evaluate their performance in several ways, from asking for immediate feedback after completion of a session to determining how the learning intervention has affected the business. This systematic process of learning evaluation is commonly known as Kirkpatrick's four levels of evaluation (see sidebar). There is a divide between how learning professionals and how business leaders evaluate learning. Learning professionals are traditionally comfortable and can easily complete Level 1 (reaction or feedback from participants) and Level 2 (learning retention or testing). Management, however evaluates learning at Level 3 (application of learning and change in employee behavior) and Level 4 (how the learning intervention impacted the business), although they do not refer to the levels. If learning professionals want to build credibility and be able to demonstrate learning's value, then in the coming years they will have to move from Levels 1 and 2 and evaluate learning performance from management's perspective at Levels 3 and 4.

Kirkpatrick's Four Levels of Evaluation

Over fifty years ago, Donald Kirkpatrick wrote his thesis on the four levels of training evaluation. Prior to Kirkpatrick's model, training evaluations were not given a second thought. Half a century later, Kirkpatrick's methodology is now more important than ever before. This simple model (see Table 11.1) is widely used in a variety of learning environments.

Table 11.1. Kirkpatrick's Four Levels of Evaluation

Level	Description
Level 1: Reaction	Obtaining participants' evaluation of the training immediately after the session is complete (smile sheets).
Level 2: Learning	Testing participants to determine whether they learned what was taught (pre- and post-testing)
Level 3: Application/Behavior Change	Determining whether participants are doing things differently back on the job as a result of the training. Are they applying the knowledge gained?
Level 4: Business Impact	Determining how the organization benefits from this new behavior.

Source: Terrence L. Gargiulo, Ajay M. Pangarkar, Teresa K. Kirkwood, and Tom Bunzel. (2006). *Building Business Acumen for Trainers: Skills to Empower the Learning Function*, pages 83–84. San Francisco: Pfeiffer.

(continued)

Level 1: The Reactions of the Training Participants

Evaluation at this level measures how participants in a training program react to it. It attempts to answer questions regarding the participants' perceptions. According to Kirkpatrick, every program should at least be evaluated at this level to provide for the improvement of a training program. In addition, the participants' reactions have important consequences for learning (Level 2).

Level 2: The Evaluation of What Participants Learned (Testing)

To assess the amount of learning that has occurred due to a training program, Level 2 evaluations often use tests conducted before training (pre-test) and after training (post-test). Assessment at this level moves the evaluation beyond learner satisfaction and attempts to assess the extent to which students have advanced in skills and knowledge.

Level 3: The Application or Transfer of the Learning to the Participants' Jobs

This level measures the change that has occurred in learners' behavior due to the training program. Evaluating at this level attempts to answer the question, "Are the newly acquired skills, knowledge, or attitude being used in the everyday environment of the learner?" For many trainers this represents the truest assessment of a program's effectiveness. However, measuring at this level is difficult, as it is often impossible to predict when the change in behavior will occur, and thus it requires important decisions in terms of when to evaluate, how to evaluate, and how often to evaluate.

Level 4: The Measurement and Impact of the Training on the Business
Level 4 evaluation attempts to assess training in terms of business results. This is the level that is the focus of management and decision-makers in your organization. Frequently thought of as the bottom line, this level measures the success of the program in terms that managers and executives can understand—increased production, improved quality, decreased costs, reduced frequency of accidents, increased sales, and even higher profits or return on investment. From a business and organizational perspective, this is the overall reason for a training program, yet Level 4 results are not typically addressed.

The biggest challenge for workplace learning is overcoming the tendency to evaluate at only Level 1 or Level 2. Many learning professionals believe that it is not possible to evaluate the impact of learning on the organization (Level 4). There are two reasons why this is the case: (1) workplace learning professionals are not sufficiently knowledgeable on how to conduct a Level 3 or Level 4 evaluation or (2) learning professionals are uncertain about the true results their solutions have to offer the organization. In either case, resolving these issues is essential if workplace learning professionals are to build management's confidence in their capability.

We as learning professionals need to address common misconceptions we have about the evaluation process. Our own preconceived notions limit the impact the learning process can have on the organization and result in our presenting programs that demonstrate no results. Let's address some of these notions:

- *Evaluation is conducted only after training is complete.* This may have worked years ago, but learning must be tied to business and strategic objectives. Learning professionals will need to identify business issues relevant to the organization and make learning evaluation an integrated and progressive process. Evaluations will need to increasingly focus on the business areas of concern to management.

- *Level 4 evaluations must show a direct financial impact.* Although financial measures are important and often expected by management, there may be none for many learning initiatives. Learning's "ROI" will be the impact it has on the business issues the learning solution addresses.

- *Management wants a "quick fix."* Management's time is limited and dispersed. So when a problem arises, they seek the quick fix. It is human nature to address the symptom of an issue and not necessarily the cause. Learning professionals must begin to leverage their analytical and assessment abilities. Rapid needs assessments must become a habit. Knowing what is needed will help management to achieve their goals and lead to sustainable results.

Learning professionals must begin thinking in a business sense if they are to gain management's respect and credibility. Begin with the following points to lead workplace learning to becoming a more valued member of the organization.

Evaluate Based on Corporate Values

Every organization has a culture, a philosophy, and entrenched values. Do you know what the values are? Have you made attempts to determine what they are? How are you building what you learn into your learning initiatives? The organization's values are based on its people and strategic objectives. By incorporating these values into your learning solutions, you will develop more focused evaluations.

Business values are very different from workplace learning values. Workplace learning evaluates its worth based on feedback from participants and knowledge retention, whereas business values performance, tangible results, and knowledge application. Part of every learning professional's responsibility is to continually develop his or her own professional skills. And one of these is the ability to determine exactly what is of value to your organization. Having regular conversations with a cross-section of people in the organization allows you to learn what is important to other departments, to the employees, and to senior management. By doing this you will be able to develop solutions that are practical and relevant to the organization.

Keep Evaluation Simple and Quick

Today's decision-makers are placing tremendous pressure on workplace learning to deliver Level 4 results. In reality, a Level 4 evaluation is not necessary for every learning effort. Evaluation must be kept simple, quick, and relevant to the proposed solution. The more complex the process becomes, the less it will be relevant to the individuals and stakeholders involved. Evaluations also deliver the best results when the metrics already exist, are accepted by management, and relate directly to the desired outcomes. (These components exist within a balanced scorecard.) Using theses metrics for Level 4 evaluations will also reduce the cost of the evaluation process and directly impact how much needs to be improved. Using what is readily available, tangible, and important to the organization will help workplace learning become a more strategically aligned business partner.

Provide Evidence, Not Proof

In business it is not about proof; it is about evidence of change. Managers will never give learning professionals full credit for resolving a business concern, so stop trying to convince them. It is time-consuming and expensive to provide undeniable proof for anything. Even training evaluation experts are unable to deliver undeniable proof that any learning solution actually contributes to the desired improvements. It is also difficult to isolate how a learning effort contributes to business results, since an initiative is often an integrated part of a larger solution. So how can you prove that learning delivers on its expectation? You can't. You only look for evidence that supports learning's effort.

Don't get caught up in how critical learning is to the organization. Workplace learning will always be an important part of an organization's growth, but you must accept that it is not the sole contributor. Work together with business managers to agree on how much learning is expected to contribute to improvements. Workplace learning is only one part of a complex, interrelated management system, as evidenced in the balanced scorecard. Proving results is not crucial, as decision-makers are usually satisfied with tangible evidence of performance.

Understand Organizational Interactions

Management expects to see a direct link between the learning initiative and its impact on the business. Finding this direct link is difficult, since training is only one of many factors contributing to improving operational issues. It is unfair to have learning and performance bear all of the responsibility for organizational improvement, as they are not in control of many other factors. If possible, determine in advance the relationships and interaction of other issues on desired outcomes. Project managers recognize this process as finding the "critical path" to reaching an objective. Thinking in this manner is important, as it can help you to be more effective:

- Understand the interactions among parts of your organization.
- Design learning programs to maximize impact on the critical links in the path.
- Evaluate outcomes and impacts throughout the process.

MANAGING LEARNING FOR A GENERATIONAL WORKFORCE

Currently there are four generations in the workforce. This is the first time in history that this has happened. Organizations need to focus primarily on the younger generations, generation X and generation Y. Generation X is seen as the "sandwich" generation because the older ones relate more to their baby boomer counterparts and the younger ones align themselves with the generation Y group. Generation Y are the most recent entering the workforce and are the children of the baby boomers.

These two generations, especially generation Y, are unlike any workforce of the past. This generation was raised differently and possesses very different attitudes toward work and learning. The learning solutions currently in place and so popular with past generations are slowly becoming outdated. The methods used to transfer learning will also have to evolve and adapt to the how new generations learn. Generation Y is the first truly digital generation. They have been influenced by digital media such as the Internet, video games, and portable digital assistants. They were often raised in isolated environments. With both parents being career driven, they had to cope with and handle situations by themselves and communicate and learn via digital media such as their computers and video game consoles.

In the next few decades, the way the workplace functions will change dramatically as a result of the incoming workforce. Workplace learning must evolve and adapt to how these generations prioritize issues and assimilate new skills and abilities. The traditional methods of learning, such as instructor-led courses and individual coaching, will be replaced with virtual learning environments and e-learning-based methodologies.

Of all of the workplace trends taking place, the entrance of these new generations will have the most profound impact on organizational strategy and on workplace learning. Business leaders will depend increasingly on their learning teams to help them manage and harness the capabilities of the workforce. Learning professionals will need to develop flexible and innovative learning solutions that meet the needs of this new workforce.

DEVELOPING THE ENTREPRENEURIAL EMPLOYEE

Some traditional concepts are on their way out or have been eliminated altogether. Concepts such as life-long employment (or similarly, the single employer-employee relationship), the forty-hour work week, hierarchical management, and salaried employees are seen as passé or outdated by many. Largely a result of the high demand for skilled workers and an aging workforce, the age of the entrepreneurial employee is here. This presents many opportunities as well as many challenges for organizations.

Increasingly, employees are seeking more control over their work and their environment, and many seek opportunities in smaller entrepreneurial-driven organizations rather than in the historically sought-after Fortune 500 companies. Organizations of every type seek to become more flexible and adaptable and are trying to compete with the threat of smaller, more agile and innovative entrepreneurial start-ups.

Developing and working with entrepreneurial employees requires a strategic management process. This helps to build an effective and sustainable innovation strategy and capacity. A dynamic management environment allows an organization to foster innovative and creative ideas, essential if an organization wants to capture emerging ideas in the workplace.

Learning will play a large role in helping to make the entrepreneurial enterprise come about. Reinventing the management process will require a new set of skills and knowledge framework. An entrepreneurial environment is a somewhat informal structure in which ideas flow freely. Those who develop new ideas must be supported by a dynamic learning strategy. Entrepreneurial employees perform best in environments that stimulate creativity and team cohesion. Learning will have to take the lead in fostering initiatives to help make this happen.

The combination of a flexible management team and a dynamic learning strategy will help organizations to create entrepreneurial cultures and encourage innovative climates.

DEVELOPING SPECIALISTS, NOT GENERALISTS

An organization is in constant flux. Employees must know how to react and know what to do to keep the organization on track and successful. Having an employee know only a slice of what is going on in the organization is no longer acceptable. Employee must know more than just the responsibilities of their own jobs. They must be aware of changes happening in their function and be current in their professional skills.

A delay in responding to market and business changes can be detrimental. Reacting too soon or inappropriately can be equally harmful. Think about recent private- and public-sector scandals that adversely affected and even brought down some large organizations. Having employees learn and understand all there is to know about their roles puts an organization in a stronger position to respond appropriately to market changes and breaking news.

Learning professionals are the ones who will develop these employee specialists. The learning team must help to develop individual learning plans that contribute to each employee's professional development, the learning strategy, and the organizational objectives. Within the balanced scorecard framework, the corporate-level scorecard should cascade all the way down to the employee level.

INCREASING TREND FOR CUSTOMER INTIMACY

In our discussion about strategy and strategic concepts in Chapter 1, we brought up the three value disciplines (product leadership, customer intimacy, and operational excellence) organizations factor into the strategy development process. Of the three value disciplines, the one gaining the most attention is customer intimacy.

A customer intimacy orientation requires an organization to build strong connections with their customers and understand the needs of the marketplace. The organization must know everything about the individuals they are selling to and what is expected from them. A few years ago, organizations may have had a choice about whether to be "customer intimate." However, organizations no longer have a choice. Technology has changed the environment so that customers are empowered to make choices. Of course, strategically, customers are always part of the balanced scorecard and are essential for the organization's survival.

What does this mean for workplace learning? This is where learning professionals can earn their worth and demonstrate tangible results for their learning efforts.

Meeting customer needs is at the center of the organization's focus, and support is required both internally, for employees, and externally, for customers. Internal support is needed for each of the business units that interact in some way with the customer. Think of all of the areas within your organization that interact with and support customer requirements. Areas such as the sales team, the customer support group, the technical support team, the after-sales support processes, the repair and servicing department, and many other areas all require some type of learning support.

Externally, the focus is on the customer and the marketplace. With organizations driving to develop innovative products and services, "educating" customers and the market falls upon the shoulders of the learning team. Learning has the opportunity to partner with other business areas; developing a close relationship with the external customer-focused business areas to develop learning solutions is a critical step to ensure customer acceptance and satisfaction.

The cost and demand on resources for the organization to obtain new and retain existing customers is significant. Business leaders must find ways to facilitate the customer intimacy process and elicit the help of their learning professionals to do so.

MANAGING KNOWLEDGE FOR MAXIMUM BENEFIT

One of the hottest topics in business today is knowledge management. Knowledge management describes a range of strategies and tools that try to capture the valuable knowledge within organizations, to deliver it to other people who can benefit from it, and to ensure that information can be acted on swiftly to the firm's advantage (Know How, 2005).

When the term "knowledge" is brought up, learning professionals quickly assume that it refers to human intellectual capital. But knowledge can be any relevant information within the organization. Sometimes this knowledge is hidden within databases, reports, and information systems. In other cases, knowledge is locked in someone's head and is lost to the organization when the person leaves the business (Know How, 2005).

Workplace learning plays a big role in knowledge management. As technology, globalization, and people increase and become more complex, so do the decisions senior management has to make. Having the right information at hand in a timely manner alleviates some of the stress of the decision-making process. An effective knowledge management process can deliver the right knowledge, information, and abilities to the right people at the right time.

In their recent book, *Alignment*, Kaplan and Norton (2006) refer to learning and growth synergies as:

- Enhancing human capital through excellent HR recruiting, training, and leadership development practices across multiple business units;
- Leveraging a common technology, such as an industry-leading platform or channel for customers to access a wide set of company services that is shared across multiple product and service divisions; and
- Sharing best-practice capabilities through knowledge management that transfer process quality excellence across multiple business units.

Workplace learning is a critical part of the overall knowledge management process, and knowledge management is an integral component of an organization's strategy. For workplace learning to be successful, it must work closely with others involved with knowledge management and deliver timely information and abilities when required.

FINAL THOUGHTS

Workplace learning is about the development of new skills and abilities to overcome current and coming challenges. Learning professionals are the catalyst to developing real solutions in the face of continuous change. Organizations face many challenges in the 21st century, and learning professionals must be knowledgeable about what will affect and benefit their organizations and how their departments fits.

The list of issues provided in this chapter is not exhaustive; some of these areas directly impact workplace learning, whereas others indirectly affect it. It is safe to say that, for every new influence an organization incorporates, workplace learning will be called upon to facilitate its integration with the organization's strategic direction and objectives. Decision-makers will expect this integration to be rapid and seamless.

The most significant concerns for business leaders at this time are the rapid evolution of technology, the effective development of people, and managing the business issues around globalization. Factors such as these are in constant flux and often cause a considerable amount of stress among managers. In business, nothing remains static. These three areas are changing rapidly. Learning professionals must develop dynamic solutions that integrate with other business initiatives and that support the organization's strategic framework.

As business environments become more dynamic, workplace learning will play more of a central role in management's decision-making process. But like every other investment management makes, learning is under close scrutiny. It is accountable for workplace learning and must demonstrating clear relationships between its proposed solutions and organizational results. The challenge for learning is in evaluating any learning initiative. Even the gurus of workplace learning and performance struggle with finding the answers. Some believe results should be demonstrated through proving a financial return on investment, but business leaders are hard-pressed to understand how an intangible learning result can be measured against a tangible financial measure. Instead, business leaders want to see results for their investment in learning. The results they seek are not in the lagging financial performance measures but in non-financial performance measures related to business performance. This requires workplace learning to move from focusing on participant evaluations (Level 1) and knowledge retention (Level 2) to measuring application of new skills (Level 3) and the impact on the business (Level 4). The balanced scorecard can be used to help learning professionals ask the right questions, incorporate the right performance metrics, and address the business issues necessary for achieving the organizational strategy.

Another area of concern is the new generation of employees. Incoming generations are changing the way that knowledge is transmitted, and thus the workplace itself. Newer generations work and learn differently, which means that learning professionals must develop learning initiatives that work for their learning styles.

Organizations must also leverage the capabilities of their employees. To respond to smaller, more agile organizations and global competition, organizations need to develop the entrepreneurial capabilities in their people. Business leaders demand specific and immediate knowledge to make sound and timely business decisions. This means that workplace learning must develop learning plans and strategies that focus on specific subjects.

In the knowledge age, naturally knowledge is the driving force for success. Being able to effectively manage all types of knowledge is essential for an organization's immediate and long-term growth. The topic of knowledge management is a popular one nowadays. How learning professionals handle the knowledge management process can be successful if required knowledge is leveraged, or prove detrimental if the process is not aligned with other knowledge processes.

We have discussed only a few of the many current trends in the organizational strategic planning processes. These are all items to consider when developing the balanced scorecard and aligning a useful learning and growth strategy. One thing is for certain: workplace learning's role is secure as long as the learning strategy developed is properly aligned with organizational objectives and is able to deliver tangible results through improved business performance—and as long as learning builds credibility by working with management to resolve specific business concerns and integrates itself into the organizational fabric. This is possible at this time only through the balanced scorecard's learning and growth perspective.

and abilities of their employees, and align all critical aspects of the business with a systematic, results-driven, forward-looking strategy.

Not all involved in the learning profession will be fortunate enough to work for one of these progressive-thinking organizations. But that does not mean that the role of learning is any less significant. Learning professionals must strive to build organizations that will become members of this exclusive club. Intellectual and knowledge capital are the currency for gaining a competitive advantage. Nothing this valuable in the history of modern business is more elusive and more noteworthy than intellectual capital.

What does learning have to do to leverage knowledge and build a learning organization? As we have discussed in this book:

- Build your business acumen as it relates to both workplace learning and how workplace learning relates to your organization's strategic framework.
- Learn as much as possible about strategy and the strategic framework your organization utilizes, such as the balanced scorecard.
- Communicate in a language that your business counterparts understand. They want to see results and care little about the process taken to get to those results.
- Identify the strategic areas of the business that will provide the most impact for your learning initiative and on the organization's objectives.
- Become a proactive partner within your organization. Learn everything that is important and critical to your internal partners'/customers' business needs.
- Push the limits into the unknown and continually learn new subjects related to both workplace learning and, more importantly, to what makes an organization successful.

The steps are simple, although the process of making it happen is somewhat more complex. We have a strategy tool available that helps to incorporate intellectual and knowledge capital—the balanced scorecard. Although this book has focused on how to integrate a learning strategy into the balanced scorecard, your organization may adapt this or other types of scorecards to their specific requirements. Whether it is Kaplan and Norton's balanced scorecard or any other scorecarding process, the workplace learning and other knowledge-driven strategies must be aligned with your organization's strategic objectives.

Stop playing a functional role in your organization. Start being an operational department that works within the organization to harness and leverage the intellectual capital of employees in building a knowledge-driven, learning-focused environment. Help your organization achieve this and become part of the exclusive club of the leading and innovative group of businesses.

WE WANT TO HEAR ABOUT YOUR EXPERIENCES

We have provided some case examples of using the balanced scorecard in the appendices to this book, but we also want you to share *your* stories with us. Please send us descriptions of your efforts and applications within your organization and a release from your organization. We will be compiling these cases and applications to use in the next edition of this book and on our supporting website. We are looking for examples of:

- Successful applications of linking learning strategies to the balanced scorecard;
- Completed learning and growth perspectives with linkages to performance metrics;
- Partnering initiatives with internal business units and internal customers;
- Completed balanced scorecards that incorporate a completed learning and growth perspective;
- Challenges and unsuccessful attempts to develop the learning and growth perspective; and
- Any experiences or applications you would like to share with us with respect to strategy application, the balanced scorecard, and the learning and growth perspective.

You may be published in the next edition of this book or asked to be part of the next series of strategic learning application publications.

Please send your experiences to:

CentralKnowledge Inc.

Email: trainersbsc@centralknowledge.com

www.centralknowledge.com

866-489-7378, ext. 1

- Create an optimal learning environment capable of supporting business and individual performance, growth, and change
- Create a structure to measure L&D's efficiency and effectiveness

The resulting strategy focused on maximizing L&D's value to the corporation. Value was accomplished through both efficiency and effectiveness strategies. Efficiency was accomplished by optimizing the cost of L&D (productivity strategy) and maximizing L&D value contribution through effectiveness (growth strategy).

Strategy maps had already been chosen by human resources (HR) as the structure for managing and aligning HR initiatives. Building off of this, L&D created their own map to help manage and execute the new L&D strategy. This allowed L&D to:

- Align people with the new direction and focus L&D was taking
- Focus on key strategic objectives
- Clarify strategies and aid in communication to all staff
- Establish metrics and ongoing evaluation of progress towards goals

DEVELOPING THE STRATEGY MAP

Several key steps were required in the development of the L&D strategy map.

Step One—Identify Key Objective

It was essential for L&D to understand the business context that the organization was working in. This step was critical, as it allowed L&D to identify where they could have the greatest impact to the organization. L&D identified their key objective as "Maximizing Learning and Development Value"—meaning having the right people with the right skills.

Step Two—Create Value Proposition

The question, "What do customers truly value?" had to be answered, as it drove the development of the strategy map itself.

Two value propositions were created:

1. Customer solutions—This is a customer intimacy strategy focused on building strong relationships with our customers. Determining true needs and providing solutions through our products and services was critical. It was about understanding our customers and helping them to achieve their goals.

2. Operational excellence—It was about delivering products and services at high quality and low cost—and doing it with ease.

Having a value proposition made the creation of the strategy map easier as it clarified the direction that L&D needed to go. This step was the foundation for developing the financial, customer, internal processes, and enablers (learning and growth) perspective on the map.

Step Three—Develop Financial and Customer Perspectives

In the Financial perspective, the two main strategies were growth and productivity.

Customer solutions drove the *growth* strategy—Maximize Learning and Development Value Contribution. This involved the continuous development of a portfolio of products and services that provide solutions to our customers. An intimate knowledge of our customers was required to develop unique solutions that would meet their needs.

Operational Excellence drove the *productivity* strategy—Optimize Cost of Learning and Development. This meant lowering the cost of products and services and improving the utilization of resources. The short-term objective focused on cost reduction and productivity improvements.

The Customer perspective focused on establishing relationships and understanding our customers' strategies.

Providing appropriate customer solutions was the key driver to the customer perspective. This involved providing competitive solutions (products and services) to our customers and developing relationships to build credibility and loyalty. In essence, this was about establishing the L&D image—credible, delivers the right solutions, quality, and timely programs.

Dofasco's L&D strategy map in Figure A.1 illustrates the customer strategies that would be implemented to achieve our value proposition. A key theme is developing effective solutions. L&D assigned a Specialist to work with HR's Business Partner to better identify learning and development gaps within the business units. This

Figure A.1. Dofasco's L&D Strategy Map

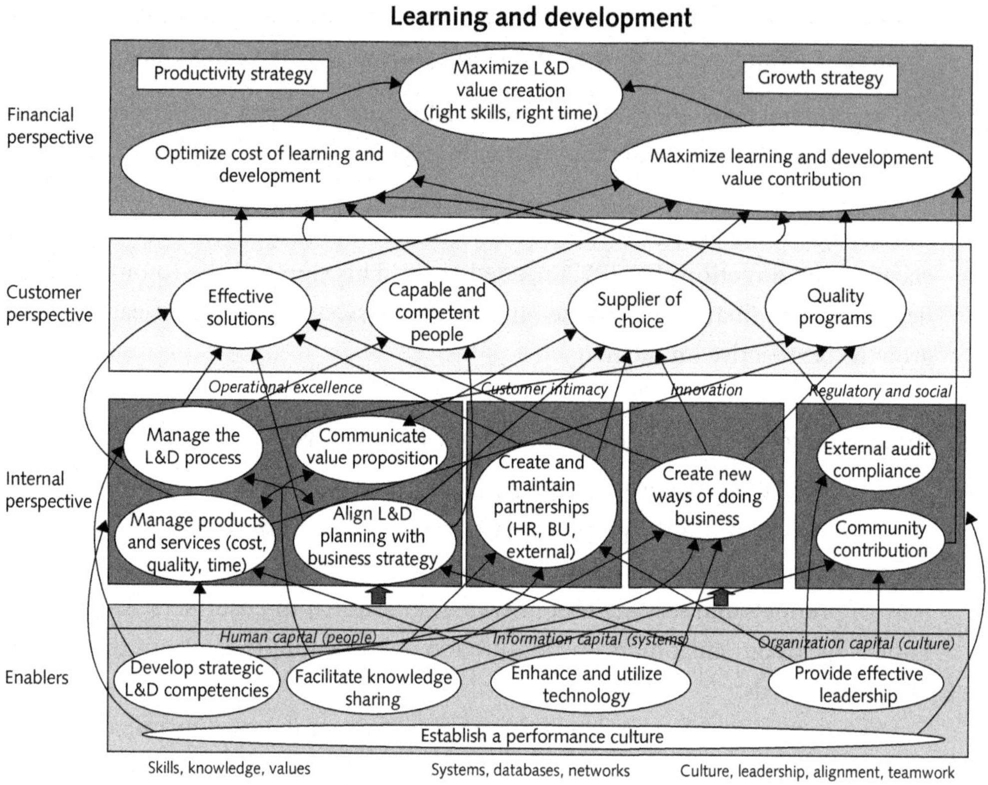

Learning and development

is an example of where the L&D strategy map aligned with the HR strategy map. Working together, the HR Business Partner and L&D Specialist gain a better understanding of the needs of the various areas across the company. They can then create value-added solutions that address corporate and unique area needs.

Step Four—Identify Actions for Success—Internal Perspective

The internal perspective looked at the business processes L&D had to excel at to satisfy both customer and financial perspectives. The value propositions of customer solutions and operational excellence provided the necessary guidance for completing this section. Some of the key objectives within the internal perspective were:

- Communicate value proposition
- Align L&D planning with business strategy
- Manage products and services (cost, quality, time)
- Create and maintain partnerships (HR, business units, external)

Delivering on these internal process objectives would result in achievement of the customer and financial strategies.

Step Five—Establish Enablers (Learning and Growth)

The Enablers perspective had an overall theme for L&D employees around establishing a performance culture. Internal learning and growth strategies were created to ensure the successful execution of the internal perspective. They fell into three areas:

- Human capital—L&D employees require the right skills, competencies, and knowledge to deliver products and services. They must also be willing to continually develop and transfer knowledge.
- Information capital—Efficient IT support and high availability of information is required.
- Organizational capital—Fostering a culture of continuous improvement, innovation, and customer service is important.

The Dofasco map in Figure A.1 clearly highlights its learning and growth strategies for the L&D department. One theme focused on capability. To successfully deliver programs and activities aligned to the business strategy highly competent and capable L&D practitioners was critical. An initiative was launched to identify the key positions and core competencies required by the new L&D organization. Once these were developed, all L&D employees were assessed to determine gaps. A development plan was created to close identified gaps.

IMPLEMENTING THE STRATEGY MAP

Step Six—Build Scorecard

Once the strategy map was developed and communication was underway, a scorecard was put in place to monitor the extent to which specific financial, customer, internal process, and learning and growth objectives were being met. Some of these measures were rolled up to become part of the HR balanced scorecard. For every identified objective, a performance measure, target, and initiative were aligned with it. The map was highly useful in determining what the critical L&D measures should be.

For example, one strategic measure at the customer level was ensuring L&D programs were aligned and relevant. If L&D was partnering with their customers, they should be delivering the right programs and achieving a high satisfaction rating. If the scorecard indicates customer complaints are frequent or there is no return business, this should trigger a review of the processes that support achievement of this objective.

To help measure this activity, a common evaluation form was created for all L&D courses. From this, we were able to report back on several key indicators, including course relevance, usage back in the workplace, that learning objectives were met, etc.

REVIEWING THE STRATEGY MAP

The L&D strategy map communicates Dofasco's need to maximize learning and development value. To be successful, L&D must provide learning and development products and services to meet the strategic needs of the organization. L&D will achieve its overriding objective by relying on the two value propositions—customer solutions and operational excellence. Because L&D does not generate revenue, the financial focus is on productivity (optimize costs) and growth (maximize value contribution). The customer-related strategies to meet the financial perspective focused on establishing relationships and understanding customer needs. To deliver this, L&D must identify, design, and implement key internal processes. On the productivity side, internal processes consist of managing the L&D process and products and services. On the growth side, internal processes consist of maintaining partnerships and creating new ways of doing business. Finally, Dofasco recognizes the importance of developing strategic competencies, enhancing technologies, and establishing a performance culture. As L&D supports the organization moving forward, these elements are critical to ongoing success.

CONCLUSIONS

The strategy map was used in several ways:

- L&D leadership used the map to communicate to staff the direction of the department, expectations, and roles in executing the strategy. The pictorial nature of the strategy map helped achieve a common language and understanding.
- The scorecard measures that came from the strategy map helped to facilitate discussions about implementing and executing strategy.
- It helped to create an awareness in the gaps of individual contributors in the department as to the knowledge, skills, and ability required by staff and created a plan of action to develop them.
- It helped to drive L&D/HR/business alignment. Strategy maps eliminate both the problem of lack of dialogue and talking in different languages by creating a single language to proactively communicate strategy and objectives.

The L&D strategy map is less than a year old as we write this. The goals and measures that support the strategy have been identified, but verifying the cause-and-effect links between the perspectives must be completed. With time, data will be collected through tracking the measures to see whether they contribute to improvements in other parts of the map and ultimately are contributing to the key objective.

Theresa O'Halloran is manager of development at ArcelorMittal Dofasco. Theresa is responsible for the development and implementation of programs to support the development, retention, and knowledge capture/sharing of employees. Theresa is currently on an assignment with ArcelorMittal USA, supporting leadership development and talent management activities. Theresa has been with ArcelorMittal Dofasco for twenty-four years, holding various positions, including operations manager and help desk manager.

Tracy MacPherson is a learning and development specialist in ArcelorMittal Dofasco's Human Resource Department. Tracy is currently responsible for consulting, analysis, and recommendation of solutions to close identified training-related performance gaps, facilitation and integration of learning and development best practices, and metrics and strategy for L&D. Tracy has been with ArcelorMittal Dofasco for twenty-four years, holding various positions in metallurgy, research, and human resources.

managers, learning consultants, and operations. Instructional designers and measurement analysts are organized at "The Centre." The partners across business unit L&D's and Corporate L&D establish strategy. A centralized design group supports and executes the strategy, bringing thought leadership and design/measurement and technology expertise.

TDBFG L&D introduced a balanced scorecard in 2004. It is based on the Norton and Kaplan business scorecard model that integrates Financial, Customer, Internal Processes, and Learning and Growth data.

WHAT IS A BALANCED SCORECARD?

The balanced scorecard is a *management system* (not only a measurement system) that enables organizations to clarify their vision and strategy and translate them into action. It provides feedback around both the internal business processes and external outcomes in order to continuously improve strategic performance and results.

Modern businesses depend on measurement and analysis of performance. Performance measures or indicators are measurable characteristics of products, services, processes, and operations the company uses to track and improve performance. The balanced scorecard provides a view for the organization from these four perspectives: Financial, Learning and Growth, Customer, and Internal Business Processes. The goal is to develop metrics, collect data, and analyze it relative to each of these perspectives. The measures or indicators should be selected to best represent the factors that lead to improved customer satisfaction, and to financial and operational performance.

Our Strategy

TDBFG's vice president of corporate L&D championed the case for an enterprise L&D balanced scorecard in early 2004. Our strategy included having a mission that aligned with the objectives of our organization: increase shareholder value and exceed customer satisfaction. Our mission is *"The right learning for the right people at the right time in support of business objectives."*

An enterprise learning council (ELC) was formed in September 2004 with a dotted line reporting structure to corporate L&D and a solid line out to seven business units. This newly formed council was assigned the task of supporting the

Figure B.1. The Enterprise Reporting Hierarchy

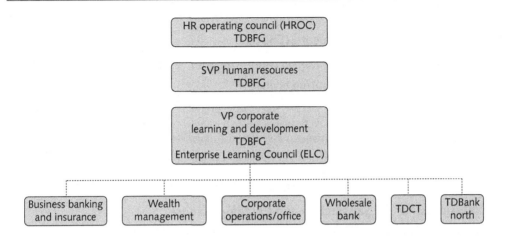

vision and ensuring open communication was in place at both the management and operational levels. Each of the balanced scorecard measures were agreed to by the ELC and approved by the HR Operational Council (HROC). The reporting hierarchy is shown in Figure B.1.

Each business had its own measures and understandably moving to a unified measurement tool that not only demonstrated financial data, but also subjective performance data was a new concept. A clear vision and strategy had to be communicated to ensure buy-in across all business lines.

By contributing to the EBSC, each of the business units had the opportunity to build a scorecard of its own. Balanced scorecard measures cascade down into business unit reporting. Each business unit has the option of reporting additional content if the value added to the business is warranted.

The Enterprise Balanced Scorecard (EBSC) Strategy Map

The enterprise balanced scorecard (EBSC) translated the enterprise L&D mission into tangible objectives and measures representing a balance across all four components: Financial, Business Partners, Internal Business Processes, and Learning and Growth. The EBSC is

- Mission aligned
- Strategic

- Operational
- Action oriented

The Enterprise Balanced Scorecard (EBSC)

Following the Norton and Kaplan model, the four perspectives were aligned to the Bank's objectives and operating needs.

Financial

The Financial measures monitor fiscal responsibility to our shareholders and are against budget planning. Financial measures help identify opportunities that result in cost savings while maintaining optimal allocation of the operational budget.

Business Partner Satisfaction and Customer Service

Business partners seek learning solutions from L&D. Business partner measures monitor satisfaction. If business partners are not satisfied, we are not meeting the needs of the business and therefore cannot exceed customer expectations. These measures are leading indicators of success: ensuring we meet or exceed quality of our products (design), timelines, and budget. The ELC was given the task of defining performance and operational excellence. The measurement team was given the task of designing the business partner index. An existing enterprise employee satisfaction measure was used for overall learner satisfaction. These became known as partner and learning satisfaction indices. Input and signoff were obtained from the ELC. Once these indices were set, it was up to the ELC to determine what its action strategy would be based on the EBSC statistics.

Internal Processes

Internal process measures ensure L&D services meet departmental and business needs while integrating innovative learning solutions. The measure allows L&D to continually assess and identify opportunities to enhance efficiency. Measuring the use of online training was a key objective over the last three years. Training effectiveness is measured through our learner satisfaction survey (Level 1).

Learning and Growth (L&D Employees)

Learning and growth measures include employee training and development as well as ensuring a positive work environment is in place that encourages innovation, creativity, and collaboration.

Figure B.2 shows a sample tracking form for the EBSC.
The Financial measures are

- **Total Training Investment:** captures operating costs combined with direct training and education costs
- **Operating Costs:** amount spent to design, develop, deliver, measure, and support training for business partners
- **Direct Expenses J-11:** an educational and training expense category (general ledger) on the finance platform
- **Total Training Investment/FTE:** represents the proportional investment per average TDBFG FTE
- **FTE (Learning and Development) Allocation:** average FTE of staff involved in L&D functions for TDBFG

The Business Partner measures are

- **Learner Development:** represents an employee's satisfaction with having the opportunity to develop. Data is taken directly from Question 12 on each of the business unit's TD Pulse report: *In the last six months, I have had opportuni-ties to develop my skills and abilities.* Results are weighted to provide equal representation.
- **Business Partner Satisfaction Index:** indicates the business partner's level of satisfaction with L&D's ability to prepare comprehensive training solutions that meet client objectives through the following three restraints: meeting or exceeding our quality benchmarks, timeframes, and budget estimates. Results for this metric are compiled by distributing a Business Partner Satisfaction Survey. Results are measured against our mission statement: "*The right learning for the right people at the right time to achieve business objectives.*" This data is captured in the cumulative sum of the "*Agree*" and "*Strongly Agree*" categories of Questions 13 and 14. The final score is an average of all business unit scores. See the sample survey in Figure B.3.

Business Partner Satisfaction Index Results

As noted below, each business unit's BPSI scores are weighted and added to the overall score in the EBSC. Each business unit contributes its own scorecard for each of the fourteen metrics that feed into the overall EBSC. On a hierarchical level, each subdivision within a business unit contributes to the overall reporting. In doing so, the strategy and vision create synergy and become a shared focal point across the organization. By example, the TD Canada Trust (TDCT) Personal Banking Scorecard is broken out into three scorecards representing e.Bank, Retail Distribution, and Retail Banking. Each scorecard acts like a building block in a pyramid, channeling data to the top. A sample BPSI scorecard is shown in Figure B.4.

Figure B.2. Sample Tracking Form

	Q1-Q2 2006	Q3-Q4 2006	Fiscal 2006	Fiscal 2005
Financial				
Total Training Investment				
Operating Costs				
Direct Expenses J-11				
Training Investment /FTE				
FTE (L&D) Allocation				
Customer Service				
Learner Development *Pulse Question #12*				
Business Partner Satisfaction Index				
Internal Processes				
Total Training Days				
Training Days/FTE				
e.-Learning				
Training Effectiveness				
Learning and Growth (L&D Employees)				
Pulse Results *Employee Experience Index*				
Professional Development/FTE				

Figure B.3. Business Partner Satisfaction Index

Learning and Development:

OPERATIONAL EXCELLENCE

1	Is quick to respond to the training needs of my business.
2	Consistently delivers project(s) within budget.
3	Consistently delivers project(s) on time.
4	Communicates in a clear and concise manner.
5	Meets the needs of my business.

BUSINESS IMPACT

6	Understands my business.
7	Provides employees with practical skills for their jobs.
8	Helps to prepare employees for their next role.
9	Provides a balance of training across all accountabilities for our employees.
10	Provides a balance of training across all accountabilities for our employees.
11	Provides training which assist in driving business results.

OVERALL

12	The amount of time employees spend in training each year is.

OVERALL

13	I am satisfied with the overall quality of training services provided by Learning and Development.
14	Learning and Development provides the right learning to the right people at the right time.

OVERALL

15	What recommendations would you make to help us improve our operational effectiveness and quality?
16	What recommendations would you make to help us improve training's impact on your business objectives?
17	What other recommendations would you make to help us improve our service?

- **Professional Development/FTE:** captures the actual budget spent per average L&D FTE. It can be used strategically to gauge whether actual spending is on target with planned budget. Results are weighted to provide equal representation.

PLANNING FOR SUCCESS

Corporate L&D formed a Measurement Department in 1997 and introduced a comprehensive measurement strategy solely aligned to defining and supporting training metrics. This included yearly planning that integrated business needs with industry best practices; such as Kirkpatrick's and Phillips' models. TDBFG's measurement team not only employs industry best practices, but modifies them to suit business needs, an evolutionary process. A natural progression to the balanced scorecard strategy ensued using the Norton and Kaplan model.

Coupled with a strong measurement department and the support of the HR executive, the planning stages for the inclusion of an enterprise balanced scorecard went relatively smoothly. Our timeline is shown in Figure B.5.

EBSC PILOT

Following the pilot with TD Canada Trust, a post-implementation review (PIR) was conducted to adjust the EBSC process. A result of the PIR was the exclusion of across-the-board benchmarks and the decision that reporting would occur on a semi-annual basis. The EBSC was rolled out in 2005 across the L&D business units, after which a second post-implementation review was conducted.

Process Improvement

The success of the development and implementation of the scorecard can be attributed to:

- Executive championing of the new methodology
- Consistent executive focus on the scorecard
- Formation of an enterprise learning council through which each business line could contribute to one enterprise balanced scorecard while maintaining individual scorecards that met their specific business needs

- Establishment of a process that could be managed by each contributing business line

- Inclusion of other areas of the Bank that already had metrics in place that we could align to

- Conducting a pilot with a business line that championed the scorecard

- Process and analysis documentation (standard)

- Annual maintenance review of the metrics and the process

- Online data collection

For example, the Fiscal 2004 scorecard took four months to complete, while the June 2005 scorecard took thirty days to complete.

From Q1 to Q2 2006, three measurement analysts and one learning consultant were assigned to manage and report on the EBSC. Through operational excellence, there was a 42 percent decrease in project hours in Q3-Q4 (128 hours versus 75 hours), with only one analyst and one learning consultant now assigned to manage the process. This time savings was also noted across other L&D business units, with an average 40 percent decrease in project hours.

During the Q3-Q4 reporting cycle, only two meetings were required, compared to eight in Q1-Q2. These gains in operational efficiency can be contributed to:

- Consistent reporting methods and static metrics

- Detailed and updated process documentation

- Improved alignment of the LMS reporting schema

- Consistent project management practices

NEXT GENERATION

The next generation begins. Does TDBFG have room for improvement? Of course!

For 2008:

- Measurement analysts continue to track industry best practices. A strategic L&D team attended the most recent Norton Breakfast hosted by the Management School of Business and the CSTD to learn how to take TDBFG's measures to the next level.

- Identify ways to compress timelines and ensure accurate analysis of data sets.
- Corporate L&D will align the EBSC with the Bank's emerging talent management strategy. Research is already underway to support this key objective. We have prototyped our leadership and management development scorecards to align to the EBSC that aligns to the HR scorecard.
- Focus on maximizing the full potential of the LMS reporting capabilities. Reporting in 2008 will be sorted by learning category type: leadership and management development, sales, and technical, to name but a few.
- Establish targets for the EBSC.
- Pilot facilitator-led workshop surveys online to have a faster, more cost-effective process in place.
- Include qualitative analysis to complement the quantitative; "tell the story."
- Continue to report J-11, break out categories that align to L&D, implementing a more consistent approach in Q1-Q2 2007 EBSC for reporting of J-11.
- Re-assess annual Business Partner Satisfaction Survey.

SUMMARY

The EBSC is now part of the L&D culture. L&D measures its financials as well as its performance. The "simple fast and easy" method captures training data from across the enterprise. In addition, TDBFG corporate L&D has created an open forum for dialogue and action through the EBSC with our ELC. The ELC partners now sit at the table looking for performance measures with more impact. Four years ago, the concept was certainly met with some reservation. It seemed like an impossible undertaking to have all L&D business units aligning their measures to a one-page fourteen-metric deep scorecard!

A scorecard is a flexible "message board." From 2004 to 2007 a key objectives was to establish the enterprise learning management system. Mission accomplished! Having the focus on this priority enabled our management team to deliver this message across the ELC and down into the operating teams.

A valuable reflection point from the creation of a balanced scorecard is that, once you have all the players at the table and an established process in place, it is fairly easy to insert new strategic objectives.

Connie Karlsson has more than seventeen years of experience as a learning and performance professional, with over ten years of measurement and evaluation experience. Connie received her ROI Certification from Dr. Jack Phillips in 1997 and her CTDP–Evaluation (Certified Training & Development Professional) in 2000 through the Canadian Society for Training and Development. She co-authored *Implementing ROI: Creating a Strategic Framework to Link Training to Business Results* for the In Action Series: Implementing Evaluation Systems and Processes, 1998. Connie is a past member of the ASTD ROI Advisory Committee and current member of the CSTD ROI Network. Connie received her Training and Development Certificate from Ryerson University in 1995, Courseware Design and Production Certificate from Sheridan College in 1990, and Applied Social Research Diploma from Sheridan College in 1989. She has had several articles published and is a sought-after speaker for presentations on such topics as bench strength and results-based training.

Several standing committees of the board as well as ad hoc operational committees assist the board and national office staff with the work of the Association.

When the CPA board approved a new, three-year strategic plan in November 2004, to extend over the three years from 2005 to 2008, it also approved using a "balanced scorecard" (BSC) approach to monitor and measure outcomes. Developed in 1990 by David Norton and Robert Kaplan, this approach is intended to move beyond financial measures—the traditional "bottom line"—and more effectively evaluate the broader performance of an organization. Although more frequently used in the private sector, more and more not-for-profit organizations are seeing the value in this type of comprehensive assessment.

The balanced scorecard approach asks an organization to answer four basic questions, covering four key elements of performance. These performance areas are referred to as "quadrants." Adapted to CPA's needs, these questions/quadrants have been defined as follows:

- *Membership:* How do our members see us? Do we provide value?
- *Learning and Growth:* Do we have momentum? How will we sustain our ability to change and improve?
- *Internal Processes:* Are we being efficient? To satisfy our members, what must we excel at?
- *Financial:* Are we on target?

A balanced scorecard approach develops over time, allowing the organization to add indicators as developed/available and drop others that prove not to be useful in evaluating progress. It requires all staff to link their day-to-day activities to identifiable performance measures and the organization's strategic plan. Ultimately, a successful BSC produces meaningful data and information that can be used for ongoing decision making. It is a tool to ensure the customer—in our world, the member—truly receives value for his or her investment.

This document provides a summary report, including an environmental scan, key highlights from the evaluation, and implications for 2007. It follows with a technical report, which will include a quadrant-by-quadrant presentation of key indicators and outcomes.

The reader is asked to keep in mind that, while this report focuses on initiatives being advanced under the guidance and direction of CPA's three-year strategic plan, considerable ongoing activities continue unabated. While many of these significant pieces of work do contribute to strategic directions, they are recognized as integral to the long-term needs of the Association, rather than being specifically tied to any particular three-year plan. Examples of these sustaining activities include congresses (including, in 2007, hosting WCPT's four-year international conference); the member newsletter, *Contact;* our peer reviewed journal, *PT Canada;* secretarial support for HEAL (Health Action Lobby); daily component support (branches, divisions, National Student Assembly, National Support Worker Assembly); NPAG projects (National Physiotherapy Advisory Group); board support; fiscal viability initiatives, and many more.

LEARNING AND GROWTH

Here we ask the questions: Do we have momentum? Can we continue to improve and create value?

Marketplace Recognition and Perception

- General public awareness of CPA, its mission, its brand (media coverage statistics)
- Government awareness of CPA (number of invitations to participate in government meetings)
- Member participation in events

Leadership/Community

- Number of members/staff on key government health care committees
- Number of partnerships with other relevant quality organizations
- Internal
- Participation rate in external meetings
  - CPA presence on non-physiotherapy meetings/events
  - Representation on committees
- External presentations given/requested

Professional Development

- Teleconferences
  - Evaluations

- Increasing trends
- Repeat registrations
- Number of new sites
- Number of participants
- Number of events
- Congress
  - Trends in submission rates
  - Participation by members
  - Number of abstracts
  - Number of volunteers
  - Three of organizations represented
  - Number and dollars of exhibitors
  - Number and dollars of sponsorships
- Awards
  - Number of nominations
  - Number of recipients
- AGM
  - Number of members attending
  - Percent of Congress registrants

ENVIRONMENTAL REVIEW

Any strategic plan is only as effective as its owner's ability to read the environment and assess potential implications for the future. While not a perfect science, being at least conscious of the elements that can have an impact on decision making, and may well influence organizational viability and effectiveness, is critically important. Understanding as best we can the world in which we live positions us to better withstand and plan for the challenges at our door—as well as take advantage of opportunities.

Monitoring reports, in turn, are best suited to tell us where we've been—not necessarily where we're going. To add meaning and relevance to such an assessment, and to guide our interpretations, we need to be able to consider a "best guess" at what the future holds. Such activities contribute to defining the implications and future directions of the organization.

The environment that we review must, these days, be quite comprehensive. While our natural first step would be to consider physiotherapy and Association-specific developments, we would be remiss if we did not extend our review to issues of domestic importance—both health and non-health related—as well as to global issues.

Notable Global Factors

- **The Environment**—Around the world, the environment, in its broadest sense, has become a top priority and is replacing health as the number-one concern of many citizens. Few would definitively say one is truly more important than the other, and both deserve our attention. Politically, tying health to the environment, which is not much of a stretch, would serve our advocacy efforts well.

- **Pandemic**—The threat of pandemic influenza continues to loom and brings with it the possibility of economic instability and monumental health human resource shortages.

- **Health Human Resources (HHR)**—Even without a pandemic, HHR has been recognized worldwide, including by the World Health Organization, as one of the great health crises of the moment.

Pan-Canadian Issues

- **Politics**—Canadian political realities tend to subordinate health concerns. With a still relatively unstable federal government in place and continuing federal/provincial/territorial tensions, it is difficult to achieve momentum in addressing the needs of the country. The current minority government, which has had some "staying power" at the time of this writing, does not appear to view health as its priority, sending a message that health has been "done." Efforts to bring greater attention to issues such as health human resources have not been met with great success. Strategies must be developed to link health with the current environmental focus.

- **Population Diversity**—The increasing diversity of Canada's population provides both opportunities and challenges that must be assessed, and addressed.

Pan-Canadian Health Issues

- **Funding**—Despite the ongoing F/P/T tensions, there has certainly been an increase in health funding at all levels in specific areas over recent years. Physiotherapy is as well-positioned as many other professions to take advantage of this.

- **Funding Models**—The debate over public/private funding of the health system will likely only escalate in 2007, particularly with the incoming president of the Canadian Medical Association being closely connected with private health delivery. HEAL (Health Action Lobby) is also particularly interested in exploring this grey area in more detail. As a profession with a foot in both camps, we will continue to be heavily involved in the discussions.

- **Wait Times**—Within the context of today's emphasis on reducing wait times for treatment/service is an expectation that by 2011 Canadians will have access to the care they need on a "24/7" basis. How this translates to a profession which, in recent years, is more accustomed to essentially a "9 to 5" context, will be a challenge in many ways.

- **Current Health Issues/Focus**—Many of the key areas of focus within the broader health field have direct links to physiotherapy, including primary health care, community/home-based care, obesity and physical (in)activity, chronic disease management, and the aging population.

- **Prevention**—In addition, there appears to be a greater willingness to include health promotion/prevention/public health in discussions and funding allocations. These are areas in which physiotherapy needs to better define itself as a player.

- **Illness Focus**—Conversely, even with an indication of greater willingness to consider prevention activities as important, the focus remains on treating illness, and there is still a great deal of work to be done to remind decision-makers and policy developers that working upstream has critical implications for costs and outcomes downstream.

- **Advanced Practice**—In the last year, this "language" has become commonplace and is being explored in various ways within many health professions. With a shortage of many health professionals, one proposed solution is to ensure all existing professionals are working not only within their full range, but also, perhaps, within an expanded scope.

- **Health Human Resources**—HHR is a priority for the entire health world and, within Canada, a major focus of activity at the federal and provincial levels. Physiotherapy has great data needs in this area, and these must be addressed for the profession to have a more meaningful part in the supply/demand debate. Despite the progress made in 2006, much more remains to be done to achieve even a basic understanding of "who, what, and where" Canada's physiotherapists are.

- **Technology**—The world is increasingly driven by new technologies, and the health field is not immune. We will need to grapple with everything from electronic health records (EHR) and e-billing to many as yet unknowns, a particular challenge for a profession that is not desk/computer-bound.

Physiotherapy-Specific Issues

- **Funding**—Physiotherapy has been targeted for special federal funding on a number of fronts related to HHR. It is up to CPA to ensure we can access that and other funding to good end.

- **Data Needs**—Today's world is driven by quantitative information, and the profession does not have comprehensive data to address its needs, whether HHR-related, for treatment outcomes, for advocacy efforts, or to enhance business practices.

- **Delisting**—Across the country, physiotherapy continues to be considered not "medically necessary" and has been taken off provincial funding lists. Minor victories are few, and the challenges many.

- **Third-Party Payers**—Insurers and the physiotherapy profession have not yet identified sound means of communicating with one another. Therefore, attempting to develop approaches to issues that respect both the business needs of one and the patient outcome needs on the other is challenging. Issues such as the imposition of preferred provider models, insisting Canadians see a physician for a referral to a physiotherapist when not legislatively required, business decisions that seem to infringe on scope, disallowing CPA's accreditation process, over-reliance on evidence versus best practice for funding decisions, and so on, all contribute to a rather adversarial environment. Given the economic pressures on both sides, these issues are more likely to escalate in the coming year than to recede.

- **Challenges to Scope**—There are ongoing issues of concern with established professions and disciplines (e.g., chiropractic; kinesiology; acupuncture; exercise physiology; massage therapy), as well as the need to be aware of emerging areas of practice. All require vigorous responses to protect the integrity of physiotherapy.

- **Advanced Practice**—Within physiotherapy, efforts are underway in certain parts of the country to allow physiotherapists to communicate a diagnosis, order x-rays, and prescribe non-steroidal anti-inflammatory pharmaceuticals. NPAG is involved in a national initiative to explore this area.

- **Evidence-Based Practice**—Although there is broad support to equally value "best practice" in the absence of rigorous scientific data, the demand for research-based evidence is only increasing, and putting pressure on all health professions to enhance their capacity in this area. A significant issue for physiotherapy is the utilization of these data by third-party payers in designing and funding treatment plans, to the exclusion of other sources of information.

- **Knowledge Transfer and Uptake**—It is not enough to produce data/information. The profession must ensure this material is passed on for clinical application. We must ensure that our members are not only aware of new developments, but also implement the directions offered.

- **Leadership**—As in other worlds, physiotherapy has not been immune to a tendency for many of its members to view their work as a job, rather than a career. This lack of professional ethos leads to limited involvement in leadership activities/opportunities and a loss of role models and mentors for next generations. A profession—or an association—is only as strong and capable as its membership. Critical mass is just that—critical—in ensuring the long-term viability of any profession, and physiotherapy is not an exception.

CPA-Specific Issues

- **50 percent Membership Base**—While membership numbers have been creeping steadily upward year after year, membership as a portion of full market share has decreased. The ability to "stand tall" and speak loudly about the needs of the profession lies in having as many physiotherapists as possible staking their futures on unity with their fellow professionals.

- **Governance Structure**—CPA enjoys a skilled and professional board, with an eye keenly fixed on its responsibilities of policy, strategy, and finance.

Relationships with key components—branches, divisions, National Student Assembly, and National Support Worker Assembly—are open, frank, and strong. All of this provides a sound foundation from which to advocate and further develop the profession. However, these structures and relationships require thoughtful attention to ensure viability on an ongoing basis.

- **Staffing/Culture**—Great efforts have been made to build a workplace culture that leads to stability and growth among staff. While CPA is not unlike others in the not-for-profit world, experiencing regular comings and goings, staff reflect an understanding of their value to the organization and participate actively in ensuring their work experience regularly improves.

- **Financial Status**—CPA has consistently performed soundly over time and is extremely well positioned to thrive on many fronts, particularly on the goal of increasing non-membership dues revenue. However, the pressure is always present to do even better, and this is the goal of staff on behalf of members.

- **Values and Ethics**—CPA is fortunate to have a board and staff that highly prize ethical judgment and decisions, and this has led to sound policies being developed, as well as solid day-to-day operations. This kind of reliable infrastructure positions the organization for every other decision that comes its way.

SUMMARY

There are as many opportunities as perceived threats for CPA in the next few years. It is up to us to plan accordingly and to be in the right place at the right time to take advantage of them. Maintaining focus on voice and profile, in particular, will be critical to ensuring we are on the health field radar. Specific opportunities include increasing our activity level around public awareness—of the value-added of physiotherapy, as well as what it "*is*"—and ensuring the profession is well-positioned to be involved in the two ends of the wellness/illness spectrum. Specifically, primary health care and the chronic disease/obesity issue on everyone's minds of late provide two meaningful opportunities for engagement of our profession.

Learning and Growth

- **Requests for Involvement**—Whether it is invitations to attend meetings and consultations, requests to provide letters of support, solicitations for experts in various areas of practice/research, international requests for Canadian physiotherapy subject-matter experts, or some other area of need, the visibility of physiotherapy involvement on all fronts has never been higher.

- **Knowledge Transfer**—More than just words on a strategic plan, 2006 saw evidence of the significant opportunities available to the Association and progress on many fronts, establishing a strong foundation for 2007.

- **Who, Where, What Are We**—Recently, physiotherapy has been selected as one of five professions for focus on several national health human resource initiatives in 2006. With progress on many fronts (for example, minimum data set, internationally educated), we are starting to scratch the surface of just who, what, and where physiotherapists "are."

- **Professional Development**—Consistent and growing uptake by members of teleconferences, clinical courses, and Congress indicate a thirst for knowledge, a view of CPA as a credible provider of professional development, and an area in which the Association must become more strategically involved.

- **Accreditation**—Dropping numbers in accreditation indicate it is an area requiring priority assessment and action in 2007.

Implications for Learning and Growth

- **Balancing Supply and Demand**—As CPA's (and physiotherapy's) profile has continued to rise in health debates and discussions, multiple external requests for our input have become an increasing challenge to which to respond. While in the past every request was viewed as an opportunity and accepted, this mode of operation now needs to shift to a more selective one in 2007 and beyond.

- **Professional Development**—With advanced technology and an education coordinator now in place, as well as data to support our members' desire for continued learning, CPA is now well positioned to further develop its educational offerings, and this needs to be given a focus in 2007, as well as in the next strategic plan.

- **Environmental Monitoring**—Staff, board, and members alike have been consistent in paying attention to the environment. However, as our capacity has developed in multiple related areas over the past two years, it is the time to approach this activity in a more strategic and coordinated manner, heading into the final year of our strategic plan. A process needs to be developed in 2007.

- **Advocacy**—Essentially all of our activities underpin the advocacy role CPA has been building for itself over the past few years—ensuring we are at important policy/research and other "tables," overhauling all position statements, creating a media presence, developing knowledge transfer options, creating new partnerships, and so on. In 2007, concrete steps must be taken to further solidify CPA's role as an advocate for its members, including the further adaptation of its advocacy strategic plan and development of an advocacy training module.

Answers to the Questions: Do We Have Momentum? Can We Continue to Improve and Create Value?

The Learning and Growth quadrant of the balanced scorecard reflects the organization's ability to adapt and change in response to evolving trends and changing environments. The Association's ability to maintain its value to members is dependent on identifying members' needs through a variety of communication channels, reflecting on gaps, and developing innovative mechanisms to respond to these identified challenges. This is an ongoing and iterative process.

Highlights from the Data
- **National Voice of Physiotherapy**—CPA continues to be a highly sought-after resource to represent the voice of physiotherapy in national and Pan-Canadian initiatives, with sixty-six requests for involvement. The voice of physiotherapy is becoming an expected and regular presence around tables of discussion related to health care issues.

- **Partnerships Continue to Flourish and Strengthen**—CPA continues to be involved in a wide diversity of partnerships that are ongoing and flourishing. The Enhancing Interdisciplinary Collaboration in Primary Health Care Initiative (EICP) ended in April 2006 with all steering committee members signing on to the principles and framework. CPA, in partnership with the other three members of the National Physiotherapy Advisory Group (NPAG), finalized *Vision 2020* for the profession, and developed a strategic framework to guide its implementation.

- **CPA a Strong Voice in National Advocacy Efforts**—CPA continues to serve as the Secretariat of the Health Action Lobby (HEAL), a coalition of over thirty organizations. Since CPA took over this essential function, there has been a significant increase in membership, with eight new applicants over the past two years and five more about to join in 2007. HEAL has been active in responding to the 2006 budget release, in sponsoring a Newsmakers' Breakfast to highlight the release of a discussion paper entitled "Core Principles and Strategic Directions for a Pan-Canadian Health Human Resources Plan," in participating in Health Canada initiatives related to health human resources planning, in contributing to a national communications strategy for Pandemic flu, and in CHLNet, an emerging network for Canadian health leadership.

- **Research and Knowledge Transfer**—CPA has partnered with a number of health organizations such as the Canadian Cochrane Collaboration, the Canadian Working Group on HIV and Rehabilitation, and the Knowledge Exchange Task Force of the Institute of Musculoskeletal Health and Arthritis of the Canadian Institutes for Health Research. CPA has provided letters of support for research projects relevant to Canadian physiotherapists, participated as expert consultants providing input into several research initiatives, and is developing strategies to fulfill its role as a partner in the knowledge transfer and exchange process.

- **Primary Health Care**—The Enhancing Interdisciplinary Collaboration in Primary Health Care (EICP) was completed and the CPA board endorsed the principles and framework developed by this initiative. A discussion paper titled "Primary Health Care and Physical Therapists—Moving the Profession's Agenda Forward" was completed and posted on the CPA website. As part of CPA's change management plan around primary health care, a series of four teleconferences was offered in the fall.

- **Health Human Resources Planning**—CPA has been an ongoing partner in the Canadian Institute for Health Information's project to develop a minimum data set for physiotherapists. The first data will be collected in 2007, with the initial report to be released in 2008. CPA has partnered with the Canadian Alliance of Physiotherapy Regulators in the Integrating Internationally Educated Physiotherapists project, which is aimed at facilitating the entry of internationally educated physiotherapists to the Canadian health system. CPA has also worked with Statistics Canada in their efforts to identify the information needed related to health provider students within the broader health human resources planning framework. Finally, CPA has been an active participant in sector health human resources planning initiatives related to physicians and nurses.

- **Professional Development**—The indicators below demonstrate there is a continuing demand by the membership for professional education activities. In 2006 CPA offered a total of eighteen teleconference sessions in a wide range of topics, including one in French and a series of four related to physiotherapy and primary health care, with 964 sites participating. Congress registration also continued the increases demonstrated in past years. PT Canada experienced sustained numbers of quality manuscripts submitted for publication in 2006. There was also a continuing interest in Shirley Sahrmann course participation in 2006, which was the first year that a Level III course was offered, with an impressive number of fifty-five registrants.

- **Accreditation**—The CPA accreditation program experienced a decline in 2006. Only two facilities were accredited in this time period, including one re-accreditation review. It appears that new facilities are not coming forward to participate in the CPA accreditation process or are deciding not to renew with CPA when their awards expire. There are currently thirty-one CPA-accredited facilities in Canada, down from forty-one in 2005. Of these facilities, some are single-site accreditations, while others received accreditation awards for multiple sites. CPA is continuing to monitor these trends.

- **Awards**—Nominations decreased significantly from 2006 levels and were lower than they were in other years in general. However, the number of prizes awarded was consistent with previous years, indicating those nominations received were of high caliber.

- **Clinical Specialization Process**—Major advances were made in this area. The report from the Joint Advisory Committee was finalized, the competencies of the clinical specialists were developed through a consultative and iterative process, and a business plan was elaborated to outline the project's financial and administrative framework.

How the Data Advances the Strategic Plan

The data from the learning and growth quadrant of the scorecard indicate that there has been steady and sustained progress towards the outcomes outlined in the strategic plan. In terms of *voice*, the data support that CPA is an established and recognized voice by governments, policy and health organizations, components, and members, and viewed as an important contributor and partner within the health debate in Canada. The commitment on the part of members to represent the profession in a variety of forms, advocate for the profession, and identify peers for professional recognition provides evidence of building *unity* within the physiotherapy profession. The proliferation of partnerships and policy statements, coupled with sustained and increasing member participation in learning activities, reflects the movement toward *excellence* in physiotherapy practice in Canada.

CONCLUSIONS AND INDICATIONS FOR THE FUTURE

CPA's reputation as the voice of the profession is increasingly acknowledged by internal and external stakeholders as well as national and international sources. Opportunities for collaboration continue to increase, and the nature of the collaborative participation is becoming more substantive and sustained. The Association and the membership will continue to be required to rise to the challenge of meeting multiple and varied requests for participation and partnerships to ensure that the voice of physiotherapy continues to be heard within the health care debate. The health care environment is rapidly changing and evolving, and CPA must be constantly attuned to emerging issues—listening to the public and members to ensure that relevant information, position statements, and discussion papers are developed and disseminated in a timely fashion and that best practice evidence in physiotherapy is readily available and utilized.

Analysis of the learning and growth indicators shown in the figures below reveals that members are looking increasingly to CPA to provide professional development opportunities, to facilitate the transition of evidence into best practices, and to support physiotherapy research initiatives in a variety of ways. These findings indicate that, in the future, CPA must continue to monitor closely members' emerging needs and to develop innovative mechanisms and activities to fulfill expectations in this area. As technology advances, innovations should be integrated into professional development activities to provide flexibility and choice in meeting members' needs.

Figure C.1 represents the total number of requests for participation, consultation, and input from CPA from external agencies such as governments, policy agencies, and health professional associations. It also represents ongoing partnership activities with groups such as NPAG, IMHA KETF, CIHI Minimum Data Set

Figure C.1. External Requests for Participation

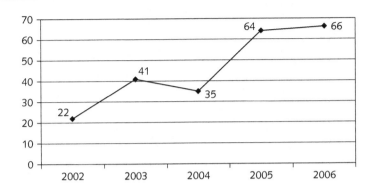

for Physiotherapists, and CWGHR. CPA has been involved in a number of initiatives related to health human resources (HHR) planning, including Task Force Two (physicians), the development of a Pan-Canadian HHR planning framework (Health Canada), and Building the Future (nurses). CPA has been asked for input related to a broad variety of initiatives such as a Canadian Cancer Society educational document for breast cancer survivors and driving for seniors. The CEO was involved in initiatives related to quality workplace, wait times alliance, and pandemic planning. Finally, CPA is increasingly being asked to provide representatives to participate in international initiatives related to setting standards in chronic obstructive lung disease, private practice, and neck injuries.

CPA is increasingly recognized as an important partner and supporter of research initiatives. There is emerging demand by funders for knowledge translation and dissemination strategies to be built into funding proposals. Through our varied communication mechanisms, CPA is recognized by researchers as a valued partner in the research process. CPA received a number of requests for letters of support from individual researchers, research partnerships, and inter-professional initiatives see Figure C.2).

2006 was a significant year in the updating and development of policy and discussion papers. Nine new position statements were developed and one additional statement was updated (see Figure C.3). All were approved by the CPA board of directors within this timeframe. In addition, to set the framework for the development of a strategy around caseload guidelines, a background paper and three annotated bibliographies were developed to present a comprehensive and easily

Figure C.2. Letters of Support from Outside Sources

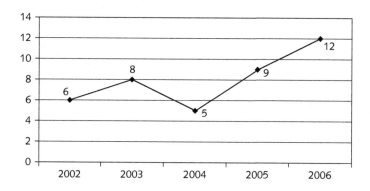

Figure C.3. Number of Discussion/Position Statements

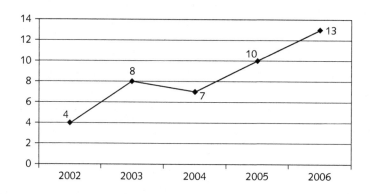

accessed overview of the evidence related to this complex topic. A discussion paper, "Primary Health Care and Physical Therapists—Moving the Agenda Forward," was completed, and annotated bibliographies related to the evidence behind the use of those were posted on the website.

Eighteen programs were offered in winter and fall sessions, with a total number of 964 sites participating. It is important to note that at each site the number of participants ranged from five to approximately thirty. There was a modest drop in the subscription to the teleconference program in 2006 (see Figure C.4). It is possible that increased competition from other sources may have had an impact on this series. In addition, a four-program series on primary health care and physiotherapy

Figure C.4. Aggregate Number of Sites Participating in CPA Teleconference Program

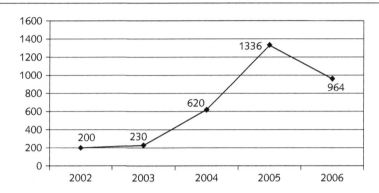

was included in the 2006 program, which had somewhat limited appeal to potential participants.

Congress 2006 continued on the upward trend experienced since 2002, with over 450 registrants attending this event. Although registration was down slightly from 2005 (see Figure C.5), it is suspected that many potential registrants were postponing Congress 2006 participation in favor of attending the WCPT Congress in Vancouver in 2007, and unfortunately New Brunswick was not seen as a popular Congress destination. It is also important to note that, even with the decline in attendance; the event was a financial success.

The quality and quantity of submissions to PT Canada was sustained through 2006. A new scientific editor and additional expert peer reviewers were secured, and the editor-in-chief role was established to further develop the peer-review journal. The number of submissions and the acceptance rate are shown in Figure C.6.

The CPA accreditation process experienced a decline in growth over the past year, as shown in Figure C.7. Only two facilities went through accreditation and received awards. Several facilities' accreditation awards expired, and they chose not to renew their accreditation with CPA.

CPA has seven national awards: Life and Honorary Membership, International Health, Mentorship, National Clinical Education, Student Leadership, and the Enid Graham Memorial Lecture (an eighth award, the Maryann Jefferies Leadership Award for Support Personnel, commenced in 2007 and will appear on the 2007 Monitoring Report). Only one award, the Enid Graham Lecture, is strictly limited

Figure C.5. Congress Registration Numbers

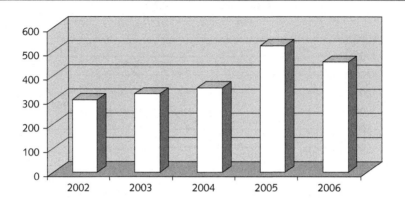

Figure C.6. Submissions to PT Canada for Publication

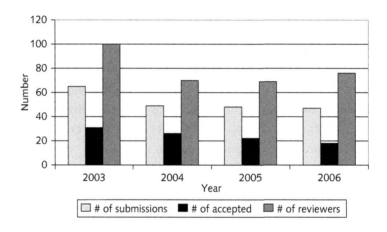

to one recipient. Several others are normally restricted to one recipient (e.g., International Health), while others such as Life Membership are commonly given to more than one individual if the nomination materials support such a decision. Nominations and awards from 2002 through 2006 are shown in Figure C.8.

There has been a sustained member participation rate in continuing professional development activities such as the Shirley Sahrmann courses. When CPA sponsored the first courses in 2004, there were 211 registrants in the Level I course.

Figure C.7. Number of CPA-Accredited Organizations

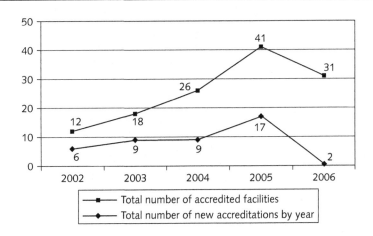

Figure C.8. Total Nominations and Awards, 2002–2006

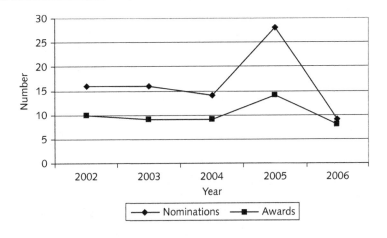

In 2005, member response peaked with a total of 312 registrants—257 in Level I and 55 in Level II. While the total number of registrants diminished somewhat in 2006 (229), this year is marked by the first year that Level III was offered (see Figure C.9). All three levels of courses demonstrated substantial registration in 2006.

Figure C.9. Shirley Sahrmann Course Participants

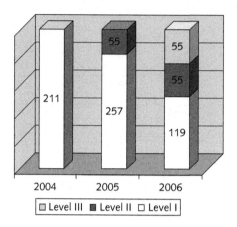

Edward Orendorff, BComm, CMA, FCMA, is the director of finance and administration for the Canadian Physiotherapy Association, the fifth-largest health profession in Canada. He has worked in Canada and the United States in both the non-profit sector and private industry over his career. He has served on the Board of Governors of the Society of Management Accountants of Ontario, the CMA Canada Board of Directors, and several community boards of directors. He has also received the Fellowship Award from CMA Canada.

—

with another local United Way within the region to review and synthesize local research to determine joint, regional priorities. They are:

- All children and youth reach their potential;
- All families are strong;
- All neighborhoods are inclusive and thriving;
- All newcomers are welcomed and supported; and
- All people are economically secure.

In the context of her mandate, the regional priorities, and the organization's new strategic plan, Jan undertook an initiative to develop a robust strategic performance management system that would be based on a series of standards of excellence (SOE) put forth by UW-CC. From this, detailed action plans were developed with each senior manager.

THE STRATEGY MAP

UW K-W developed its strategy map to communicate and monitor the success of its strategy and aggressive plans. Jan also looked to the strategy map to assist in the training and engagement of new employees as the organization continued its plans for growth (see Figure D.1).

EMPLOYEE LEARNING AND GROWTH

One of Jan's primary objectives was to key in on the Employee Learning and Growth perspective (EL&G). Each of the four EL&G objectives was derived in part from the UW-CC SOEs, so not surprisingly both were well aligned.

Objectives 1 and 4: Maximize Staff Potential; Promote Work/Life Balance

These two objectives aligned well with Standard 4.3 from the SOE: Commit to People. UW-CC cultivates a culture that strives to continuously improve performance by assessing and adapting to the changing environment. The culture of the organization—behaviors, language, customs, problem solving, inclusiveness, office

Figure D.1. United Way of Kitchener-Waterloo and Area Strategy Map

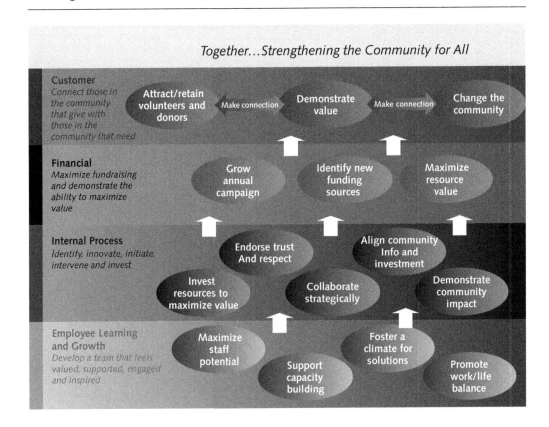

design and technology, the management of knowledge, learning and development, work/life balance—is one that leads to fulfillment of the mission.

Four key practices were developed to achieve the strategy map of these two objectives:

1. *Monitor organizational culture:* Establish formal and informal assessment tools.

2. *Define key competencies:* Determine the competencies needed to deliver our mission; listen to communities; engage and connect with them; focus on root causes; mobilize and leverage resources; build the capacity of the communities; measure and report on progress.

Cam Scholey, MBA, CMA, Ph.D., has been a speaker, author, and consultant for the past decade, focusing on the strategic concepts of balanced scorecard and strategy mapping. His specific areas of interest are communication, risk management, and board governance. Cam has also been a faculty member at The University of Waterloo. He was heavily involved in designing and teaching in the new master's of business, entrepreneurship, and technology (MBET) program, now in its fourth year at The University of Waterloo. He now works at McMaster University, teaching their CMA/MBA courses.

A facilitator of the new CMA Strategic Leadership Program, Cam is also an experienced writer and is the author of *A Practical Guide to the Balanced Scorecard* (CCH Canadian). He is also the author of several articles, including "Strategy Maps: A Step-by-Step Guide to Measuring, Managing, and Communicating the Plan" (*Journal of Business Strategy*, May/June 2005). He co-authored the management accounting guideline titled Using Strategy Maps to Drive Performance (2007) and has recently authored a new management accounting guideline, Using Strategy Maps to Drive Performance in the Not-for-Profit Sector (2008).

- *Pillar 3. Support.* Lead agents to autonomy by assuring transfer of skill and knowledge post-learning intervention quality (support team, methods writers, and communication prime).
- *Pillar 4. Post-Training/Scorecard Analysis.* Measure the effectiveness of learning event and provide essential data to stay focused on the business strategies.
- *Pillar 5. Audits and Evaluation.* Ensure that our trainers and support team continue to meet accreditation results expectations and put in place necessary actions to close any gaps.

LEARNING RESULTS OWNERSHIP: YOUR SUCCESS IS MY SUCCESS!

Our second step was to bring back specific accountabilities of the learning experience results to all levels by establishing a dynamic working environment centralizing all resources. The goal was to make our designers, trainers, methods writers, communication primes, quality team, and the support team accountable to the entire learning experience and evaluate their work as a team (not as individuals) based on the company key metrics (that is, agent sales, order quality, call quality, product knowledge, agents' anticipated behavior).

In this way, learning objectives, knowledge transfer, and application were everybody's priorities, and since the conceptual model is based on the company objectives, we were making sure we were walking in the same direction.

BRING ANALYTICAL SKILLS IN!

The third key for us was to establish a pillar we called: "post-training/scorecard analysis." Since the other pillars are implicit to every organization (training delivery, accreditation, support, and audits), this one was a never-explored area because of the lag time, accountabilities, money, and interest.

For our learning group, this area is the most important. This is what made us step back for a moment and think about the training experience as a whole. It also brought the reconciliation of two worlds: performance metrics and business objectives.

Basically, we tell everyone in the learning chain to now become an expert on company objectives and key performance metrics in order to analyze their training intervention value. We pushed to bring analytical skills into the learning chain.

In order to get there, we put in place a tool in our process we called a post-training package. This package resulted from all the training objectives (themselves linked to the company objectives) connected directly to their proper evaluation methods. Those methods had to be measurable and tangible (for example, scores, observations, call monitoring reports, coaching sessions, calls to the help desk, etc.).

All those involved had to take ownership and contribute (designers, trainers, methods writers, communication primes, quality team members, and the support team) to populate and deliver the analysis through the organization's scorecard.

The post-training package has three steps for the learning team to follow:

1. Gather the data/metrics (sales, knowledge results, help desk calls, knowledge database usage, order quality, call quality, etc.) and measure training event impacts and ROI expectations from the training objectives.

2. Populate and analyze an overall scorecard to compare, measure, and follow the effectiveness of behavior scores, productivity scores, and sales.

3. Discuss the results with training peers and bring recommendations based on results.

This tool and process were designed to be systemic and give immediate feedback and lead to an action plan (if required).

BUILD TOOLS TO MEASURE

The fourth step for our learning team is about building a dashboard that measures the training organization itself. This "performance training index" regroups many different elements, such as:

- Training type (communication, refresher, initial training)
- Design productivity
- Training time
- Methods error feedback
- Help desk calls

The goal is to isolate the training event and determine the possible trends or redundancy (for example, new product launch, behavior training, refreshers, initial training, and news articles) and their effects on the key performance indicators (financial or not).

We shared our performance training index with our executive management team in order to gain their support in relation to their specific demands, such as marketing and financing pressures. This way we were able to evaluate the productivity of the individual parts of the learning chain and use the scorecard to track their performance on training events.

LESSONS AND LEARNINGS

As a very vertical and silo organization that also ensures the leadership of key individuals, the process took us almost two years to bring together the teams, craft the model, and build the tools.

One of our biggest challenges was bringing back synergies and accountabilities among all of the elements of the learning chain that traditionally considered one another to be potential enemies. We underestimated the organizational culture and the difficulties in working through the change management process. New forms of accountabilities are often viewed with scepticism and can be more daunting when people are being evaluated as a team.

An additional challenge was integrating the required analytical skills in the existing learning team, which was not held accountable for their results, but who were well acclimated in their comfort zone. We had to rework and redesign the learning roles and associated job profiles in our human resource plan to bring new talent with the appropriate skills. Even after two years, we were facing skills issues with the most tenured employees.

On the positive side, our Five Pillar Model brought direct linkage to the business's tactical objectives and was used by our senior managers to better translate performance into their operations. It did help to enhance the majority of management's results (mainly around quality and sales) and help some major organizational change to happen . . . but remember that this is a long-term journey.

Mathieu Campeau, associate director–Awareness/Knowledge Management/Initial and Continuous Training, has been working for Bell Canada for more than twelve years, holding various organizational learning responsibilities. Mr. Campeau was influential in implementing the company's learning and awareness strategies and supporting multiple lines of businesses with offices throughout Canada and off-shore. Mr. Campeau is responsible for the entire learning strategy, consisting of program development, continuous training, knowledge management, strategy development, and execution. During the past four years, Mr. Campeau has been developing strategies on linking knowledge and specific key performance indicators by implementing a corporate-wide knowledge management tool; implementing a team's architecture by combining the key elements (design, training, knowledge management, support); and designing and implementing productivity, capacity, impac, and satisfaction analysis methodology. Mr. Campeau holds a bachelor of science degree in mathematics from Université du Québec à Montréal and is also a Six Sigma green belt holder.

and the national partner is monitored by the Council of Chairs (the Council). Normally, the chair for each partner serves as a voting representative on the Council. The CMA Canada Board approved a strategic plan for all thirteen partners of the CMA partnership in February 2006. In conjunction with the strategic plan, a risk management framework and long- and short-term business plans were also developed.

The CMA Canada Board and Council immediately recognized the importance of measuring the progress of the initiatives in the strategic plan. A *"multi-jurisdictional"* balanced scorecard was therefore developed; its role is to measure the progress of the initiatives for CMA Canada, as well as the collective initiatives of all partners. Figure F.1 presents an overview of the balanced scorecard, its central vision and strategy, perspectives, and the related major success factors.

Figure F.1. CMA's Balanced Scorecard

Balanced Scorecard

Risk Management
- Financial Stewardship
- Model Governance
- Risk Mitigation

Stakeholder
- Designation Relevancy/Differentiation
- Understand and Respond to Stakeholder Needs
- International Relevance
- Advancement of Management Accounting

Internal Business Processes
- Operational Excellence
- Effective Strategic Plan, Measures, Targets, Initiative Setting
- Product Quality

Learning and Growth
- Employee Involvement and Learning
- Organizational Learning
- Board and Volunteer Member Growth

CMA

Vision and Strategy

Fiscal Accountability
- Fiscal Capacity
- Model Governance
- Risk Mitigation
- Technological Infrastructure

Stakeholder
- Brand Stewardship
- Heighten Profile, Influence and Image
- Member Learning and Growth
- Membership Satisfaction
- Effective Relationships

Partnership Effectiveness
- Strategic Alignment
- Mutual Communication, Consultation and Collaboration
- Staff Learning and Growth
- Standards

THE LEARNING AND GROWTH PERSPECTIVE

The CMA Canada balanced scorecard contains the *"Learning and Growth"* perspective. This perspective is the most important one in the model, as it fuels the stakeholder and internal business processes. Dr. David Norton, co-creator of the balanced scorecard, describes the learning and growth perspective as representing the root system of a tree. The roots are what keep the tree alive and provide for the growth of branches and fruit. The more the roots are nourished, the more fruit the tree yields. The strategic performance of the organization is therefore directly correlated to the level of learning and growth of governance and staff.

The partners of CMA Canada have implemented a number of initiatives designed to increase the amount and effectiveness of the *"nourishment"* for the tree. Just as it is important that the staff of CMA Canada have learning objectives in order to achieve the stakeholder and internal business processes objectives, it is critical that the volunteers, especially the governance of the organization, also have established learning objectives in order to ensure that their fiduciary responsibilities are being effectively carried out. The CMA Canada Board and partner boards fully support volunteer and staff learning, as continuous learning is one of the tenets related to the success of any profession.

Learning and Growth—Volunteers

The volunteers are responsible for the governance of CMA Canada and the partners, since the boards are accountable directly to the members. They are therefore responsible for ensuring that, through the board, the objectives of CMA Canada and its partners are achieved. Due to these responsibilities, a policy has been established whereby volunteers who serve on the CMA Canada Board or Council or chair the standing committees must successfully complete the following three modules in the Chartered Director Program, The Directors College, McMaster University:

- Module 1: Accountability and Change
- Module 2: Leadership and Strategy
- Module 4: Communication and Corporate Social Responsibility

It is also highly recommended that the chair and vice chair of the CMA Board complete the Chartered Director designation. The chair of the Audit and Finance

Committee is encouraged to attain the appropriate certification related to the governance of audit committees.

The strength of the volunteer learning objective is that the governance of the CMA partners is more focused on the strategic direction of the CMA partnership. Volunteers are also in a position of recognizing the importance of their fiduciary responsibilities related to governance.

Learning and Growth—Employees

One of the features of the balanced scorecard is that the initiatives must cascade to all staff to ensure that everyone understands how they contribute to the organization and its success. Each staff member therefore has a *"Personal Balanced Scorecard"* and is rewarded after achieving the measures. Figure F.2 reflects how the goals of the editor-in-chief, *CMA Management* magazine, align with the key strategy, *"CMA is positioned in the market as the owner of strategic management accounting."*

After each staff member had developed a personal balanced scorecard, it was recognized that certain competencies are core to all employees of CMA Canada. Seventeen competencies were identified. In addition to the core competencies, each

Figure F.2. Sample Personal Scorecard

Perspective	Stakeholder
Objective	• Advancement of Management Accounting

Board — Key Strategy 1 – CMA is positioned in the market as the owner of strategic management accounting

President — Non-Member Revenue from Products and Services

Vice President — Increase non-member CMA Magazine subscriptions 20%

Editor — CMA Magazine content – very useful 65%

position also requires individual competencies. The list of the core competencies and individual competencies follows:

Core Competencies
- Action Oriented
- Approachability
- Communication
- Customer Focus
- Ethics and Values
- Functional/Technical Skills
- Informing
- Integrity and Trust
- Interpersonal Savvy
- Learning on the Fly
- Listening
- Organizational Agility
- Peer Relationships
- Planning
- Priority Setting
- Time Management
- Timely Decision Making

Individual Competencies
- Building Effective Teams
- Business Acumen
- Comfort Around Higher Management
- Composure
- Conflict Management
- Creativity
- Decision Quality
- Delegation

- Developing Direct Reports and Others
- Drive for Results
- Hiring and Staffing
- Managerial Courage
- Managing Vision and Purpose
- Motivating Others
- Negotiating
- Organizing
- Perspective
- Political Savvy
- Presentation Skills
- Problem Solving
- Process Management
- Self-Development
- Standing Alone
- Strategic Agility
- Technical Learning

The core competencies and individual competencies combine to create a competency-based DNA for each position. Staff may therefore identify the required competencies related to their current positions and ones for which they may aspire. A sample competency-based position description is shown in Figure F.3.

The following principles are imbedded in the staff learning model:

- The core competencies were developed by the staff.
- The learning model is completely separate from job performance.
- The employee and supervisor agree to the employee's placement on the competency continuum.
- The employee and supervisor agree to a learning plan that enables the employee to further develop certain competencies.

Figure F.3. Sample Competency-Based Position Description

POSITION DESCRIPTION

1. IDENTIFYING INFORMATION

Title:	**Manager**	Reports to:	**Vice President**
Department:			
Incumbent's Name:	**Sally Smith**	Position(s) supervised:	Nil

2. POSITION OUTCOMES

The position's primary purpose and focus
The manager ensures that governance responsibilities are facilitated and streamlined by providing duties to the vice president.

3. POSITION DUTIES AND RESPONSIBILITIES

Major responsibilities of the position
Manager functions: • Supports the vice president in the timely preparation and issue of high-quality and accurate meeting agendas, minutes, manuals, supporting documents, and other resource materials   • Contributes to the effective utilization of volunteer members through accurate meeting arrangements and organized travel itineraries   • Ensures the vice president is fully supported and informed on all material issues and items   • Contributes to member satisfaction by ensuring that inquiries are responded to in a timely and professional manner   • Contributes to the effectiveness of the vice president through well-organized scheduling of appointments and travel itineraries   • Uses technology, enters and manipulates data, and interprets information for reports   • Performs all other duties required by the vice president to ensure expected results

4. CMA CANADA CORE COMPETENCIES

CMA Canada Core Competencies required for all positions

- Action Oriented

- Communication

- Customer Focus

- Ethics/Values/Integrity and Trust

- Functional/Technical Skills

- Informing/Peer Relationships

- Interpersonal Savvy/Listening/Approachability

- Learning on the Fly

- Organizational Agility

- Planning/Time Management/Priority Setting

- Timely Decision Making

5. KEY COMPETENCIES

The key and critical competencies required for this position are:

- Composure

- Conflict Management

- Decision Quality

- Drive for Results

- Organizing

- Problem Solving

- Technical Learning

6. CERTIFICATIONS

I have read the foregoing and understand it is a description of the duties assigned to my position.		
Employee's Signature		Date

I certify that this is an accurate description of the responsibilities required of the position and that it forms the basis for the performance appraisal of the incumbent. The incumbent has received a copy of this position description.

Supervisor's Signature		Date

Meeting minutes will be prepared for review within two weeks of the meeting.Requests for committee meeting travel will be distributed at least three weeks before each meeting.

DEVELOPMENT PLANS FOR THE YEAR

List specific self-development plans: A one-day course on Conflict ResolutionParticipation in the NQI Workshop— Mapping Process Attend the Disney Storyboarding course Enroll in the Certificate Program on Customer Service and Organizational Success	*Timeline:Before Dec. 31, 2007 February 2008 August 2008 September 2008 to June 2010*

Additional detail for each of the principles follows.

The Core Competencies Were Developed by the Staff

A competency model will achieve greater success if the staff is consulted through-out its development. For that reason, management did not review the competencies and determine which ones were core and which would apply to certain employees. Instead, a small group of employees was given the responsibility of selecting the competencies that apply to all staff.

A staff meeting was held, and the competencies and their respective definitions were reviewed. Buy-in with respect to the competencies every staff member should possess was therefore ensured.

The process of identifying each staff member's unique competencies was facilitated through a professional. This individual met with the staff and his/her supervisor to identify which competencies, in addition to the core competencies, would be required.

The Learning Model Is Completely Separate from Job Performance

It is important to recognize that competency development should not be related to staff performance. If the two are perceived as relating to each other, the message would be one of forcing individuals to learn and either compensating them or penalizing them based on their learning success. The competency development plan and review processes are therefore held during a different period than the performance reviews. The performance reviews focus on the initiatives related to each individual's *"cascaded"* personalized scorecard, and success is recognized through a pay increase. The competency development meetings, on the other hand, are designed to achieve greater employee competency growth.

The Employee and Supervisor Agree to the Employee's Placement on the Competency Continuum

Each competency has a continuum, which varies among employees. The continuum ranges from no knowledge of the competency to full knowledge of the competency. Each employee is asked to identify where he or she fits on the continuum and this is verified by the supervisor. In the case of disagreement, the employee and supervisor engage in dialogue and agree on the point on the continuum where the specific employee will be ranked. Since the competency development is not related to remuneration and job performance, the anxiety level of having to perform at the continuum's upper extreme is greatly reduced.

The competency for each employee is ranked in the following categories:

- Outstanding—has fully mastered the competency.
- Achieving—significant progress in the competency has been achieved.
- Growing—significant development is required.

It should be noted that no employee is likely to be outstanding in more than six competencies. This reduces the pressure of trying to achieve an "outstanding" score in all competencies.

Normally, the competencies in the "Growing" and "Achieving" categories are identified for additional learning. The employee and supervisor develop a plan that determines which competencies require improvement and the learning methodologies that will be employed. The costs related to all employee learning plans are incorporated in the annual business plan. Significant and long-term learning costs, such as post-graduate degree programs or professional designations, are included in the long-term business plan.

LESSONS LEARNED

CMA Canada recently initiated the competency-based position descriptions and personalized balanced scorecard; thus, it is therefore very difficult to measure its success at this point. The two models have provided employees with a greater learning focus that is directly related to the strategic objectives of the organization, however. Prior to the introduction of the model, employee learning was on a best-efforts basis.

Employees are now able to relate what they learn to improvements in their specific competencies. If a large number of employees require learning related to a specific competency, in-house training can be explored as an alternative.

Initially, the measurement of each staff member's personalized balanced scorecard and the competency learning plan and evaluation were designed to occur concurrently. It was recognized, however, that a potentially dangerous message could be communicated, as employees could perceive their remuneration as being related to the level of their competencies. Learning initiatives would therefore decrease because staff would be tempted to make the case that no additional learning was required. By separating the two processes, learning is being pursued without any relation to remuneration.

Steve F. Vieweg, MBA, C.Dir., CMA, FCMA, president and CEO, has extensive experience in the management accounting, education, and association management sectors. Steve joined the CMA partnership in 1990 and has held positions as director of education–CMA Manitoba; executive director–CMA Manitoba; vice president–professional cervices, CMA Canada; and his president position as president and CEO–CMA Canada

Steve earned his CMA designation in 1984 and received an MBA from Syracuse University in 1990. In September 2003, he was named a Fellow of The Society of Management Accountants of Canada (FCMA). In 2007, he received the Chartered Director (C.Dir.) from The Directors College, McMaster University.

Steve works closely with CMA Canada's National Board of Directors in setting the strategic direction for CMA Canada, developing and implementing business strategies, and building partnerships with allied professional organizations in Canada and globally.

Cam Scholey, MBA, CMA, Ph.D., has been a speaker, author, and consultant for the past decade, focusing on the strategic concepts of balanced scorecard and strategy mapping. His specific areas of interest are communication, risk management, and board governance. Cam has also been a faculty member at The University of Waterloo. He was heavily involved in designing and teaching in the new master's of business, entrepreneurship, and technology (MBET) program, now in its fourth year at The University of Waterloo. He now works at McMaster University, teaching their CMA/MBA courses.

A facilitator of the new CMA Strategic Leadership Program, Cam is also an experienced writer and is the author of *A Practical Guide to the Balanced Scorecard* (CCH Canadian). He is also the author of several articles, including "Strategy Maps: A Step-by-Step Guide to Measuring, Managing, and Communicating the Plan" (*Journal of Business Strategy*, May/June 2005). He co-authored the management accounting guideline titled Using Strategy Maps to Drive Performance (2007) and has recently authored a new management accounting guideline, Using Strategy Maps to Drive Performance in the Not-for-Profit Sector (2008).

- All the potential metrics are evaluated using parameters/criteria that are discussed and jointly agreed to by the executive team. This is to ensure that the metrics on the balanced scorecard represent the company strategies accurately and are feasible and useful for ongoing management decision making.
- The list of potential metrics is narrowed down through a three-stage process: (1) elimination of metrics for which better alternatives are available based on the assessment; (2) short listing of a vital set based on discussions with the executive team; and (3) finalization based on discussion with the board of directors.
- The metrics thus chosen (financial/non-financial) form the Infosys balanced scorecard, which is then used for target setting and quarterly reporting and review.

The Infosys balanced scorecard is then converted into an "alignment matrix" for all the members of the executive team. This exercise drives clarity in the individual (primary) and shared (secondary) responsibilities of the executive team and also leads to the design of a balanced scorecard for each member. Individual scorecards inherit corporate targets, if applicable, or the executive team members define targets, which are approved by the CEO.

COMPETENCY DEVELOPMENT

During the annual strategy planning exercise of 2004, keeping in mind the anticipated growth of the organization, the company decided to develop a strategy for deepening the competencies of Infosys employees (a term used to refer to the employees of Infosys). This was linked to the overall strategy of achieving global leadership.

As a first step, a cross-functional team was formed to develop the strategy. The team comprised members from business units and business enabling functions. The competency development team first worked to identify various factors related to employee skill development in the context of Infosys. This was done by analyzing annual client satisfaction results, employee satisfaction results, interviews with leaders in the organization, and brainstorming sessions with a cross-section of employees across the organization.

Identifying four dimensions of competencies, having point persons for competency development across the organization, explicit linkage of career progression to competency development, and creation of a governance structure were some of the recommendations made by the competency development team.

Four Dimensions of Competency

The first recommendation required that competencies be viewed along four parameters, and that all employees be required to develop competencies in four key areas (see Figure G.1): technology, domain, behavioral and process.

The relative emphasis on these dimensions will vary by role based on the expectations of the role. Thus, while the technology component may be the highest for a software engineer, project management process may form a significant component for the project manager.

Pilot

The next step was to pilot the recommendations in one of the business units. During the pilot, which involved more than 1,500 people, competency champions were identified across the business unit and a process for creating a competency development plan for each individual was established.

At the end of the four-month pilot program, the outcomes were very encouraging. Every software engineer had identified two technology areas in which to become competent over the next two years. Technology training was conducted in every development centre to enable this. Moreover, an initial domain training was established as part of the standard new hire-induction programs, and one

Figure G.1. Four Dimensions of Competency

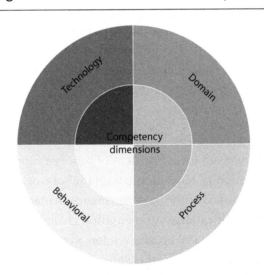

business-domain-specific workshop was conducted in the United States and in European offices. The customer satisfaction results for the unit were among the highest in the company.

The competency development team then discussed the strategy and the pilot outcome with the management council. As a next step, recommendations were rolled out across the organization. Creating the network of competency champions and creation of the unit-level competency plans were the first set of visible outcomes.

Competency Council

In the second phase of this journey, a competency council with representatives from various functions and the head of customer delivery as the chairperson was created. A competency framework that linked certifications to roles was formulated. This framework identified three levels of certifications for technology, business domain, and process dimensions recommended by the competency development team. Training programs for each certification were developed by the learning units in the company. Competency champions communicated the framework to their respective units.

Rollout of the certifications were done in a phased manner. A top-down approach was used at the direction of the chairperson of the competency council. As a result, compensation and career progression of senior members of the client delivery teams were first linked to certifications. Bridge certifications were created for existing people, and the framework was rolled out in its entirety for new joinees. Over the next twenty-four months the entire delivery organization was covered by the certification framework. A combination of internal and external certifications were rolled out. External certifications, primarily in the business domain, were offered through global industry bodies.

Systems and Process

The third phase involved the refinement of processes and the creation and integration of information systems to help with the scale of operations. Competency plans were tightly linked with the performance management systems to ensure the link between certifications, compensation changes, and career progressions. Assessment centers were scaled up, and vendors were identified to provide proctored certification environments across the globe.

On a bi-annual cycle, Infoscions are assessed through self- and manager appraisals using a data capture tool called Performagic. Following the assessment, a targeted competency development plan specific to the employee's role profile is created through the online tool iLite. In the develop stage, employees engage in the actual training programs. Upon demonstration of the newly acquired skills and positive evaluation, the certifications are released and updated in a central tracking system.

SCORECARDS

As indicated earlier, scorecards constitute the key performance measurement and management tools at Infosys. Given our client focus and the nature of business, learning and competency development is critical to our success.

In cognizance of this, as per the process shown in Figure G.2, competency development constitutes a key metric under the talent management perspective. Besides being a metric in the corporate scorecard, the competency development metrics find a mandatory place in the scorecards of each of the units.

Further, the unit with the key mandate for training and competency development also has a set of metrics reflecting the unit's key mandate. In addition, this is a key metric in the personal goals of individual employees and is measured as part of the annual appraisals.

Figure G.2. Translating Strategies to Business Units

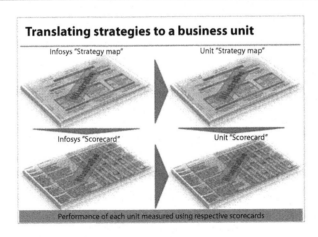

Translating strategies to a business unit

Infosys "Strategy map"   Unit "Strategy map"

Infosys "Scorecard"   Unit "Scorecard"

Performance of each unit measured using respective scorecards

Thus the alignment of the metric is complete, being driven through multiple levels.

- Corporate
- Unit
- Individual

RESULTS

The last three years have seen the certification programs stabilize, due in large part to the linking of competency development with career progression and appraisals.

During the period January to December 2007 over 125,000 certification exams had been created across technology, business domain, and process. Certification has now become part of the DNA of the organization and has helped in the growth of the organization. A clear process for rolling out new certifications has been laid out, making the entire system very responsive and agile. This strategy, coupled with flawless execution in linking competency development to individual growth, has led to a sustainable program to ensure continuos development of its professionals.

Infosys Technologies Ltd. (NASDAQ: INFY) defines, designs, and delivers IT-enabled business solutions that help Global 2000 companies win in a flat world. These solutions focus on providing strategic differentiation and operational superiority to clients. Infosys creates these solutions for its clients by leveraging its domain and business expertise, along with a complete range of services. With Infosys, clients are assured of a transparent business partner, world-class processes, speed of execution, and the power to stretch their IT budgets by leveraging the Global Delivery Model that Infosys pioneered.

V. Ganapathy Subramanian heads the Corporate Performance Management function at Infosys Technologies Ltd. In this role, he drives alignment through the goal setting and scorecard processes across the organization. He has nine years of experience in the areas of strategy, planning, and finance in industries spanning banking, insurance, management consulting, and IT services. Before joining

Infosys he set up and headed business planning and financial planning functions in two private-sector general insurance companies. Prior to his stint in insurance, he also consulted for Indian companies, primarily in the areas of strategy and finance. Ganapathy has a post-graduate degree in management from the Indian Institute of Management, Lucknow, and holds a bachelor's degree in engineering. Ganapathy's professional areas of interest include measurement and management of corporate performance.

Tan Moorthy, vice president and head, Education and Research, oversees the various competency development programs at Infosys: (a) Campus Connect to increase the employability of students at engineering colleges in India, (b) the Foundation Program, a sixteen-week residential program for new graduates joining Infosys, and (c) certifications, a continuous development program for employees across Infosys. Tan has more than twenty-two years of global experience in the IT industry, during which time he has gained an extensive background and hands-on experience in technology, project and people management, and customer interaction. Tan's experience ranges from systems and applications programming on a variety of computing platforms to client partnering, operations management, business development, and strategy definition. Tan has been a key contributor to the competency development initiative at Infosys and is a core member of the organization-wide competency development and Malcolm Baldrige-based excellence programs.

Bernard Marr. (2006). *Strategic Performance Management: Leveraging and Measuring Your Intangible Value Drivers.* London: Butterworth-Heinemann.

Paul R. Niven. (2003). *Balanced Scorecard Step-by-Step for Government and Nonprofit Agencies.* Hoboken, NJ: John Wiley & Sons.

Paul R. Niven. (2005). *Balanced Scorecard Diagnostics: Maintaining Maximum Performance.* Hoboken, NJ: John Wiley & Sons.

Nils-Goran Olve, Jan Roy, & Magnus Wetter. (1999). *Performance Drivers: A Practical Guide to Using the Balanced Scorecard.* Hoboken, NJ: John Wiley & Sons.

Nils-Goran Olve, Carl-Johan Petri, Jan Roy, & Sofie Roy. (2003). *Making Scorecards Actionable: Balancing Strategy and Control.* Hoboken, NJ: John Wiley & Sons.

Theodore H. Poister. (2003). *Measuring Performance in Public and Nonprofit Organizations.* San Francisco: Jossey-Bass.

Michael E. Porter. (1998). *Competitive Advantage: Creating and Sustaining Superior Performance.* New York: The Free Press.

Michael E. Porter. (1998). *Competitive Strategy: Techniques for Analyzing Industries and Competitors.* New York: The Free Press.

Michael E. Raynor. (2007). *The Strategy Paradox: Why Committing to Success Leads to Failure (and What to Do About It).* New York: Currency.

Theresa Seagraves. (2004). *Quick! Show Me Your Value.* Alexandria, VA: ASTD Press.

Diane C. Vanenti. (2003). *Training Budgets Step-By-Step: A Complete Guide to Planning and Budgeting Strategically-Aligned Training.* San Francisco: Pfeiffer.

RECOMMENDED WEBSITES

- 2GC Performance Management Resource Centre.
  www.2gc.co.uk/resource.asp

- Army Business Transformation Knowledge Center.
  www.army.mil/armybtkc/enablers/pm/ibp.htm

- Balanced Scorecard Development for the Government Shareholder.
  www.adb.org/Documents/Books/Balanced-Scorecard/chap4.pdf

- Balanced Scorecard resources (non-biased site).
  http://faculty.css.edu/dswenson/web/525ARTIC/balancedscorecard.html

- Canadian Management Centre. Linking Learning Strategy with the Balanced Scorecard Certification.
  www.cmctraining.org/reg/course.asp?sid=0&course_id=91005-XCNE&cat_id=8

- Implementing the Balanced Scorecard in State Government.
  www.ksg.harvard.edu/visions/performance_management/salmon%201999.
  pdf
- Memphis City Schools (sample).
  www.mcsk12.net/scorecard/index.html
- Strategy and Performance Management in the Government.
  www.exinfm.com/workshop_files/strategy_pm_gov.pdf
- The Balanced Scorecard Collaborative.
  www.thepalladiumgroup.com
- The Balanced Scorecard Institute.
  www.balancedscorecard.org
- The Balanced Scorecard: Beyond Reports and Rankings.
  http://oaa.osu.edu/irp/balancedscorecard.pdf
- The Conference Board of Canada. Developing a Balanced Scorecard Approach
  to Measure the Performance of Your e-Learning Initiatives.
  www.conferenceboard.ca/education/reports/pdfs/elearning_presentation.pdf
- The Trainer's Balanced Scorecard. CentralKnowledge Inc.
  www.centralknowledge.com
- Using the Balanced Scorecard for Ranch Planning and Management: Setting
  Strategy and Measuring Performance.
  http://agbiopubs.sdstate.edu/articles/EC922.pdf

Huselid, Mark A., Brian E. Becker, & Richard W. Beatty. *The Workforce Scorecard: Managing Human Capital to Execute Strategy.* Cambridge, MA: Harvard Business School Press, 2005.

Gartner Survey of 1,400 CIOs Shows Transformation of IT Organization Is Accelerating. Stamford, CD: Gartner, 2006.

Kaplan, Robert S., & David P. Norton. *The Balanced Scorecard: Translating Strategy into Action.* Cambridge, MA: Harvard Business School Press, 1996.

Kaplan, Robert S., & David P. Norton. Having Trouble with Your Strategy? Then Map It. *Harvard Business Review*, September/October 2000.

Kaplan, Robert S, & David P. Norton. *Strategy Maps: Converting Intangible Assets into Tangible Outcomes.* Cambridge, MA: Harvard Business School Press, 2004.

Kaplan, Robert S., & David P. Norton. *Alignment: Using the Balanced Scorecard to Create Corporate Synergies.* Cambridge, MA: Harvard Business School Press, 2006.

Kim Chan W., Renée Mauborgne. *Blue Ocean Strategy: How to Create Uncontested Market Space and Make the Competition Irrelevant.* Cambridge, MA: Harvard Business School Press, 2005.

Know-How: Managing Knowledge for a Competitive Advantage. (2005, June). *The Economist.*

Koch, Richard, & Peter Nieuwenhuizen. *Simply Strategy: The Shortest Route to the Best Strategy.* Englewood Cliffs, NJ: Pearson Education, 2006.

McManus, John. *Leadership: Project and Human Capital Management.* London: Butterworth-Heinemann, 2006.

Niven, Paul R. *Balanced Scorecard Step-by-Step for Government and Nonprofit Agencies.* Hoboken, NJ: John Wiley & Sons, 2003.

Niven, Paul R. *Balanced Scorecard Diagnostics: Maintaining Maximum Performance.* Hoboken, NJ: John Wiley & Sons, 2005.

Niven, Paul R. *Balanced Scorecard Step-by-Step: Maximizing Performance and Maintaining Results.* Hoboken, NJ: John Wiley & Sons, 2006.

Nonaka, Ikujirō. *Knowledge Management: Critical Perspectives on Business and Management.* London: Routledge, 1998.

Phillips, Jack J., & Ron Drew Stone. *How to Measure Training Results: A Practical Guide to Tracking the Six Key Indicators.* New York. McGraw-Hill, 2002.

Porter, Michael E. *Competitive Advantage: Creating and Sustaining Superior Performance.* New York: The Free Press, 1985.

Seagraves, Theresa. *Quick! Show Me Your Value: A Trainer's Guide to Communicating Value; Connecting Training and Performance to the Bottom Line.* Alexandria, VA: SHRM/ASTD Press, 2004.

Senge, Peter M. *The Fifth Discipline: The Art and Practice of the Learning Organization.* New York: Currency Doubleday, 1990.

Tanaszi, Margaret, & Duffy, Jan. *Measuring Knowledge Assets.* Mississauga, ON: The Society of Management Accountants of Canada, 2000.

Treacy, M., & Wiersema, F. (1993). Customer Intimacy and Other Value Disciplines. *Harvard Business Review.*

Treacy, Michael, & Fred Wiersema. *The Discipline of Market Leaders: Choose Your Customers, Narrow Your Focus.* New York: Basic Books, 1995.

Zeinstra, B. (2004, December). Converting from a Training Department to a Profit Center. *CLO Magazine.*

C

C-level (or C-suite) decision-makers: comments on workplace learning by, 30; commitment to workplace learning by, 36; description of, 5; learning to think like they do, 83*e*; making learning relevant to, 39–40; understanding language and mind-set of, 99. *See also* Management

Campeau, M., 345, 349

Canadian Physiotherapy Association (CPA) case study, 319–338

Canadian Telecommunication Company case study: Non-financial performance measures of, 124–128; SMB learning team measuring process, 125–128

Cascading scorecards: description and benefits of the, 68–69; development process of, 254*fig*; "granularizaton" of strategic objectives within, 69–71; illustration of, 70*fig*; to personal scorecards, 71–72

Case studies: Bell Canada, 345–348; Canadian Physiotherapy Association (CPA), 319–338; Canadian Telecommunication Company, 124–128; CMA Canada, 351–361; Dofasco, Inc., 297–303; Infosys, 363–368; Sky Air Limited (SAL), 13, 215–251*fig*; Toronto-Dominion Bank, 305–316; United Way-Centraide Canada (UW-CC), 339–343. *See also* Balanced Scorecard (BSC)

Cash flow statement: description of, 155; structure of, 164*t*

CMA Canada case study, 351–361

Communication: customer perspective context of, 102*e*; financial perspective context of, 102*e*; internal business perspective context of, 103*e*; language of learning and performance for good, 99–102; language of management used in, 98–99; learning perspective context of, 103*e*

Corporate strategy: business strategy vs., 24–25; description of, 22*fig*, 24; focal points of, 28*fig*; fundamental questions related to, 27*t*

Cost recovery, 87

Covey, S., 106

Customer intimacy orientation, 286–287

Customer perspective: defining the, 58–59; of learning department's BSC, 261–263, 268–269; learning and growth performance measures for, 211*e*; management expectations and, 102*e*; performance targets related to, 183*t*; sample BSC and, 67*fig*; sample initiatives and, 66*t*; sample measures and, 64*t*; sample objectives and, 63*t*; sample targets and, 65*t*; Sky Air case study on, 227–229*e*, 231*t*, 233*t*–234*t*, 237*t*, 239*t*–240*t*, 244*t*–245*t*, 247*t*; as strategic framework component, 50*fig*, 51; strategy map build around, 53; summary of, 60*fig*. *See also* Balanced Scorecard (BSC); External management expectation perspectives

Customer service department: initiative selection template for, 185*e*; initiatives on improving, 204; performance objective and targets related to, 184; skills gaps in, 182*t*

Customer service representative (CSR), 116

Customers: developing learning and growth initiatives related to, 180–182, 184–188; skills gaps related to, 182*t*; value chain's proposition to the, 136, 138

D

Daniels, M., 125, 127, 128

"Dashboard," 45

Decision making, 114

Design value, 143*e*

Distribution value, 144*e*

Dofasco, Inc. case study, 297–303

Duffy, J., 21

E

Employee knowledge/skills: gaps for customer support, 182*t*; gaps for manufacturing, 182*t*; people-based learning initiatives, 202, 212*e*–213*e*; relationship between value chain and, 146*e*–147*e*; reskilling matrix, 172*fig*; technological revolution affecting, 275. *See also* Kirkpatrick Level 3 (application of skills); Knowledge; Learning and growth perspective

Employees: developing the entrepreneurial, 285; developing specialists and not generalists among, 286; increasing trend for customer intimacy orientation of, 286–287; managing learning for a generational workforce, 284–285; technological revolution affecting, 275

Entrepreneurial employee, 285

Evaluation: based on corporate values, 282; challenges related to, 281; common misconceptions regarding, 281–282; keeping it simple and quick, 282–283; providing evidence and not proof during, 283; understanding organizational interactions during, 283–284. *See also* Kirkpatrick's evaluation model; Training and development (T&D); Workplace learning and performance (WLP)

Expense-investment differentiation, 154

External management expectations perspectives, 102*e*. *See also* Customer perspective; Financial perspective

F

Financial performance: BSC to translate strategic plan into, 37; learning and growth performance measures for, 212*e*; Workplace learning and performance (WLP) relationship to, 11, 153–165

Financial performance objectives: 1. increase organizational value, 155–157; 2. increase organizational profitability, 157, 160–161; 3. increase organizational liquidity, 162, 164; 4. aligning investment with strategic objectives, 164

Financial perspective: defining the, 57–58; "How Do We Look to Our Stakeholders?" worksheet on, 260*e*; learning department's BSC, 258–260*e*, 268; of learning and growth performance measure, 212*e*; management expectations and, 102*e*; sample BSC and, 67*fig*; sample initiatives and, 66*t*; sample measures and, 64*t*; sample objectives and, 63*t*; sample targets and, 65*t*; Sky Air case study on initiatives for, 239*t*, 240*t*; Sky Air case study on strategic linkages to, 227; of stakeholders, 57–58, 258–260*e*; as strategic framework component, 50*fig*, 51; strategy map build around, 53; summary of, 60*fig. See also* Balanced Scorecard (BSC); External management expectation perspectives

Financial statements: balance sheet, 155, 156*t*, 157, 158*e*–159*e*; cash flow statement, 155, 164*t*; income statement, 155, 160*t*, 162*e*–163*e*; management objectives tied to, 155–157, 160–162, 164–165; types of, 155; value of organization, 154–155

Ford, H., 3

Ford Motor company, 1–2

G

Gargiulo, T. L., 58, 84, 279

Gartner Survey (2006), 112

General Electric, 35

General Motors, 3

Globalization factor, 275

Google, 35

Gross margin (GM), 161

H

"How Can Learning Continue to Improve and Create Value?" (worksheet), 267*e*

"How Do Our Customers See Us" (worksheet), 262*e*

Human capital, 52

I

Image and reputation, 138

Income statements: definition of, 155; structure of, 160*t*; value creation of, 162*e*–163*e*

"Information age," 35

Information capital, 52

Information as driver, 2–3

Infosys case study, 363–368

Initiative Selection Template, 185*e*

Innovation management, 204

Institute of Management Accountants (IMA), 48

Intangible assets: human, information, and organizational capital as, 52; identifying and aligning, 56

Internal processes perspective: of learning department's BSC, 263–264, 265*e*, 269; learning and growth performance measures for, 211*e*; management expectations and, 102*e*, 103*e*; performance measures and, 10–11; performance targets related to, 183*t*; process-based learning initiatives, 202, 213*e*; sample BSC and, 67*fig*; sample initiatives and, 66*t*; sample measures and, 64*t*; sample objectives and, 63*t*; sample targets and, 65*t*; Sky Air case study on, 228, 230*e*, 232*t*, 233*t*, 235*t*, 238*t*, 239*t*, 241*t*, 245*t*, 246*t*, 248*t*; as strategic framework component, 50*fig*, 51; strategy map build around, 53. *See also* Balanced Scorecard (BSC); Learning and growth perspective

International Monetary Fund List, 275

Investment-expense differentiation, 154

K

Kaplan, R., 3, 44, 52, 56, 60, 61, 71, 138, 168, 171, 288

Karlsson, C., 305, 317

Key performance indicators (KPI): Canadian Telecommunication Company's, 127; flow from strategic objectives, 124, 130*fig*; measures of, 131*e*

Kim, C. W., 21

Kirkpatrick, D., 279

Kirkpatrick Level 1 (reactions): customer perspective on, 261; learning objectives for, 174; needs assessment for, 101; overview of, 279*t*, 280

Kirkpatrick Level 2 (retention/testing): demonstrating results for learning through, 205–207; internal process perspective on, 263; learning objectives for, 175; needs assessment for, 101; overview of, 279*t*, 280

Kirkpatrick Level 3 (application of skills): connecting learning to, 35; demonstrating results for learning through, 206; establishing learning and growth measures, 177; internal process perspective on, 263; learning objectives for, 175; needs assessment for, 101; organizational value of, 168; overview, 279*t*, 280. *See also* Employee knowledge/skills

Kirkpatrick Level 4 (learning): demonstrating results for learning through, 206–207; establishing learning and growth measures, 177; financial perspective

Kirkpatrick Level 4 (learning) (*Continued*)
on, 259; learning objectives for, 175;
misconceptions regarding, 282; organizational
value of, 168; overview of, 279*t*, 281
Kirkpatrick's evaluation model: description of, 101,
278–281; level 1 (reactions), 101, 174, 261, 279*t*,
280; level 2 (retention/testing), 101, 175, 205–207,
263, 279*t*, 280; level 3 (application of skills), 35,
101, 168, 175, 177, 206, 263, 279*t*, 280; level 4
(learning), 168, 175, 177, 206–207, 259, 279*t*, 281,
282. *See also* Evaluation; Learning and growth
measures; Performance metrics
Kirkwood, T. K., 58, 84, 279
Know How (2005), 287
Knowledge: as competitive driver, 2–3; managing for
maximum benefit, 287–288; "people," 56. *See also*
Employee knowledge/skills; Learning
Knowledge-workers learning imperative, 169
KPMG, 44

L
Learning: ADDIE model approach to, 100*fig*; based
on operational data, 116–117*fig*, 119*e*; based on
strategic data, 115, 117*e*–118, 117*fig*; based on
tactical data, 115–116, 117*fig*, 118*e*–119*e*; building performance value chain and, 148–150*fig*;
deconstructing the value change around the BSC
and, 137*fig*, 139–148; demonstrating results for,
205–207; determining initiatives affecting,
201–202; evaluating, 281–284; Ford example of
strategic planning is impacted by, 1–2; as knowl-
edge-worker imperative, 169; made relevant to
management, 39–40; managing for generational
workforce, 284–285; understanding language of
performance and, 99–102. *See also* Knowledge;
Learning; Strategic learning solutions
Learning concerns: conducting a needs assessment
for, 84; management expectations context of,
80–96; management questions about, 104–110;
workplace learning and performance (WLP)
context of, 97*e*
Learning culture, 36
Learning department's BSC: cascading scorecard
development process, 254*fig*; customer perspective of, 261–263, 268–269; financial perspective of,
258–260*e*, 268; "How Can Learning Continue
to Improve and Create Value?" worksheet, 267*e*;
"How Do Our Customers See Us" worksheet, 262*e*;
"How Do We Look to Our Stakeholders?"

worksheet on, 260*e*; internal process perspective of,
263–264, 265*e*; learning and growth perspective
of, 264, 266, 267*e*, 269–270; purpose of the,
253–255; questions to ask before developing,
255–256; questions used to help develop, 270*fig*;
rapid development process for, 266, 268–270;
sample, 271*t*; sample performance metrics of,
257*fig*; unique perspective of, 256–258; "What Must
Learning Excel At?" worksheet, 265*e*
Learning department's BSC steps: 1. completing
the financial perspective, 268; 2. completing the
customer perspective, 268–269; 3. completing the
internal process perspective, 269; 4. completing the
learning and growth perspective, 269–270
Learning and growth: developing performance metrics for, 173; gaps for manufacturing and customer
support, 182*t*; initiatives for, 66*t*, 180–182, 181*t*,
184–188; measures of, 64*t*, 176–178, 188–191*e*;
objectives for, 63*t*, 174–176; targets for, 65*t*,
178–180, 181*t*
Learning and growth measure templates: BSC
initiatives, 212*e*–213*e*; BSC and learning initiatives, 213*e*–214*e*; BSC learning initiatives and
performance metrics, 214*e*; customer perspective
performance measures, 211*e*; financial perspective
performance measures, 212*e*; identifying objectives,
210–211; identifying strategically critical areas,
209*e*–210*e*; internal process perspective performance measures, 211*e*–212*e*; steps with corresponding exhibits, 208*t*; strategic linkages
analysis, 210*e*
Learning and growth measures: application of,
188–190; criteria used for development of,
176–178; facilitating development of, 207; improving and creating value through, 191*e*; sample of
BSC, 64*t*; templates for developing, 208*t*–214*e*. *See
also* Kirkpatrick's evaluation model
Learning and growth perspective: application of,
193–214; BSC context of, 171–188; cause-and-
effect relationship to, 69*e*; defining the, 60–62;
developing the, 12, 194–195; examining application
of, 12–13; importance of developing, 168–169;
learning department's BSC, 264, 266, 267*e*,
269–270; management expectations and, 103*e*;
organizational value chain alignment with, 136*fig*;
performance targets related to, 183*t*; sample BSC
and, 67*fig*; Sky Air case study analysis of,
242*e*–243*e*, 244–250*e*; as strategic framework component, 50*fig*, 51–52; strategy map build around,

53; summary of basic principles of, 196*t*. *See also* Balanced Scorecard (BSC); Employee knowledge/skills; Internal perspectives

Learning and growth perspective application: basic principles of, 196*t*; demonstrating results for learning, 205–207; executing learning strategy, 196–205; facilitating development of learning and growth metrics, 207; understanding learning and growth for, 194–195

Learning initiative templates: initiative description, 187*e*–188*e*; initiative development, 185*e*; initiative prioritization, 186*e*

Learning initiatives: ADDIE model approach to, 110*fig*; alignment between overall vision and, 104–106; determining how learning is affected by, 201–202; determining the, 202, 204; developing, 66*t*, 180–182, 184–188; expected outcomes of, 106; gaining buy-in from affected departments/individuals, 107, 110; linking organizational core values to, 106; people-based and process-based, 202, 212*e*–213*e*; performance metrics of BSC, 214*e*; perspective levels of, 213*e*–214*e*; Sky Air Limited (SAL) case on, 236–241*t*, 249*e*; tangible benefits of the, 106–107; two types within BSC framework, 107; worksheets for asking/answering management questions on, 108*e*–109*e*

Learning needs: Kirkpatrick levels 1, 2, and 3 establishment of, 101; reconciling business and, 139*fig*

Learning peers, 5

Learning strategy execution: 1. assess and analyze the strategy map, 197*fig*–198; 2. determine the objectives, 198–199; 3. determine performance measurement tools utilized, 199, 201; 6. determine the learning initiatives, 202, 204; determine initiatives affecting learning, 201–202; issues related to, 196–197

M

Macpherson, T., 297

Malleret, V., 45

Management: defining T&D target audience/needs among, 93*t*; differentiation between investment and expense by, 154; of knowledge for maximum benefit, 287–288; language of, 98–99; making learning relevant to, 39–40; moving from performance measurement to strategic, 76–80; perspective on the value chain by, 140*fig*; Porter's five forces awareness by, 24–25; talent management (TM), 35; what they want to know about WLP, 32–33. *See also* C-level (or C-suite) decision-makers

Management expectations: answer questions about learning initiatives tied to, 103–110; BSC alignment with, 9; closing the communication gap between T&D and, 98–103; critical questions to ask about, 82*e*; internal and external perspectives of, 102*e*–103*e*; learning concerns vs., 80–97; learning to think like they do to understand, 83*e*; marketing T&D in context of, 85–96; Sky Air Limited (SAL) case study on, 224–226

Management questions: how is learning strategy aligned with overall vision?, 104–106; how will we gain necessary buy-in for learning strategy?, 107, 110; what are expected outcomes of learning strategy?, 106; what are tangible benefits of learning strategy?, 106–107; worksheet for answering, 108*e*; worksheet for responses to, 109*e*

Marketing value, 144*e*

Mauborgne, R., 21

Measures. *See* Performance measures

Microsoft, 35

Mission: fundamental questions to ask about, 27*t*; learning objectives aligned to, 175; primary points of strategy related to, 29*fig*. *See also* Vision

Moorthy, T., 363, 369

N

Niven, P. R., 61, 167

Non-financial performance measures: Canadian Telecommunication Company case study of, 124–128; description of, 120–121; growing need for accountability in, 121–123; limitations to, 123–124

Norton, D., 3, 44, 52, 56, 60, 61, 71, 138, 168, 171, 288

N¢reklit, H., 45

O

Objectives: BSC perspectives and examples of, 63*t*, 64*t*, 65*t*, 66*t*; definition of, 61, 62, 174; financial statements tied to financial, 155–157, 160–162, 164–165; for learning and growth, 174–176, 210*e*–211*e*; learning strategy execution by determining, 198–199; sample BSC and, 67*fig*; Sky Air Limited (SAL) case on, 221–223, 228–229

O'Halloran, T., 297

Operational data: learning based on, 116, 119*e*; WLP's impact on decision making using, 117*fig*

Operational decisions, 114

Orendorff, E., 319, 338

Organizational capital, 52

Organizational change process, 4*fig*

Organizational decision making, 114

Organizational learning culture, 36

Organizations: BSC context of learning in, 171–188; defining expectations of your, 34e; how strategic framework links to, 38fig; knowledge as driving, 2; knowledge and information as driving, 2–3; linking learning to core values of the, 106; mission of, 27t, 29fig, 175; strategic framework of, 48–52; strategy map value for, 53, 555; vision of, 27t, 29fig, 104–106. *See also* Strategy

Organization's Strategic Expectations (worksheet), 34e

P

Pangarkar, A. M., 58, 84, 279

People knowledge, 56

People-based initiatives: description of, 202; financial perspective of, 212e–213e; internal process perspective of, 213e

Performance: benchmarking, 207; BSC perspectives and sample, 63t, 64t, 65t, 66t, 67fig; BSC thinking versus traditional approach to, 169–171; building the learning and value chain of, 148–150fig; definition of, 61, 62–63; key performance indicators (KPI) of, 124, 127, 130fig, 131e; pitfall of using only lagging, 72–73; specific factors driving, 128–131; understanding language of learning and, 99–102; WLP relationship to financial, 11, 153–165

Performance measures: definition of, 62–63; learning and growth, 64t, 176–178, 181t, 188–191e, 208t–214e; moving to strategic management from, 76–80; non-financial, 120–128; pitfalls of using only lagging, 72–73; sample of BSC perspectives and, 64t, 65t, 66t, 67fig

Performance metrics: BSC vs. traditional, 46–47; business processes and, 10–11; developed for learning and growth, 173; importance of business data and, 9–10; initiatives as, 63t–64t, 65t–66t, 67fig; learning and growth, 64t, 176–178, 181t, 188–191e, 208t–214e; measures, 62–63t, 64, 65t–66t, 67fig; objectives, 62, 63t–64, 65t–66t, 67fig; pitfall of using generic, 73; sample of balanced scorecard, 257fig; sample learning scorecard, 258fig; Sky Air Limited (SAL) case on, 229e–230, 237t, 249e; targets as, 63t–64, 65t–66t, 67fig. *See also* Kirkpatrick's evaluation model

Performance targets: definition of, 61, 63; examples of learning and growth, 65t, 181t; learning strategy execution by determining, 201; related to customer, internal process, and learning perspectives, 183t; sample BSC and, 67fig; setting learning and growth, 178–180; Sky Air Limited (SAL) case on determining, 230–236, 237t, 238t

Porter, M., 20, 24, 134

Porter's five forces model, 24–25

Process-based initiatives: description of, 202; financial perspective of, 213e; internal process perspective of, 213e

Product manufacturing department: initiative selection template for, 185e; learning objectives and targets for, 184; skills gaps in, 182t

Products: value chain role of, 143e–144e; as value proposition, 138

Projected time line, 55–56

Prototype creation, 204

R

R&D (research & development): initiatives to improve, 204; value of, 142e–143e

Reputation and image, 138

Reskilling matrix, 172fig

Responses to Management's Questions (worksheet), 109e

ROCE (return on the capital employed), 268

ROI (return on investment): expectation of workplace learning investment, 276fig–278; fostering a learning culture to move beyond, 36; moving beyond and toward strategy, 37–39

S

"Sacred cow," 36

Sales process improvements, 202

Scholey, C., 339, 351, 362

Services: value chain role of, 145e; as value proposition, 138

The Seven Habits of Highly Effective People (Covey), 106

Skills gaps: customer support, 182t; for manufacturing, 182t

Skills to Empower the Learning Function (Pangarkar and Kirkwood), 5

Sky Air Limited (SAL) case application: 1. assess and analyze strategy map, 219–228; 2. determine the objectives, 228–229; 3. determining performance measurement tools utilized, 229e–230; 4. determining the performance targets, 230–236; 5. determining the initiatives affecting learning, 236–241t; 6. determining learning initiatives, 241–250

Sky Air Limited (SAL) case study: background information on, 217–219; BSC learning initiatives and performance metrics in, 249e; completed strategy map and BSC for, 249e; identifying strategically critical areas in, 222e; incomplete strategy map and BSC for, 220fig; introduction to, 13; learning and growth analysis of, 242e–243e, 244–250e; management expectations in, 224–226; reviewing learning and growth steps to apply to, 215–216t; steps for BSC and strategy development at, 219–251fig; strategic linkages analysis in, 226–228; strategy map developed for, 221fig

SMB (small medium business) learning team, 125–128

The Society of Management Accountants of Canada, 68

Stakeholders: defining current value gap for, 55; financial perspective of, 57–58, 258–260e; "How Do We Look to Our Stakeholders?" worksheet, 260e

Strategic data: learning based on, 115, 117e–118e; WLP's impact on decision making using, 117fig

Strategic framework: BSC role in the, 49fig–51; customer perspective of, 50fig, 51; description of, 48; financial perspective of, 50fig, 51; internal business processes of, 50fig, 51; learning and growth perspective of, 50fig, 51–52

Strategic learning solutions: based on strategic data, 115; using business data to develop, 112–113; workplace learning and performance (WLP) role in, 113–120

Strategic linkages analysis: of financial, customer, and internal process perspectives, 227–228; relevant to objectives, 228; Sky Air Limited (SAL) case study on, 226–228

Strategic planning: BSC to translate into financial performance from, 37; Ford example of how learning impacts, 1–2; model for, 1

Strategic themes, 56

Strategy: business context of, 22fig; corporate vs. business, 24–25; defining your organization's, 31e; defining your organization's expectations for, 34e; definitions of, 7, 20, 22, 23, 29fig; differences between tactics and, 23t; executing learning, 196–205; factors affecting, 25–32; focal points of general, 28fig; fostering a learning culture to enhance, 36; fundamental questions related to general, 27t; importance and description of, 20–22; moving beyond ROI toward, 37–39; pitfalls of lacking well-defined, 72; primary points of, 28, 29fig; "realized" or "emergent," 23; relationship between

WLP and, 28, 30–32; sample of fundamental questions to ask about, 27t; specifying and funding initiatives to execute, 56; three basic forms of, 22fig–23; WLP professional focus on specifics of, 32–33. *See also* Organizations

Strategy factors: listed, 25–26; three basic "value disciplines," 26t; understanding of the questions as, 26–28

Strategy map: assess and analyze learning, 197fig–198; comparing BSC to, 37–38; definition and characteristics of, 52–53; five main principles behind, 55; functions of, 53, 55; how to use, 55–57; illustrated sample of, 54fig; Sky Air Limited (SAL) case on, 219–228, 221fig, 251fig

Subramanian, V. G., 363, 368–369

Sun Tzu, 21

T

"Tableau de bord," 45

Tactical data: learning based on, 115–116, 118e–119e; WLP's impact on decision making using, 117fig

Tactical decisions, 114

Tactics, 23t

Talent management (TM), 35

Tanaszi, M., 21

Targets. *See* Performance targets

Technological revolution: impact on business by the, 275; impact on customers by, 286

Templates: learning and growth metrics development, 208t–214e; learning initiative, 185e, 186e–188e; summary of steps with corresponding, 216t. *See also* Worksheets

Toronto-Dominion Bank case study, 305–316

Toyota, 35

Training and development (T&D): answering seven essential questions about, 92, 94–96; challenges of "selling," 85–86; closing the communication gap between management and, 98–103; defining target audience and their needs for, 93t; description and benefits of, 5; expectation on ROI of, 276fig–278; knowing your audience to gain buy-in, 88–89; mistakes made when marketing, 89–92; now referred to as learning and performance, 75; proving worth of, 87–88. *See also* Evaluation; Workplace learning and performance (WLP)

U

United Way-Centraide Canada (UW-CC) case study, 339–343

V

Value chain: BSC perspectives aligned with, 135*fig*; deconstructed around the BSC and learning, 137*fig*, 139–148; identifying your, 142*e*–145; illustration of, 135*fig*; learning department's BSC on improving and creating, 264, 266, 267*e*; learning and growth initiative to improve, 191*e*; learning and growth perspective alignment with, 136*fig*; proposition to the customer, 136, 138; real value provided through, 134–136; relationship between employee skills and, 146*e*; workplace learning and performance (WLP) role in, 148–150*fig*, 291–293

Value chain deconstruction: around BSC and learning, 137*fig*; management's perspective of the, 140*fig*; process of, 139–148; reconciling business and learning needs, 139*fig*

"Value disciplines," 26*t*

Value gap, 55

Value propositions: categories of the, 138; defining your organization's, 142*e*; reconciling current value, 55; strategies of, 59*t*

Varner, J., 339

Vieweg, S. F., 351, 361

Vision: explaining how learning strategy is aligned to, 104–106; fundamental questions to ask about, 27*t*; primary points of strategy related to, 29*fig*. *See also* Mission

W

Wal-Mart, 35

What Is Management Asking You? (worksheet), 108*e*

"What Must Learning Excel At?" (worksheet), 265*e*

Widget, Inc. BSC, 200*fig*

Workplace learning and performance (WLP): also known as talent management (TM), 35; Balanced Scorecard and relationship with, 6; C-level (or C-suite) decision-maker comments on, 30; factors affecting BSC, strategy, and, 14–15; financial performance relationship to, 11, 153–165; learning concerns of, 97*e*; organizational decision making and role of, 117*fig*; performance value chain role of, 148–150*fig*, 291–293; relationship between strategy and, 28, 30–32; specifics of organizational strategy required for, 32–33; strategic learning solutions and role of, 113–120; strategy development role of, 33, 35–36; what management wants to know about, 32–33. *See also* Evaluation; Training and development (T&D)

Worksheets: defining your organization's expectations, 34*e*; defining your organization's strategy, 31*e*; "How Can Learning Continue to Improve and Create Value?," 267*e*; "How Do Our Customers See Us," 262*e*; "How Do We Look to Our Stakeholders?," 260*e*; Organization's Strategic Expectations, 34*e*; responses to management questions, 109*e*; what is management asking you?, 108*e*; "What Must Learning Excel At?," 265*e*. *See also* Templates

Z

Zeinstra, B., 87

Ajay M. Pangarkar, CTDP, learning strategist, speaker, and author, is president and co-founder of CentralKnowledge Inc., leaders in comprehensive strategic learning solutions, assessment management systems, and just-in-time e-learning tools. With a wealth of experience in creating and implementing learning strategies, Ajay's focus is to ensure that workplace learning interventions are always aligned with an organization's business and strategic objectives. Ajay is a foremost authority on integrating organizational learning strategies with the Balanced Scorecard and is an industry-leading learning strategist in building results-driven learning solutions. Ajay works closely with leading Fortune 1000 companies and non-profit and governmental organizations that seek his expertise in developing innovative and results-oriented learning solutions. Ajay regularly writes for many prominent publications, including *CLO, Talent Management Magazine, HR Reporter, HR Professional, and CMA Management*. Other publications include *Building Business Acumen for Trainers: Skills to Empower the Learning Function* (2006) and *The Trainer's Portable Mentor* (2008). Ajay serves as the vice chair of the Canadian Society for Training and Development (CSTD) National Board of Directors. He holds CSTD's industry-recognized Certified Training & Development Professional (CTDP) designation. Ajay is highly involved with non-profit community groups. Ajay was nominated for the Ernst & Young/Canadian Business of the Year award and is regularly interviewed by business and news media. Contact Ajay at ajayp@ centralknowledge.com.

Printed in the United States
By Bookmasters